INTERNATIONAL LAW AND THE SIGNIFICANCE OF DISCIPLINARY BOUNDARIES

Over the last thirty or so years, international law and legal practice have become increasingly more specialized and diversified. These developments come with an increasingly divergent legal practice, in what has been coined 'special regimes'. This book proposes a new understanding of the concept of a special regime to explain why specialists in different fields of international law do similar things differently. It argues that special regimes are best conceived as communities of practice, in the sense of Etienne Wenger's theory of communities of practice. It explores how the theory of communities of practice translates to the context of international law and the concept of a special regime. The authors draw up an innovative methodology to investigate their theory, focused on the conduct of community members, and apply this method to selected case studies, offering an original approach to the understanding of the special regimes in international law.

ULF LINDERFALK is Professor of International Law at Lund University. He is a 'specialized generalist'. His research has examined issues such as normative conflict, legal hierarchy, legal interpretation, intertemporal law, legal principles, legal concepts, good faith, abuse of rights, proportionality, and the international legal system as such.

ERIC DE BRABANDERE is Professor of International Dispute Settlement at the Grotius Centre for International Legal Studies at Leiden University's Law School. He also practises in international law and (investment) arbitration (as partner with DMDB Law in Brussels).

INTERNATIONAL LAW AND THE SIGNIFICANCE OF DISCIPLINARY BOUNDARIES

Special Regimes as Communities of Practice

ULF LINDERFALK
Lund University, Sweden

ERIC DE BRABANDERE
Leiden University, Netherlands

CAMBRIDGE
UNIVERSITY PRESS

CAMBRIDGE
UNIVERSITY PRESS

Shaftesbury Road, Cambridge CB2 8EA, United Kingdom

One Liberty Plaza, 20th Floor, New York, NY 10006, USA

477 Williamstown Road, Port Melbourne, VIC 3207, Australia

314–321, 3rd Floor, Plot 3, Splendor Forum, Jasola District Centre, New Delhi – 110025, India

103 Penang Road, #05-06/07, Visioncrest Commercial, Singapore 238467

Cambridge University Press is part of Cambridge University Press & Assessment, a department of the University of Cambridge.

We share the University's mission to contribute to society through the pursuit of education, learning and research at the highest international levels of excellence.

www.cambridge.org
Information on this title: www.cambridge.org/9781009543200

DOI: 10.1017/9781009543194

When citing this work, please include a reference to the DOI 10.1017/9781009543194

First published 2025

A catalogue record for this publication is available from the British Library

A Cataloging-in-Publication data record for this book is available from the Library of Congress

ISBN 978-1-009-54320-0 Hardback

CONTENTS

AUTHOR NOTES

This book is a joint project by the authors. Chapters 1, 2 and 6 were written by Ulf Linderfalk. The following sections were written by Ulf Linderfalk: 'The Organization of Conferences and Workshops', 'Further Specialization', 'Scholars are Unequally Prone to Argumentative Legal Research', 'Scholars are Providers of Legal Knowledge in Different Senses', 'The Exercise of Discretion', 'The Effect of Invalid Declarations and Reservations', 'Interpretation in International Law', 'Proportionality Assessment', 'Teleological Reasoning in Treaty Interpretation', 'The Concept of a Jus Cogens Norm', 'The Concept of a Conflict of Two Rules', 'Terms That Have No Use Outside of the Activities of a Group of Specialists', 'The Clean Slate Principle' and 'The Theory of Autonomous Concepts'. The following sections were written by Eric De Brabandere: 'Specialized International Law Journal', 'The Creation of Intergovernmental Organization', 'The Work of NGOs', 'The Specialized Research Profile of International Scholars and Description of Chairs', 'The Function Ascribed to the Judiciary: Judicial Activism', 'The Function Ascribed to the Judiciary: Developing the Law', 'Predictability and Legal Certainty', 'The Principle of Sustainable Development', 'Amicus Curiae Briefs', 'Jura Novit Curia', 'Incidental Jurisdiction', 'The Concept of Effective Control', 'Compensation and the Ways of Calculating Interest', 'Arguments of "Soft Law" in Legal Reasoning' and 'Arguments of Justice'.

ABBREVIATIONS

AB	World Trade Organization Appellate Body
ACCA	Associations communales de chasse agréées
BBNJ	Biodiversity of Areas Beyond National Jurisdiction
BIT	bilateral investment treaty
CIEL	Centre for International Environmental Law
CoE	Council of Europe
DSU	World Trade Organization Dispute Settlement Understanding
ECHR	European Convention on Human Rights
ECJ	European Court of Justice
ECOSOC	Economic and Social Council
ECtHR	European Court of Human Rights
EJIL	*European Journal of International Law*
ESIL	European Society of International Law
FYROM	Former Yugoslav Republic of Macedonia
ICC	International Criminal Court
ICCPR	International Covenant on Civil and Political Rights
ICJ	International Court of Justice
ICSID	International Centre for Settlement of Investment Disputes
ICTY	International Criminal Tribunal for the Former Yugoslavia
IHL	international humanitarian law
IIA	international investment agreement
ILC	International Law Commission
IPCC	Intergovernmental Panel on Climate Change
ISDS	investor–state dispute settlement
IUU	illegal, unreported and unregulated
JICJ	*Journal of International Criminal Justice*
MoU	memorandum of understanding
NGO	non-governmental organization
PCIJ	Permanent Court of International Justice
RFMO	regional fisheries management organization
SCC	Stockholm Chamber of Commerce
UN	United Nations

UNCITRAL	United Nations Commission on International Trade Law
UNCLOS	United Nations Convention on the Law of the Sea
UNCTAD	United Nations Conference on Trade and Development
VCLT	Vienna Convention on the Law of Treaties
WG III	UNCITRAL Working Group III
WILNET	Women in International Law Network
WTO	World Trade Organization

1

The Concept of a Special Regime

1.1 There Can Be No Special Regime Without a Theory of Law

Over the last thirty or so years, international law and legal practice have become increasingly more specialized and diversified. As stated by the ILC Study Group on Fragmentation of International Law in its Final Report of 2006:

> What once appeared to be governed by 'general international law' has become the field of operation for such specialist systems as 'trade law', 'human rights law', 'environmental law', 'law of the sea', 'European law' and even such exotic and highly specialized knowledge as 'investment law' or 'international refugee law' etc.[1]

In response to these developments, international lawyers have coined a new term. They now widely refer to international trade law, international human rights law, international environmental law and many others as 'special regimes'.[2]

[1] Fragmentation of International Law: Difficulties Arising from the Diversification and Expansion of International Law, Report of the Study Group prepared for the Fifty-eighth session of the International Law Commission, 1 May–9 June and 3 July–11 August 2006, U.N. Doc. A/CN.4/L.682, Corr. 1 and Add. 1, at 10.

[2] See, for example, Gerhard Hafner, 'Pros and Cons Ensuing from Fragmentation of International Law' (2004) 25 *Michigan Journal of International Law* 849–863; Stephen Humphreys, 'Climate Change: Too Complex for a Special Regime' (2016) 34 *Journal of Energy & Natural Resources Law* 51–56; Daniel Joyner and Marco Roscini (eds.), *Non-Proliferation Law as a Special Regime: A Contribution to Fragmentation Theory in International Law* (Cambridge: Cambridge University Press, 2012); Martti Koskenniemi, 'The Politics of International Law' (2009) 20 *European Journal of International Law* 7–19; Marie-Thérèse Lanquetin, 'L'égalité entre hommes et femmes dans le régime spécial de retraite de fonctionnaires' (2002) 2 *Droit social* 178–199; Daniel Moeckli, 'The Emergence of Terrorism as a Distinct Category of International Law' (2008) 44 *Texas International Law Journal* 157–183; Kurt Siehr, 'A Special Regime for Cultural Objects in Europe' (2003) 8 *Uniform Law Review* 551–564; Bruno Simma and Dirk Pulkowski, 'Of Planets and the Universe: Self-Contained Regimes in International Law' (2006) 17 *European Journal of International Law* 483–529; Raphaël van Steenberghe, *Droit international humanitaire.*

When lawyers refer to a legal branch such as trade law or human rights law as a 'special regime', they are thinking of it as a subpart of the international legal system. This was the approach of the ILC Study Group on Fragmentation of International Law,[3] and it has since also been the approach of the international scholars who have written on the topic.[4] Thus, for every instance in which the term is being used, it expresses an idea of the international legal system. This idea is markedly different from the one that traditionally dominated international legal thinking. International lawyers no longer conceive of the international legal system as an indivisible whole, but divide it into separate segments in their descriptions.[5] Academics are struggling to understand this new construction of the international legal system. It raises a series of critical questions. For example, what is the relationship between the different subparts of the international legal system – between the special regimes and the remainder of international law, and between the special regimes among themselves? And how can the development towards an increasingly more specialized and diversified international law be combined with the fundamental idea of international law as a single legal system? These questions prompt further inquiries into the concept of a special regime.

In an inquiry into a legal concept such as that of a special regime,[6] a researcher's focus is on two questions in particular. The first question is what it is that identifies a phenomenon as one that belongs to the *extension* of the investigated concept – that comes within its scope. According to the ontology adopted in this book, a concept is the generalized idea of an empirical or normative phenomenon or state of affairs or a class of such phenomena or states of affairs.[7] As implied by the word 'generalized', concepts are formed through a process of abstraction. They are the result of the ability of the human brain to perceive of particular

Un regime special de droit international? (Bruxelles: Bruylant, 2013); Jorge Viñuales, 'Cartographies imaginaires: Observations sur la portée juridique du concept de 'régime spécial' en droit international' (2013) 140 *Journal du droit international* 405–425. See also Fragmentation of International Law, U.N. Doc. A/CN.4/L.682, 37.

3 Fragmentation of International Law, U.N. Doc. A/CN.4/L.682, 10.

4 For references, see above, Note 2.

5 Fragmentation of International Law, U.N. Doc. A/CN.4/L.682, 10.

6 On the concept of a legal concept, see Ulf Linderfalk, 'The Concept of an International Legal Concept' (2023) 12 *Cambridge International Law Journal*, 177–189.

7 For an excellent overview of the research done in this field, see Eric Margolis and Stephen Laurence, 'Concepts', in Edward Zalta and Uri Nodelman (eds.), *The Stanford Encyclopedia of Philosophy* (Summer 2010 Edition), http://plato.stanford.edu/archives/sum2010/entries/concepts.

properties of phenomena as characteristics shared by all entities that belong to the extension of a concept.[8] For example, *footballs* are round or oval; they are made of leather or plastic; they weigh somewhere between 410 and 450 grams. Similarly, *the nationality of a ship* is an entitlement granted to a ship-owner by a state.[9] *High seas* are all parts of the sea that are not included in the exclusive economic zone, in the territorial sea or the internal waters of a state, or in the archipelagic waters of an archipelagic state.[10] A *jus cogens norm* is a norm accepted and recognized by the international community of states as a whole as a norm from which no derogation is permitted and which can be modified only by the creation of a new norm of *jus cogens*.[11] Properties such as these serve as criteria for the identification of an entity as one that belongs to the extension of a concept. Hence, if an object is round and made of leather, and it has a weight of something of 420 grams, it may indeed be a football. Similarly, if a sea area is not included in the exclusive economic zone, territorial sea or internal waters of a state, nor in the archipelagic waters of an archipelagic state, it may be a part of the high seas. Again, if a norm is accepted and recognized by the international community of states as a whole as a norm from which no derogation is permitted and which can be modified only by the creation of a norm of *jus cogens*, it may have the status of *jus cogens*.

A second question that any thorough investigation of a legal concept must address is the significance of having identified a phenomenon or state of affairs as one that belongs to its extension. A concept is not just a tool that human beings use to create a fair amount of order among their many beliefs about the world.[12] It is also crucial for the productivity of thought.[13] The concept of a football, for example, not only enables me to discriminate between footballs and non-footballs but also helps me draw

[8] Compare Stephen Laurence and Eric Margolis, 'Concepts and Cognitive Science', in Eric Margolis and Stephen Laurence (eds.), *Concepts: Core Readings* (Cambridge: The MIT Press, 1999), 3–81.

[9] Compare United Nations Convention on the Law of the Sea, Montego Bay, 10 December 1982, in force 16 November 1994, 1833 U.N.T.S. 397, Art. 91.

[10] Compare ibid., at Art. 86.

[11] See common Art. 53 of the 1969 and 1986 Vienna Conventions on the Law of Treaties. Vienna Convention on the Law of Treaties, Vienna, 23 May 1969, in force 27 January 1980, 1155 U.N.T.S. 331; Vienna Convention on the Law of Treaties Between States and International Organizations or Between International Organizations, Vienna, 21 March 1986, not in force, (1986) 25 ILM 543.

[12] See Margolis and Laurence, 'Concepts'.

[13] Ibid.

inferences about footballs.[14] If I identify some certain object as a football, I may infer from this observation that the object may be put to use in a game of football; that the object, in order to be of good use, should be inflated to a certain pressure; that the object will not seriously hurt me if I kick or head it; that the object, if I kick it hard, will easily go through a glass window; and so forth. Similarly, if I identify an area (A) as a part of the high seas, I may immediately infer that, according to international law, all states have the right to navigate in this area; that fishing in area A does not come under the exclusive jurisdiction of any state; that in area A, enforcement jurisdiction may only be exercised by the flag state, save in exceptional circumstances; and so forth.[15]

These simple observations point out the direction that any thorough investigation of the concept of a special regime must take. In this investigation, emphasis will need to be on the below two questions:

Question (1): What are the defining features that allow international lawyers to think about a segment of the international legal system as a special regime separate from other special regimes and from general international law?

Question (2): What is the significance of having identified a segment of the international legal system as a special regime?

Since, for all lawyers, a special regime is a segment of the international legal system, any answer to Question (1) presupposes some idea of how this system is constructed – it presupposes a conception of an international legal system. This close relationship between the concept of a special regime and lawyers' conception of an international legal system makes the question more difficult than it may appear at first glance. International lawyers not only have one conception of an international legal system, but several of them. These different conceptions derive from different theories of law.[16] Hence, responses to Question (1) will inevitably vary depending on the particular theory of law that the respondent presupposes.

Responses to Question (2) are similarly conditional upon the presupposition of a theory of law. This is so because the practical significance of having identified an entity as one that belongs to the extension of a concept is dependent on the defining features of this concept. Thus, it is

[14] Ibid.

[15] Compare Part VII of the United Nations Convention on the Law of the Sea.

[16] Ulf Linderfalk, *The International Legal System as a System of Knowledge* (Cheltenham: Edward Elgar Publishing Limited, 2022), 19–38.

because footballs are thought of as objects weighing somewhere between 410 and 450 grams that I may infer about an object identified as a football that it will easily go through a glass window if I kick it hard. It is because the high seas are thought of as areas open for all states to use that I may infer about an area identified as high seas that fishing in this area does not come under the exclusive jurisdiction of any individual state. The significance of having identified a segment of the international legal system as a special regime is similarly dependent on the feature or features that define it as precisely such as regime. Thus, if lawyers have different ideas of what it is that defines a segment of the international legal system as a special regime, they will also have different ideas of the practical significance of having identified such a segment as one that fits the presupposed definition.

As evident, there can be no concept of a special regime without a theory of law. Whether you are interested in establishing the criteria that define a segment of the international legal system as a special regime, or the significance of having so identified it, the theory of law that you bring to bear on this investigation will determine its outcome. In the subsequent Sections 1.2 and 1.3, we will explore the further implications of this dependence.

1.2 The Defining Features of a Special Regime

What are the features that define a segment of the international legal system as a special regime? There are essentially three different ways of answering this question. Each answer corresponds to a distinct theory of international law.

A first way of conceiving of the defining features of a special regime is that associated with exclusive legal positivism.[17] Exclusive legal positivism is founded on two fundamental tenets, sometimes referred to as the pedigree and separation theses.[18] According to the pedigree thesis, legal norms can be identified by their pedigree and source of origin.[19] According to the separation thesis, law exists irrespective of its moral

[17] On the distinction between exclusive and inclusive legal positivism, see, for example, Kenneth Himma, 'Legal Positivism', in *Internet Encyclopedia of Philosophy*, https://iep.utm.edu/legalpos.

[18] Ibid.

[19] See, for example, G. J. H. Van Hoof, *Rethinking the Source of International Law* (Deventer: Kluwer Law and Taxation Publishers, 1983), 36.

and other merits.[20] The combination of these two theses explains the positivist's conception of a legal system. For exclusive legal positivism, law exists only as part of a legal system.[21] A legal system is a system of norms. These norms serve as reasons for action and bases for the justification of legal decisions. They are organized along chains of authority – according to the way in which they confer authority upon each other.[22] For an exclusive legal positivist, since a legal system provides itself the conditions for the existence of its norms, there is nothing outside of these chains of authority that we can refer to as law.[23] Legal norms are the only constitutive elements of law.

In a chain of authority, a 'superior' norm provides only a reason of validity, but does not itself provide the contents of the norm or norms that are 'inferior' to it.[24] Hence, the relations between norms are purely formal.[25] They are conditioned only by the pedigree of norms and their logical form. This means that, ultimately, from the point of view of exclusive legal positivism, law is nothing but a logical framework. It remains to be furnished with substantial contents drawn from social facts,[26] such as the conclusion of an agreement creating an international organization, or the adoption of a resolution by an organ of this organization. Importantly, these facts are themselves not included in the concept of law.

Since, for exclusive legal positivism, the international legal system is a system of norms, a special regime too must be a system of norms, or else it cannot be a segment of the international legal system. These norms relate to each other as units in a logical system. This is not to say that a special regime is ever 'self-contained',[27] in the sense of a collection of norms that are all analytically separate from all norms that are not comprised by this regime. The way positivists conceive of a legal norm, there can be no such impermeable boundaries between collections of

[20] Ibid.

[21] See, for example, Mario Prost, *The Concept of Unity in Public International Law* (Oxford: Hart, 2012), 73.

[22] See Hans Kelsen, *Pure Theory of Law*, Max Knight (translator), 2nd edition (Berkeley: University of California Press, 1967), 221–222.

[23] Prost, *The Concept of Unity*, 73.

[24] The words 'superior' and 'inferior', in this context, have nothing to do with any hierarchy of norms.

[25] See Michael Green, 'Hans Kelsen and the Logic of Legal Systems' (2003) 54 *Alabama Law Review* 365–413.

[26] Ibid.

[27] On this concept, see *United States Diplomatic and Consular Staff in Tehran (United States v. Iran)* [1980] I.C.J. Rep. 3, para. 41.

norms.[28] Neither is a special regime self-contained, in the sense of a collection of norms, which derive from an entirely distinct set of legal sources, unknown to other parts of international law, or which have no logical connection to norms that do not belong to that collection.[29] If that had indeed been the case, we would not be able to speak any more about a special regime as an integral part of the international legal system. Instead, we would have had to deal with it as a legal system of its own.

As we have to conclude, then, a special regime is for exclusive legal positivism a collection of norms, the pedigree or logical structure of which somehow distinguishes it from other parts of international law with respect to some, *but not all,* of its several features.[30] For an example that would seem to fit this description, consider diplomatic law. This law has a very distinct form, structured, as it is, based on a relationship between a sending and receiving state.[31] Similarly, positivists would no doubt conceive of European human rights law as a special regime, if by 'European human rights' we understand the collection of all norms that come within the jurisdiction of the European Court of Human Rights. For an even clearer example, think of the law of the United Nations, which can be conceived of as a collection of norms, which all have their basis in the Charter of this organization, directly or indirectly.

A second way of conceiving the defining features of a special regime is that of American legal realism.[32] American legal realists accept the description of the international legal system as a collection of norms. By a norm, however, realists understand something other than the legal positivists. Realists reject the existence of norms in the sense of objective reasons for action and as bases for justification of legal decisions.[33]

[28] See Ulf Linderfalk, 'The Legal Consequences of *Jus Cogens* and the Individuation of Norms' (2020) 33 *Leiden Journal of International Law* 893–909. For legal positivism, a norm is complete if, and only if, it provides a description of: (i) the specific kind of conduct or state of affairs being prescribed, prohibited, or permitted (as the case may be); and (ii) each and every single condition, of which the prescription, prohibition, or permission is dependent.

[29] Compare Simma and Pulkowski, 'Of Planets and the Universe', 483–529.

[30] See Linderfalk, *The International Legal System*, 109–119.

[31] See Vienna Convention on Diplomatic Relations, Vienna, 18 April 1961, in force 24 April 1964, 500 U.N.T.S. 95; Vienna Convention on Consular Relations, Vienna, 24 April 1963, in force 19 March 1967, 596 U.N.T.S. 261.

[32] On American legal realism, see, for example, Michael Green, 'Legal Realism as a Theory of Law' (2005) 46 *William and Mary Law Review* 1915–2000.

[33] Ibid., at 1936.

For them, a legal norm is a piece of language, which guides the behaviour of its addressees because of its grammatical form and legal meaning, and not because it expresses any legal obligations.[34] This piece of language is not inscribed in any written legal instrument, such as a treaty or a resolution adopted by an international organization. It is essentially a prediction of how adjudicators and other legal decision-makers would generally decide.[35] This prediction may be based partly on the existence of a treaty or a resolution adopted by an international organization. Importantly, it may be constructed also on the basis of other social facts, if and to the extent that these can be thought to have an influence on legal decision-making – even though they do not express anything that the legal positivist would consider legally binding.[36]

With this approach to law, the relationship between legal norms cannot possibly pertain to their logical form. It can only pertain to their legal meaning. By the legal meaning of a norm, realists understand its relationship with what it refers to in the real world.[37] More specifically, while, for legal realists, the function of law is to cause adjudicators to change their opinions and behaviour, they identify the legal meaning of a norm with its referential function in this chain from cause to effect.[38]

For the realists, consequently, the meaning of a norm cannot be detached from the concrete situations of its application. To illustrate, consider the dispute between the Netherlands and Russia in the case of *The Arctic Sunrise*.[39] This dispute was brought before an arbitration tribunal by the Netherlands, instituting arbitral proceedings under Annex VII of the United Nations Convention on the Law of the Sea (UNCLOS).[40] A norm that is central to the consideration of this case is the one laid down in Article 92, paragraph 1 of the Convention, together with Article 58, paragraph 2:

[34] Ibid., at 1921–1925.

[35] Ibid., at 1934.

[36] Ibid.

[37] See Alf Ross, 'Tû-tû' (1956–1957) 70 *Harvard Law Review* 812–825.

[38] Ibid.

[39] Further information about the case can be obtained through the webpage of the International Tribunal of the Law of the Sea. 'The "*Arctic Sunrise*" Case (*Kingdom of the Netherlands v. Russian Federation*), Provisional Measures', www.itlos.org/en/main/cases/list-of-cases/case-no-22.

[40] Ibid.

> **Article 92, para. 1**
> Ships shall sail under the flag of one State only and, save in exceptional circumstances provided for in international treaties or in this Convention, shall be subject to its exclusive jurisdiction.
>
> **Article 58, para. 2**
> Articles 88 to 115 and other pertinent rules of international law apply to the exclusive economic zone in so far as they are not incompatible with this Part.

For the realists, this norm refers, on the one hand, to the facts, which serve as a condition for its application to the case of *The Arctic Sunrise*: Russian authorities exercised enforcement jurisdiction over a ship called *The Arctic Sunrise*; jurisdiction is exercised in the exclusive economic zone of Russia; *The Arctic Sunrise* is a ship sailing under the flag of the Netherlands. On the other hand, the norm refers to the predictable legal consequences of its application to the case at hand: arbitrators will decide that Russia is internationally responsible for having exercised enforcement jurisdiction over *The Arctic Sunrise*, and that it shall offer appropriate assurances and guarantees of non-repetition, and make full reparation for any injury caused.

This example helps to explain the realists' conception of a special regime. For the American legal realists, a special regime is a collection of norms, which address either a set of similar facts or a set of similar legal consequences.[41] To give a few concrete examples, for the realists, diplomatic law is a special regime, because it addresses diplomatic activities. International trade law is a special regime because it addresses trade across borders. International responsibility law is a special regime because it ensures the full reparation of injury caused to a state or an international organization, and the non-repetition of wrongful behaviour. International criminal law is a special regime, because it establishes individual criminal responsibility for certain acts.

A third way of conceiving the defining features of a special regime is that associated with legal idealism.[42] Legal idealism can be distinguished from legal positivism by the way in which it approaches the separation thesis. Contrary to legal positivism, legal idealism dismisses the idea that law can exist independently of its moral or other merits.[43] This position can be explained by the legal idealists' understanding of law as a social

41 See Linderfalk, *The International Legal System*, 109–119.

42 Ibid. On the concept of legal idealism, see, for example, Sean Coyle, 'Positivism, Idealism and the Rule of Law' (2006) 26 *Oxford Journal of Legal Studies* 257–288.

43 Ibid.

practice.[44] A social practice manifests itself in concrete action. One of the characteristic features of a social practice is the idea among its participants that there is something that makes this action worthwhile.[45] This is why social practices inevitably come with a normative element, which will always reflect upon participants' conception of how to properly think and do things.[46] This understanding of law comes hand in hand with a very particular attitude to the relationship between law and social order – one that is markedly different from that of the legal positivists. Whereas positivists see law as a form of social order valuable in its own right,[47] idealists do not. For legal idealists, no law can be self-justifying. If law exists, then this is always because of the presence of some or other idea, either of what law should be like, or what the legal project should achieve.[48] This fundamental idea – sometimes referred to as 'the connection thesis' – [49] is a necessary element of all legal idealists' theories of law.

To have an idea of what law should be like, or what law should achieve, is to set an ideal for the legal project.[50] As defined by legal philosophers, an ideal is a state of affairs presented by a person or a group of persons as something desirable and worth aspiring to.[51] Idealists are divided over the issue of what precisely are the ideals set for legal enterprise. Examples range from justice and the well-being of all members of the international community, to legality and the integrity of law.[52] These differences notwithstanding, legal idealists have a common conception of a legal system. They all think of a legal system as a system of norms arranged to accommodate for the one or several ideals set for the legal project. A legal norm is a reason for action and a basis for justification of legal decisions. Since ideals lack this prescriptive dimension, the logical form of a norm cannot explain the relationship between a legal norm and an ideal. This relationship can only be a matter of the efficacy of the norm relative to

[44] Ibid.

[45] See Etienne Wenger, *Communities of Practice: Learning, Meaning and Identity* (Cambridge: Cambridge University Press, 1998), 73.

[46] Ibid., at 81.

[47] See, for example, Coyle, 'Positivism, Idealism and the Rule of Law', 257–288.

[48] Ibid.

[49] See, for example, Torben Spaak, 'Realism About the Nature of Law' (2017) 30 *Ratio Juris* 75, 78.

[50] On the concept of an ideal, see Sanne Taekema, *The Concept of Ideals in Legal Theory* (The Hague: Kluwer Law International, 2010), 1–45.

[51] Ibid., at 4.

[52] See Ulf Linderfalk, *Understanding* Jus Cogens *in International Law and International Legal Discourse* (Cheltenham: Edward Elgar Publishing Limited, 2020), 53–59.

the ideal.[53] Interestingly, idealists conceive similarly of the relationship between the norms themselves. The one conclusive issue that in all cases determines this relationship is the degree to which norms help to bring about the ideal or ideals set for the legal project.[54]

Legal idealists have to align their definition of a special regime with this particular conception of an international legal system, or else a special regime cannot for them be a segment of the international legal system. This prompts them to think of a special regime as a community of practice, in the sense of Etienne Wenger: a group of people, who experience and continuously create their shared identity within larger society through engaging in and contributing to a more or less well-defined activity, much like footballers, carpenters, neurobiologists or dentists.[55] A community of practice presupposes the existence of a very particular kind of relationship between community members. According to Wenger, this relationship manifests itself in a distinct set of normative presuppositions. Applied to the concept of a special regime, thus, different international law specialists think of themselves as engaged in the pursuit of an enterprise together with different people; they have different ideas of what desirable state or states of affairs they are pursuing; they find different rhetorical tools appropriate; and so forth.

To illustrate, think of the difference between international environmental law and the law of international investment. International environmental lawyers generally think of themselves as pursuing the ideal of sustainable development,[56] whereas international investment lawyers generally do not.[57] Alternatively, think of the difference between international criminal law and the law of the European Convention on Human Rights. European human rights lawyers generally conceive of the concept of torture as necessarily involving an act of a state,[58] whereas international criminal lawyers generally do not impose this requirement.[59] Again, think of the difference between World Trade

53 Linderfalk, *The International Legal System*, 31–32.

54 Ibid.

55 See Wenger, *Communities of Practice.*

56 See, for example, Christina Voigt, *Sustainable Development as a Principle of International Law* (Leiden: Martinus Nijhoff Publishers, 2008).

57 See, for example, Manjiao Chi, *Integrating Sustainable Development in International Investment Law: Normative Incompatibility, System Integration and Governance Implications* (New York, NY: Routledge, 2018).

58 See, for example, Case 25803/94, *Selmouni v. France*, [1999] ECHR 66, para. 97.

59 See, for example, *Prosecutor v. Kunarac*, Trial Chamber, Judgement Case No. IT-96-23-T and IT-96-23/1-T, 22 February 2001, para. 496.

Organization (WTO) law and the law of the European Convention on Human Rights. WTO lawyers have been generally critical of the few cases, in which the WTO Appellate Body conducted a proportionality assessment to determine the legality of the imposition of a safeguard.[60] This way of approaching safeguards, they say, implies a change of the clear intention of the drafters of the relevant treaty texts.[61] European human rights lawyers have no similar qualms about the practice of the European Court of Human Rights, which regularly resorts to the proportionality principle to determine whether human rights restrictions are consistent with the European Convention.[62] Legal idealists would explain all these differences of attitude as characteristic traits of different special regimes.

1.3 The Significance of Having Identified Something as a Special Regime

What is the significance of having identified a segment of the international legal system as a special regime? Stated in utilitarian terms, what does the concept of a special regime help doing that cannot as easily be done without it? International lawyers answer this question differently, depending on the particular theory of law that they are assuming.

For the exclusive legal positivists, the international legal system recognizes only the logical form of legal norms and their function as sources of authority of other international norms.[63] This particular conception of an international legal system comes hand in hand with a very particular idea of the function of legal concepts: concepts help us understand and describe social facts in a logically coherent fashion.[64] The particular need that the concept of a special regime helps to meet presents itself when positivists find that legal decision-makers deal differently with similar issues in different parts of legal practice. Logical coherence requires that there be a sound reason for these differences. The proposition that practices pertain to different special regimes provides such a reason.[65]

60 See, for example, Andrew Mitchell, 'Proportionality and Remedies in WTO Disputes' (2006) 17 *European Journal of International Law* 985, 1004–1008.

61 Ibid., at 1008.

62 See, for example, Benedikt Pirker, *Proportionality Analysis and Models of Judicial Review: A Theoretical and Comparative Study* (Groningen: Europa Law Publishing, 2013), 187–234.

63 See Section 1.2.

64 Linderfalk, *The International Legal System*, 109–119.

65 Ibid.

Take, for example, the UN Human Rights Committee, which in General Comment No. 24 reflected on its approach to the legal effect of invalid reservations to the International Covenant on Civil and Political Rights (ICCPR).[66] Previously, in consideration of the effect of invalid reservations to treaties generally, the International Court of Justice had stressed the principle of state consent: if a reservation to a treaty is invalid, the reserving state will not be a party to the treaty.[67] The Human Rights Committee had chosen a different approach. As it had insisted, invalid reservations to the ICCPR 'will generally be severable, in the sense that the Covenant will be operative for the reserving party without benefit of the reservation'.[68] The emphasis placed by the Committee on 'the special character of a human rights treaty' such as the ICCPR would seem to have helped to secure a sufficient amount of support for this proposition.[69]

For another example, consider the judgement of the International Court of Justice in the *Tehran Hostages Case*.[70] This judgement confirmed the claim that Iran had committed a long series of breaches of diplomatic law, including many provisions of the 1961 and 1963 Vienna Conventions on Diplomatic and Consular Relations. To establish the responsibility on Iran for these breaches, the Court explored the suggestion of the Iranian Government that its conduct might be justified as an exercise of its right to take countermeasures.[71] The right to take countermeasures entitles an injured state to take action, which is itself inconsistent with international law, to induce compliance with the several secondary obligations entailed by a wrongful act taken previously by another state.[72] It applies generally, save only for those situations where the implementation of the international responsibility of a state is governed by special rules of international law.[73] As the Court found, this

[66] Human Rights Committee, General Comment No. 24, 11 November 1994, U.N. Doc. CCPR/C/21/Rev.1/Add.6, para. 18.

[67] See *Reservations to the Convention on Genocide Advisory Opinion*, ICJ Reports 1951, p 15, at 29. See also, for example, Alain Pellet, 'Article 19: Formulation of a Reservation', in Olivier Corten and Pierre Klein (eds.), *The Vienna Conventions on the Law of Treaties: A Commentary*, vol. 1 (Oxford: Oxford University Press, 2011), 442.

[68] Human Rights Committee, General Comment No. 24, para. 18.

[69] Ibid.

[70] *United States Diplomatic and Consular Staff in Tehran*, 3.

[71] Ibid., at paras. 80–81.

[72] See Articles on the Responsibility of States for Internationally Wrongful Acts, 28 January 2002, U.N. Doc. A/RES/56/83, Annex, Art. 49.

[73] Ibid., at Art. 55.

right to take countermeasures does not apply in cases of breaches of obligations provided in Articles 41 and 55 respectively of the 1961 and 1963 Vienna Conventions. '[D]iplomatic law', the Court explained, 'itself provides the necessary means of defence against, and sanction for, illicit activities by members of diplomatic or consular missions' – in effect, the right to declare a member persona non grata, and to break off all diplomatic relations with a sending state and call for the immediate closure of its mission.[74] This finding was not self-evident, as neither of the two Vienna Conventions explicitly excludes the application of the right to take countermeasures. If you approach it from the perspective of a legal positivist, the categorization of diplomatic law as a special regime may help to secure the necessary justification. The Court itself came very close to doing precisely this when describing diplomatic law as a 'self-contained régime'.[75]

American legal realists think of international norms as pieces of language, and not in terms of the legal obligations that they express. Therefore, the significance of the concept of a special regime cannot for them have anything to do with the logical relationship between norms. It can only pertain to their legal meaning. By the legal meaning of a norm, realists understand its referential function in the chain from cause to effect – that is, from the facts that form the condition for the application of the norm, to their predictable legal consequences. If the international legal system is a collection of norms in this unorthodox sense, the significance of having identified a segment of this system as a special regime must be explained accordingly. As we conclude, the concept offers a way for the realists to conceive of legal facts and legal consequences in general terms.[76] It helps them to predict future legal decision-making and to think and talk about detected differences in legal practice in a more economic fashion than they would be able to do without it.[77]

As a simple example, consider once again the approach of the UN Human Rights Committee to the effect of invalid reservations to the ICCPR. If other human rights treaty monitoring bodies follow suit,[78] it is comparably easy to say that in human rights law, if a state has formulated

[74] *United States Diplomatic and Consular Staff in Tehran*, para. 83.

[75] Ibid., at para. 86.

[76] See Linderfalk, *The International Legal System*, 109–119.

[77] Ibid.

[78] See, for example, *Belilos v. Switzerland*, [1988] ECHR 4, paras. 50–60; Case 11.816, *Hilaire v. Trinidad and Tobago*, [2001] Inter-. Am. Ct. H.R. (ser. C) No. 80, paras. 43–98.

an invalid reservation to a treaty, it will be a party to this treaty without benefiting from the reservation.[79] It is certainly more difficult to say that this is the approach of the UN Human Rights Committee, the Committee on the Rights of the Child, the Committee on the Elimination of Women, the European Court on Human Rights, the Inter-American Courts on Human Rights, and so forth. Similarly, if the categorization of 'diplomatic law' as a self-contained regime means what the Court says, not only is there no right for Iran to take countermeasures pursuant to a violation of Articles 41 and 55 of the two Vienna Conventions by the United States. There is no right for *any* receiving state to take countermeasures pursuant to *any* violation of *any* sending state of *any* provision of those two conventions. If this proposition is indeed correct, there can be no objection to the Court's way of presenting its conclusion. The alternative would be to think of the issue as one that concerns single states and single provisions of the two Vienna Conventions, which certainly requires a more elaborate description of the relationship between diplomatic law and the law of countermeasures.

For legal idealists, the mere existence of an international legal discourse manifests a commitment on the part of all its participants – a willingness to give time and energy to the realization of some presupposed legal ideal or ideals. From the point of view of legal idealists, the concept of a special regime helps to understand and describe social facts in a way that coheres with this commitment. International criminal lawyers may be using a different definition of the concept of torture than European human rights lawyers,[80] for example. Similarly, environmental lawyers may be more inclined than international investment lawyers to understand legal texts in the light of the principle of sustainable development.[81] Legal idealists would justify these differences in terms of the efficacy of international law. As they would contend, if the practice of international norms is to be of any help for the realization of the presupposed legal ideal or ideals, we have to accept that different contexts of law sometimes require different solutions to similar problems.

[79] See, for example, Bruno Simma and Gleider Hernández, 'Legal Consequences of an Impermissible Reservation to a Human Rights Treaty: Where Do We Stand?', in Enzo Cannizzaro (ed.), *The Law of Treaties Beyond the Vienna Convention* (Oxford: Oxford University Press, 2011), 60–85.

[80] See, for example, *Prosecutor v. Kunarac*, paras. 465–497.

[81] See, for example, Chi, *Integrating Sustainable Development.*

1.4 The Objective of This Book

The previous two sections of this chapter demonstrated the multifarious nature of the concept of a special regime. For the same reasons as lawyers disagree about the proper definition of the concept of international law, they conceive differently of the concept of a special regime. Sections 1.2 and 1.3 highlighted altogether three such conceptions:

1. A *special regime* is a collection of norms, the pedigree or logical form of which somehow distinguishes it from other parts of international law with respect to some, but not all, of its several features. The concept helps international lawyers to understand and to describe social facts in a logically coherent fashion.
2. A *special regime* is a collection of norms, which address either a set of similar facts, or a set of similar legal consequences. The concept helps international lawyers to think and talk about detected differences in legal practice in an economic fashion.
3. A *special regime* is a community of practice in the sense of Etienne Wenger – it is distinguishable because of the normative presuppositions of community members. The concept helps international lawyers to understand and describe social facts in a way that coheres with their commitment to give time and energy to the realization of some presupposed legal ideal or ideals.

To facilitate easy reference, we will refer to these as 'the legal positivist's', 'the legal realist's' and 'the legal idealist's' conception, respectively.

If we isolate these conceptions from the theories of law, with which they are associated,[82] they are not in all cases mutually exclusive. Thus, in single instances, when you apply two or more of the three conceptions to categorize a segment of the international legal system, it is fully possible that they lead to the same conclusion. One example would be diplomatic law, which is a special regime, whether you apply the legal positivist's or the legal realist's conception of a special regime.[83] This observation tells us something important about the deep structure of the three conceptions. If there are differences among them, it is not because they insist upon different understandings of identical facts. It is because they place their emphasis on different aspects of legal structure and because they further the realization of different results. The legal positivist's

[82] See, for example, Linderfalk, *The International Legal System*, 109–119.
[83] See Section 1.2.

conception stresses the formal relationship between legal norms. It serves to maintain the logical coherence of the international legal system. The legal realist's conception stresses the relationship between legal norms and what they refer to in the real world. It serves to facilitate thought about facts and legal consequences in general terms, which seems to be necessary if predictions of future legal decisions are to be at all possible. The legal idealist's conception emphasizes the relationship between the human beings that are engaged with understanding, discussing and applying legal norms. It serves to promote the efficacy of international law relative to the legal ideal that they assume.

The different emphasis of the three conceptions make them unequally suited to manage and control the effect of legal fragmentation – yet another phenomenon associated with the increased specialization and diversification of international law.[84] Fragmentation of international law has been a much-discussed issue among international lawyers and scholars, all since the mid-1990s.[85] Discussions led the International Law Commission (ILC) to include the topic on its agenda of work and to establish a group for the purpose of conducting a study on the topic.[86] In parallel to the work of the ILC, scholars published a long series of articles and monographs addressing particular issues raised by the trend of seeing a fragmenting international law.[87] This research – much like the

[84] Fragmentation of International Law, U.N. Doc. A/CN.4/L.682.

[85] See, for example, Mads Andenäs and Eirik Björge (eds.), *A Farewell to Fragmentation: Reassertion and Convergence in International Law* (Cambridge: Cambridge University Press, 2015); L. Barnhoorn and Karel Wellens (eds.), *Diversity in Secondary Rules and the Unity of International Law* (Den Haag: Nijhoff, 1995); Andreas Fisher-Lescano and Gunther Teubner, 'Regime Collisions: The Vain Search for Legal Unity in the Fragmentation of Global Law' (2004) 25 *Michigan Journal of International Law* 999–1046; Chiara Giorgetti and Mark Pollack (eds.), *Beyond Fragmentation: Cross-Fertilization, Co-operation and Competition among International Courts and Tribunals* (Cambridge: Cambridge University Press, 2022); Martti Koskenniemi and Päivi Leino, 'Fragmentation of International Law: Post-Modern Anxieties' (2005) 15 *Leiden Journal of International Law* 553–579; Ulf Linderfalk, 'Cross-Fertilisation in International Law' (2015) 84 *Nordic Journal of International Law* 428–455; Andreas Paulus, 'Jus Cogens in a Time of Hegemony and Fragmentation' (2005) 74 *Nordic Journal of International Law* 297–334; Serge Sur, 'The State between Fragmentation and Globalization' (1997) 8 *European Journal of International Law* 421–434; Margaret Young (ed.), *Regime Interaction in International Law: Facing Fragmentation* (Cambridge: Cambridge University Press, 2012).

[86] Report of the International Law Commission, Fifty-fourth Session, 29 April–7 June and 22 July–16 August 2002, U.N. Doc. A/57/10, paras. 492–494.

[87] See, for example, Anja Lindroos, 'Addressing Norm Conflicts in a Fragmented Legal System: The Doctrine of *Lex Specialis*' (2005) 74 *Nordic Journal of International Law*

work of the ILC Study Group – concentrated mainly on the formal relationships that exist between rules of international law, and on phenomena such as legal hierarchy, the resolution of normative conflicts, the filling of legal gaps, the systemic interpretation of treaties, and the possibility of review of international legal decisions. It paid little attention to the more acute issue of 'cross-border' communication. Because of the increasing specialization and diversification of international law, specialists are experiencing increasingly greater difficulty in understanding the reasoning of other specialists and their particular solutions to legal problems. Generalists are having similar problems in understanding the specialists, and vice versa. This is the real threat posed by a fragmenting international law and legal practice. When lawyers cannot understand each other any more, all that they will see is incorrect thought and behaviour. It is at this point that lawyers start seriously questioning the fundamental idea of international law as a single legal system.[88]

To improve communication across borders of different regimes, a doctrine must be developed that can explain why, sometimes, specialists in different fields of law do similar things differently. The legal positivist's and legal realist's conceptions of a special regime cannot perform this task. The positivist's conception directs attention to the formal relationship between legal norms. Its explanation as to why different specialists prefer different solutions is that they are dealing with norms with partly different logical structures or pedigrees. The realist's conception directs attention to the referential meaning of legal norms. Its explanation is that

27–66; Rüdiger Wolfrum and Nele Matz, *Conflicts in International Environmental Law* (Berlin: Springer, 2003); Campbell McLachlan, 'The Principle of Systemic Integration and Article 31(3)(c) of the Vienna Convention' (2005) 54 *International and Comparative Law Quarterly* 279–320; Alexander Orakhelashvili, *Peremptory Norms in International Law* (Oxford: Oxford University Press, 2006); Paulus, 'Jus Cogens', 297–334; Joost Pauwelyn, *Conflict of Norms in Public International Law* (Cambridge: Cambridge University Press, 2003); Dinah Shelton, 'Normative Hierarchy in International Law' (2006) 100 *American Journal of International Law* 291–323; Simma and Pulkowski, 'Of Planets and the Universe', 483–529; Christian Tams, *Enforcing Obligations* Erga Omnes *in International Law* (Cambridge: Cambridge University Press, 2005); Erich Vranes, 'The Definition of 'Norm Conflict' in International Law and Legal Theory' (2006) 17 *European Journal of International Law* 395–418.

[88] The International Law Commission Study Group concludes: 'International law is a legal system'. See Fragmentation of International Law: Difficulties Arising from the Diversification and Expansion of International Law, Report of the Study Group prepared for the Fifty-eighth session of the International Law Commission, 1 May–9 June and 3 July–11 August 2006, U.N. Doc. A/CN.4/L.702, at 7.

different specialists are dealing with norms that address different categories of facts or legal consequences. Both explanations beg further questions. They do not explain why the different logical structures or pedigrees of norms, or the focus of these norms on different categories of facts or legal consequences, cause specialists to prefer different solutions. They lack the depth of a sound explanation of human behaviour, for the same reason that legal positivism and legal realism do not offer any full explanations of the concept of legal obligation.[89]

The legal idealists' conception certainly does better. This conception directs attention to the relationship between the human beings that are engaged with understanding, discussing and applying legal norms. Like the legal positivist's and the legal realist's conceptions of a special regime, it provides an answer to the question of why specialists in different fields of law sometimes prefer different solutions to similar problems. The answer is that specialists operate in different social contexts. Access to the social context of human behaviour is often crucial to understanding it. Assume, for example, that in the beginning of a game of football, a TV commentator sounds off: 'United has a good bench'. Football buffs will immediately understand that the commentator is referring to the substitutes of the one team.[90] Outside of the community of football buffs, people will understand this utterance differently, and they will no doubt conceive of it as very peculiar. From the point of view of the idealist's conception, a special regime is fully comparable to the community of football buffs. If lawyers that are not themselves active in a special regime are not equipped to understand the reasoning and behaviour of those who are, this is because they do not have the same access to the social context in which these other lawyers operate. This is indeed a very plausible explanation to why different groups of lawyers have great difficulty understanding each other.

What makes the idealist's conception less appealing are the methodological problems that come with every instance of its application. Whatever conception of a special regime that you apply, your

[89] Positivists have still to answer the question: Why should a legal rule be complied with, just because it can be traced back to a source of law recognized by the basic criteria of the legal system? Realists owe an answer to an equally critical question: why should a legal decision-maker decide as the legal realists predict that legal decision-makers in a jurisdiction generally would?

[90] I admit to having used this example before. See Ulf Linderfalk, 'Proportionality and International Legal Pragmatics' (2020) 89 *Nordic Journal of International Law* 432.

categorization of a segment of the international legal system as a special regime will raise a very particular question of justification: how can you support your suggestion that this segment is a special regime? Confronted with this question, the positivist's conception will direct your attention to the pedigree and logical structure of norms. It will allow you to justify your suggestion easily by reference to legal norms and norms of deontic logic. The realist's conception, for its part, will direct your attention to legal facts and their predictable legal consequences. It, too, will allow you to justify your suggestion easily. Justification will require no more than a reference to earlier legal decisions, coupled with the assumption that future legal decision-makers will decide according to the patterns that these earlier decisions establish. The important point that we are trying to make is that the idealist's conception presupposes a methodology of a very different kind, directing attention, as it does, to social context. Many international lawyers and scholars would conceive of this focus of the conception as a problem. They would consider themselves ill-equipped to engage with any relationship between human beings and the social context in which they operate. As these lawyers would insist, such engagement requires the methodology and expertise of a sociologist.

There are strong reasons against this position. Not only does the idealist's conception have great explanatory value. It is also not correct that the application of this definition presupposes the use of sociological methods – methods that the legal scholar is not used or equipped to employ. As we, the authors of this book, maintain, the task of establishing the social context characterizing a special regime is not significantly different from many investigations that classically trained legal scholars are already conducting, more or less as a matter of course. It is the objective of this book to establish this one proposition.

The book offers an explanatory framework for understanding the significance of disciplinary boundaries in international law. As should be clearly understood, we do not as such endorse any particular theory of international law. If our preferences are with the legal idealist's conception of a special regime, it is because it helps to answer the question of why specialists in different fields of law sometimes prefer different solutions to similar problems. In fact, the legal idealist's conception of a special regime has the great advantage of being compatible with all of the legal positivist's, legal realist's and legal idealist's conceptions of an international legal system. This will transpire from subsequent chapters.

Our writing will proceed in three steps. In a first step, we will explore how Etienne Wenger's theory of communities of practice translates to the context of international law and the concept of a special regime. According to Wenger, a community of practice is defined by the presence of three structural elements: there must be a mutual engagement of community members; community members must be engaged in a joint enterprise; and they must have a shared repertoire.[91] As we will explain, this can be interpreted to mean that in different special regimes:

1. Community members think of themselves as engaged in the pursuit of an enterprise together with different people.
2. Community members think of themselves as pursuing different states of affairs than that which other international lawyers pursue, and they have a different idea of the proper way to perform assignments.
3. Community members have different opinions about the appropriateness of different intellectual tools, such as forms of argumentation, legal terminologies and legal concepts.[92]

In a second step, we will draw up the contours of a methodology that will help the classically trained legal scholars to establish such normative presuppositions. To cut the story short, our suggestion is that they be studied as implicit in the actual conduct of community members, based on the assumption that these specialists act rationally and that they recognize the appropriateness of their own action. This methodology is not significantly different from the way in which international courts establish the *opinio juris* of states, or the way in which legal scholars establish a court's understanding of rules of international law.

In a third and last step of writing, we will conduct case studies that will help to illustrate the practical operation of our proposed methodology. Case studies will be organized around the below three sets of questions:

- What is the engagement of the selected community of international law specialists? How does this engagement compare with that of other communities of international lawyers?
- What desirable states of affairs are the selected community of international law specialists pursuing? How do these states of affairs compare with those pursued by other communities of international lawyers?

[91] Wenger, *Communities of Practice*.

[92] See Section 2.2.

- What rhetorical tools does the selected community of international law specialists consider appropriate? How do these rhetorical tools compare with those that other communities of international lawyers consider appropriate?

The first and second steps correspond to Chapter 2. The third step corresponds to Chapters 3–5. In the concluding Chapter 6, we will reflect on the question of how the development towards an increasingly more specialized and diversified international law can be combined with the fundamental idea of international law as a single legal system.

2

Special Regimes as Communities of Practice

2.1 The Theory of Communities of Practice

Colleagues in the field describe Etienne Wenger as an educational theorist. He is best known for his work on communities of practice and for the book that he published on this topic, *Communities of Practice*, in 1998.[1] This book will be the focus of our further investigations of the legal idealist's conception of a special regime.

Wenger's book introduces a new perspective to the understanding and further study of the activity that people refer to as *learning*. 'Our institutions,' Wenger explains, 'are largely based on the assumption that learning is an individual process, that it has a beginning and an end, that it is best separated from the rest of our activities, and that it is the result of teaching.'[2] Wenger's perspective is another. For him, learning is a social phenomenon:[3] it is an enterprise that people pursue in the context of the activities of some or other social community. Dentistry, for example, is learned relative to the activities of dentists; law is learned relative to the activities of lawyers and adjudicators; carpentry is learned relative to the activities of carpenters. Social communities of this kind are not formed by coincidence. As Wenger argues, they come into being because of the engagement of their members in a common enterprise – dentistry, law, carpentry, and so forth – manifested, among other things, in their contributions to a practice.[4]

This idea reflects Wenger's assumptions about the nature of knowledge and what learning is eventually all about:

> (1) We are social beings. Far from being trivially true, this fact is a central aspect of learning.

[1] Etienne Wenger, *Communities of Practice: Learning, Meaning and Identity* (Cambridge: Cambridge University Press, 1998).

[2] Ibid., at 3.

[3] Ibid.

[4] Ibid., at 6–7.

(2) Knowledge is a matter of competence with respect to valued enterprises – such as singing in tune, discovering scientific facts, fixing machines, writing poetry, being convivial, growing up as a boy or a girl and so forth.
(3) Knowing is a matter of participating in the pursuit of such enterprises, that is, of active engagement in the world.
(4) Meaning – our ability to experience the world and our engagement with it as meaningful – is ultimately what learning is to produce.[5]

These assumptions form the basis for his theory, which characterizes learning as participation in the practice of a social community.

Participation in the practice of a social community is a form of belonging, Wenger argues. Not only does it affect what people do, and how they do what they do, but it is also an important factor in the development of their identities.[6] Based on this assumption, Wenger suggests that we look upon learning as a process that has altogether four necessary components:

(1) *Meaning*: a way of talking about our (changing) ability – individually and collectively – to experience our life and the world as meaningful.
(2) *Practice*: a way of talking about the shared historical and social resources, frameworks and perspectives that can sustain mutual engagement in action.
(3) *Community*: a way of talking about the social configuration in which our enterprises are defined as worth pursuing and our participation is recognizable as competence.
(4) *Identity*: a way of talking about how learning changes who we are and creates personal histories of becoming in the context of our communities.[7]

The concept of a community of practice serves to incorporate all these components, while at the same time embedding it in familiar experience. As Wenger reminds us, communities of practice are an integral part of most people's lives:

> Across a worldwide web of computers, people congregate in virtual spaces and develop shared ways of pursuing their common interests. In offices, computer users count on each other to cope with the intricacies of obscure systems. In neighbourhoods, youths gang together to configure their life on the street and their sense of themselves.[8]

[5] Ibid., at 4.
[6] Ibid.
[7] Ibid., at 5.
[8] Ibid., at 6–7.

This familiarity of the concept of communities of practice is what makes it so attractive. By systematically exploring it, Wenger has developed it into a useful tool for academic thinking.

Each of the four components of Wenger's theory requires further clarification to make it useful for our further consideration of the legal idealist's conception of a special regime. First is the concept of a *practice.* A practice, in the sense of Wenger, originates in the pursuit of a group of individuals of some common enterprise.[9] This pursuit requires that individuals interact, and this, in turn, forces them to modify, to some degree, their relations with each other to accommodate the needs of their common pursuit.[10] It also gradually changes how individuals understand and interact with their factual environment.[11] Bit by bit, they learn how to do things. Over time, this collective learning results in a practice, which reflects not only the pursuit of the many individuals involved but also how they perceive each other and their factual environment.[12] In the sense of Wenger, a practice is what dentists, lawyers, carpenters and other groups of people develop in doing their jobs.[13] This practice includes both the explicit and the tacit:

> It includes the language, tools, documents, images, symbols, well-defined roles, specified criteria, codified procedures, regulations and contracts that various practices make explicit for a variety of purposes. But it also includes all the implicit relations, tacit conventions, subtle cues, untold rules of thumb, recognizable intuitions, specific perceptions, well-tuned sensitivities, embodied understandings, underlying assumptions, and shared world-views.[14]

A second component of Wenger's theory is the concept of *meaning.* Wenger's interest is not so much in the concept of meaning as such as in its role in the process of learning. Since a practice, for Wenger, is a process by which people can experience the world and their engagement with it as meaningful, the important question for him is how a practice can bring about meaning.[15] Wenger responds by appealing once again to

[9] Ibid., at 45.
[10] Ibid.
[11] Ibid.
[12] Ibid.
[13] Ibid., at 47.
[14] Ibid.
[15] Ibid., at 51.

the social element: meaning is created through a combination of what he refers to as 'participation' and 'reification'.[16]

'Participation', in this terminology, presupposes not just action but also social connection. It stands for the experiences that come from membership in social communities and active involvement in the social enterprises that social communities pursue.[17] This definition makes participation a very wide-ranging concept indeed. In the sense of Wenger, '[i]t is a complex process that combines doing, talking, feeling, and belonging'.[18] It is not synonymous with collaboration, he explains – it 'involves all kinds of relations, conflictual as well as harmonious, intimate as well as political, competitive as well as cooperative'.[19] Neither is it limited to a direct engagement in specific activities with specific people.[20] Claims processors, for example, 'are not claims processors just while they work in the office. Of course, that time of intense engagement with their work and with one another is especially significant. But they do not cease to be claims processors at five o'clock'.[21]

As for 'reification', it is the term that Wenger uses to represent the process by which people give form to their experience of a practice by producing 'things' that congeal it, such as abstractions, tools, terms and concepts.[22] In a community of practice, he explains, such products unavoidably affect the experience of its members in their activities and pursuits.[23] If, for example, community members are given a new tool to perform an activity, this typically changes the way in which they conceive the same activity. Similarly, if community members are given a term to denote a particular relation between those who participate in an activity, this term typically changes the way in which they conceive each other. In Wenger's terminology, this is to say that reification creates new meanings.[24] This interplay between reification and participation is an ever-continuing process: new meanings lead to further developments of the community practice, which in turn inspire new processes of reification, and so forth ad infinitum. As Wenger describes it, a community

[16] Ibid., at 52.
[17] Ibid., at 55–56.
[18] Ibid., at 56.
[19] Ibid.
[20] Ibid., at 57.
[21] Ibid.
[22] Ibid., at 58.
[23] Ibid., at 56.
[24] Ibid., at 62.

practice is a process, in which products of reification are merely 'points of focus' for further negotiation.[25] They never fully determine the experience of community members. It is in this sense that participation and reification combine to create meaning, which, in the words of Wenger, is always 'potentially expanded and potentially lost'.[26]

A third component of Wenger's theory is the concept of a *community*. The very idea of a social community presupposes the existence of a very particular kind of relationship between community members. As Wenger argues, this relationship has three distinctly different dimensions.[27] First, there must be a *mutual engagement* of community members.[28] This mutual engagement, Wenger points out, may require different things depending on the particular enterprise that engages the community.[29] For some, it may be a requirement that community members come to an office and work together in a defined physical environment. For others, such as singers or carpenters, focus is more on the performance of some presupposed task than on the place in which the task is performed. Importantly, Wenger emphasizes mutual engagement does not imply homogeneity; real-life experience indicates rather the opposite.[30] Thus, when people engage in the pursuit of a common enterprise, community members specialize and make themselves known for their different ability to do whatever their enterprise requires them to do. Without these different competences of community members, a mutual engagement would often not be possible.[31] In the sense of Wenger, consequently, mutual engagement draws upon what community members do and what they know, as much as on their ability to connect meaningfully to what they do not do and what they do not know.[32]

A community of practice, as Wenger's theory goes, also presupposes the existence of an idea among community members that they are engaged in *a joint enterprise*.[33] This enterprise is not fixed at the outset but is defined and developed by community members in the course of its pursuit. Thus, Wenger explains, the enterprise that community members

25 Ibid., at 58.
26 Ibid., at 62.
27 Ibid., at 72–73.
28 Ibid., at 73.
29 Ibid., at 74.
30 Ibid., at 75.
31 Ibid.
32 Ibid., at 76.
33 Ibid., at 77.

pursue is the result of a process of negotiation in much the same way as the experiences of meaning that it creates.[34] Community members may have different opinions on how to do things and why they do them, but they may conceive of their activities as a joint enterprise nevertheless. If an enterprise is joint, it is because it is communally negotiated.[35] Such negotiations among community members do not just define the goal of their enterprise, but they also help to develop relations of mutual accountability:

> These relations of accountability include what matters and what does not; what is important and why it is important; what to do and what to abstain from doing; what to pay attention to and what to ignore; what to talk about and what to leave unsaid; what to justify and what to take for granted; what to display and what to withhold; when actions and artefacts are good enough and when they need improvement and refinement.[36]

Such relations have considerable influence on the behaviour of community members. They explain why members sometimes feel concerned or unconcerned by sudden changes in their factual environment.[37]

A community of practice, finally, presupposes the existence of *a shared repertoire*.[38] The repertoire of a community of practice provides resources for negotiating meaning.[39] As Wenger explains:

> [it] includes routines, words, tools, ways of doing things, stories, gestures, symbols, genres, actions, or concepts that the community has produced or adopted in the course of its existence, and which has become part of its practice. The repertoire combines reificative and participative aspects. It includes the discourse by which members create meaningful statements about the world, as well as the styles by which they express their forms of membership and their identities as members.[40]

An important characteristic of a repertoire is its ambiguity.[41] This ambiguity is a double-edged sword. While it no doubt impedes effective communication and coordination of activities, as Wenger emphasizes, it also makes these processes dynamic.[42] The real problem of

[34] Ibid., at 78–79.
[35] Ibid., at 78.
[36] Ibid., at 81.
[37] Ibid.
[38] Ibid., at 82.
[39] Ibid.
[40] Ibid., at 83.
[41] Ibid.
[42] Ibid., at 83–84.

communication, he says, 'is to situate ambiguity in the context of a history of mutual engagement that is rich enough to yield an opportunity for negotiation'.[43]

A fourth component of Wenger's theory of communities of practice is the concept of *identity*.[44] Wenger's theory, no doubt, presupposes a very close relationship between identity and practice. As the author explains: 'Developing a practice requires the formation of a community whose members can engage with one another and thus acknowledge each other as participants. As a consequence, practice entails the negotiation of ways of being a person in that context.'[45] More than anything else, identity forms because of the competence that community members develop from participating in a practice.[46] Wenger analyses this competence along the same three dimensions with which he earlier examined the concept of a community. For Wenger, consequently, identity inheres in a mutuality of engagement, in the accountability to an enterprise, and in the negotiability of a repertoire:

> In a community of practice, we learn certain ways of engaging in action with other people. We develop certain expectations about how to interact, how people treat each other, and how to work together ... As an identity, this translates into a form of individuality defined with respect to a community. It is a certain way of being part of a whole through mutual engagement.
>
> ...
>
> As we invest ourselves in an enterprise, the forms of accountability through which we are able to contribute to that enterprise makes us look at the world in certain ways ... As an identity, this translates into a perspective ... [and] a tendency to come up with certain interpretations, to engage in certain actions, to make certain choices, to value certain experiences [...].
>
> ...
>
> Sustained engagement in practice yields an ability to interpret and make use of the repertoire of that practice ... As an identity, this translates into a personal set of events, references, memories and experiences that create individual relations of negotiability with respect to the repertoire of a practice.[47]

[43] Ibid., at 84.
[44] Ibid., at 145.
[45] Ibid., at 149.
[46] Ibid., at 152.
[47] Ibid., at 152–153.

That said, we can return to our study of international law. In Chapter 1, we suggested that Wenger's theory will be of good use for a description of the legal idealist's conception of a special regime. We also suggested that, contrary to first impression, the operation of this theory does not presuppose any more complicated methods than those that international lawyers are already used to applying. To justify these suggestions, we need to accomplish two tasks. The first task is to explain how Wenger's theory translates to the context of international law and how it plays out, more specifically, in an investigation of the legal idealist's conception of a special regime. The second task is to identify a methodology that international lawyers can use to establish a suggestion categorizing a segment of the international legal system as a community of practice. These tasks are still ahead of us. We will use Sections 2.2 and 2.3 to accomplish them.

2.2 Communities of Practice and International Law

Wenger's theory has four necessary components: practice, meaning, community and identity. The question we need to address is how each of these four components manifests itself in the activities of lawyers with a specialization in human rights, international criminal law, diplomatic law, and so forth. Stated more specifically:

1. In what way do the activities of lawyers with a specialization in international human rights law, international criminal law, diplomatic law, and so forth represent a practice in the sense of Wenger?
2. In what way do the activities of lawyers with a specialization in international human rights law, international criminal law, diplomatic law, and so forth engage in the negotiation of meaning?
3. In what way do lawyers with a specialization in international human rights law, international criminal law, diplomatic law, and so forth represent a community?
4. In what way do the activities of lawyers with a specialization in international human rights law, international criminal law, diplomatic law, and so forth contribute to developing their respective identities?

We will respond to these four questions in turn.

In what way do the activities of lawyers with a specialization in international human rights law, international criminal law, diplomatic law, and so forth represent a practice in the sense of Wenger? Following Wenger, a practice is what international law specialists develop in doing their jobs.[48] This definition must be articulated in a more precise form to suit the needs of our investigation. International law specialists are a heterogeneous bunch. They are accredited state representatives to international organizations and their organs; they are the officers of international organizations; they are experts appointed by international organizations to perform particular missions; they are delegates at diplomatic conferences; they are legal counsellors and legal advisers; they are judges and arbitrators; international law scholars; non-governmental organization (NGO) employees; and so forth.

Depending on the particular capacity in which an international law specialist is acting, his or her job may include the performance of many different tasks. Thus, for instance, specialists negotiate; they draft and adopt international agreements, resolutions and other similar instruments; they make oral statements; they write reports and amicus curiae briefs; they deliver written submissions; they hold and participate in plenary and committee meetings and in hearings of courts and arbitration tribunals; they plead; they adjudicate; they publish articles and monographs; they participate in academic conferences; they present papers at such conferences; and they contribute to blogs. As Wenger emphasizes, practice includes the explicit as well as the tacit.[49] For the purpose of our investigation of international law, this means that we would also have to recognize the importance of the less visible parts of the job of international law specialists. For example, specialists develop certain attitudes and mindsets; they adopt certain perspectives and approaches to the world and to their fellow specialists; they endorse and maintain certain understandings; they assume and take certain things for granted.

In what way do the activities of lawyers with a specialization in international human rights law, international criminal law, diplomatic law, and so forth engage in the negotiation of meaning? Practice is a process by which people experience the world and their engagement with it as meaningful. Wenger refers to this process as the negotiation of meaning.[50] It involves the interaction of two analytically separate processes, which Wenger calls participation and reification.[51]

Participation, in a legal context, materializes as legal discourse. Lawyers argue – this is what they do: by oral and written statements,

[48] See Section 2.1.
[49] See Section 2.1.
[50] See Section 2.1.
[51] See Section 2.1.

they seek to affect the beliefs, attitudes and behaviour of other people. Participation includes active engagement in such argumentation. More subtly, it also involves the mental state or states of affairs that participants provoke or seek to affect: approval, belief, apprehension, sympathy, endorsement, satisfaction, commitment, determination, concurrence, assent, conviction, expectation, hope, suspense, impatience, ambivalence, doubt, mistrust, disbelief, suspicion, fear, misgiving, grievance, unease, reluctance, concern, dedication, hesitation, indecision, disapproval, dissatisfaction and so forth.

Reification, Wenger explains, is the process by which community members give form to their experience of a practice by producing 'things' that congeal it.[52] In a legal context, reification immediately brings to mind the sources of law. Products of reification are practically everything that the basic criteria of the international legal system prompt lawyers to consider, such as: treaties concluded by states and international organizations; established patterns of state practice; general principles of law recognized by civilized nations; unilateral declarations of states; judicial decisions; resolutions adopted by international organizations; and draft articles and other instruments adopted by the International Law Commission. Importantly, products of reification include other kinds of output of international legal discourse: terminologies, concepts, principles, axioms, maxims, instructions, regulations, guidelines, codes of conduct, model conventions, theories, doctrines, modes of operation, general approaches, methods, ways of talking, writing and behaving more generally, ways of dressing, and so on.

In what way do lawyers with a specialization in international human rights law, international criminal law, and so forth represent a community? Characteristic of a community of practice is the existence of a very particular relationship between community members. This relationship has three different dimensions: (i) there must be a mutual engagement of community members; (ii) community members must be engaged in a joint enterprise; and (iii) they must have a shared repertoire.[53]

A *mutual engagement* is an idea among community members that they are engaged in something together. This idea can be described as a feeling of 'togetherness'. In the activities of international law specialists, this feeling manifests itself in the existence of two different phenomena. The first phenomenon is the existence of a legal discourse. It is of critical importance that specialists not only take action – such as the adoption of

[52] See Section 2.1.
[53] See Section 2.1.

international instruments, the adjudication of an international dispute, or the giving of a presentation at an academic conference – but that they do this to affect the beliefs, attitudes and behaviour of other members of the community. The second phenomenon is specialization.[54] International human rights law, international criminal law, and diplomatic law are examples of enterprises that require the involvement of different competences, much like all international law. Thus, when international law specialists ascribe different functions to different categories of community members – judges, NGOs, scholars, international organizations, and so forth – this is a clear indication of their mutual engagement.

A *joint enterprise* implies the existence of an idea among community members that certain states of affairs are desirable.[55] In the activities of international law specialists, such states of affairs may include effective political democracy,[56] respect for human dignity,[57] the effective prosecution of international crimes,[58] the maintenance of international peace and security and friendly relations among nations.[59] Every idea of the desirability of a state of affairs comes hand in hand with a mutual accountability regime,[60] which is essentially an idea of the proper way to perform assignments. In a special regime, this idea entails, more specifically: an understanding of which states of affairs community members should spend efforts improving; an understanding of which legal propositions these members should take the troubling of justifying; an understanding of which legal issues they should consider important; an understanding of the proper way to ascribe importance to different assignments; an understanding of the proper way to prioritize among different outstanding assignments; and so forth.

A *shared repertoire* provides resources for the negotiation of meaning, Wenger explains.[61] In a legal context, since law is all about argumentation,

54 See Section 2.1.
55 See Section 2.1.
56 See, for example, Statute of the Council of Europe, London, 5 May 1949, in force 3 August 1949, 87 U.N.T.S. 103, preambular para. 4.
57 See, for example, *Prosecutor v. Furundžija*, Trial Chamber, Judgment Case No. IT-95-17/1-T, 10 December 1998, para. 183.
58 See, for example, Rome Statute of the International Criminal Court, Rome, 17 July 1998, in force 1 July 2002, 2187 U.N.T.S. 3, preambular para. 4.
59 See, for example, Charter of the United Nations, San Francisco, 26 June 1945, in force 24 October 1945, XV UNCIO 335, amendments in 557 U.N.T.S. 143, 638 U.N.T.S. 308 and 892 U.N.T.S. 119, Art. 1(1)-(2).
60 See Section 2.1.
61 See Section 2.1.

the bulk of this repertoire will consist of rhetorical tools of various kinds, such as:

- *Terminologies*: the terms that specialists use, and their association of terms with certain meanings.
- *Concepts*: for example, the concept of the reasonable person,[62] or the concept of incidental jurisdiction.[63]
- *Methods*: for example, the ecosystem services approach or methodology for calculating environmental damages,[64] or the historical method used for the interpretation of treaties and other similar instruments.[65]
- *Forms of argument*: for example, arguments based on analogies,[66] or on the perceived further consequences of the application of a norm generally.[67]
- *Doctrines*: for example, the margin of appreciation doctrine,[68] or the doctrine of intertemporal law.[69]
- *Theories*: for example, the dualist and monist theories of the relation between international and domestic law,[70] or the declarative theory, according to which states can exist irrespective of other states' recognition.[71]

In what way do the activities of lawyers with a specialization in international human rights law, international criminal law, diplomatic law,

62 See, for example, Valentin Jeutner, *The Reasonable Person: A Legal Biography* (Cambridge: Cambridge University Press, 2024).

63 See, for example, *Prosecutor v. Tadić*, Appeals Chamber, Defence Motion for Interlocutory Appeal on Jurisdiction Case No. IT-94-1, 2 October 1995, para. 20.

64 See, for example, *Certain Activities Carried Out by Nicaragua in the Border Area (Costa Rica v. Nicaragua)* [2018] I.C.J. Rep. 15, paras. 45–48.

65 See, for example, Odile Ammann, *Domestic Courts and the Interpretation of International Law: Methods and Reasoning Based on the Swiss Example* (Leiden: Koninklijke Brill NV, 2020), 215.

66 See, for example, Silja Vöneky, 'Analogy in International Law', in Rüdiger Wolfrum (ed.), *The Max Planck Encyclopedia of Public International Law*, vol. 1 (Oxford: Oxford University Press, 2012), 374–380.

67 See, for example, Tim Clark, 'The Teleological Turn in the Law of International Organisations' (2021) 70 *International and Comparative Law Quarterly* 533–567.

68 See, for example, Yuval Shany, 'Towards a General Margin of Appreciation Doctrine in International Law?' (2005) 16 *European Journal of International Law* 907–940.

69 See, for example, Ulf Linderfalk, 'The Application of International Legal Norms Over Time: The Second Branch of Intertemporal Law' (2011) 58 *Netherlands International Law Review* 147–172.

70 See, for example, Peter Malanczuk, *Akehurst's Modern Introduction to International Law*, 7th edition (London: Routledge, 1997), 63–64.

71 Ibid., at 83.

and so forth help to develop their respective identities? A community practice, Wenger insists, does not just entail the negotiation of meaning. Since a practice can only exist among people, who acknowledge each other as community members, a practice also entails the negotiation of ways of being a person in that community.[72] More than anything else, identity forms because of the competence that community members develop by participating in a practice.[73] This close relationship between competence and identity helps Wenger to explain what most people experience when being exposed to a practice, with which they are themselves largely unfamiliar:

> When we come into contact with new practices, we venture into unfamiliar territory. The boundaries of our communities manifest as a lack of competence along the three dimensions I just described. We do not quite know how to engage with others. We do not understand the subtleties of the enterprise as the community has defined it. We lack the shared references that participants use. Our non-membership shapes our identities through our confrontation with the unfamiliar.[74]

Wenger does not have any particular communities in mind, but this passage feeds directly into our investigation of international law and the legal idealist's conception of a special regime. It can be argued that it is precisely because international lawyers have different identities that they have trouble communicating across the borders of different regimes.[75] Even more importantly, it can be argued that it is precisely because the identity of lawyers is at stake that their different solutions to similar legal problems cause so much contention.

2.3 In Search of an Effective Methodology

When Wenger wrote his book on communities of practice, he had his focus on the process of learning. He was interested in developing a set of concepts that he and other educational theorists could use to think systematically about learning as a social phenomenon. Our focus is different. We are in search of a methodology that international lawyers can use to provide justification for their categorization of segments of the international legal system as communities of practice. To make this search successful, we need to engage with an ontological question. Unless we

[72] See Section 2.1.
[73] See Section 2.1.
[74] Wenger, *Communities of Practice*, 153.
[75] See Section 1.4.

know the object of our study, we will not be able to assess the utility of the many methodologies that we and other legal scholars could potentially use for studying it. Hence, it will have to be our first task to make perfectly clear in what sense a community of practice can exist.

This task directs our attention to the 'eminent trio'. As Wenger argued, there can be no community of practice without a mutual engagement, a joint enterprise, and a shared repertoire.[76] It is important to understand precisely what this trio represents. Its three elements are not defining features of the concept of a community. As Wenger warned, he was not suggesting that everything that anybody might call a community is a community of practice.[77] The three elements describe the relationship that always obtains between the practice and the community in a community of practice. They are the dimensions of the social relationship that defines a multitude of people participating in a practice as precisely a community of practice. This observation is of crucial importance to understand the ontology of such a community.

A community of practice exists in the sense of a set of normative presuppositions of its members. When we explored the concept of a joint enterprise in Section 2.2, we articulated it in terms that make this explicit. We referred to it as an idea among community members that certain states of affairs are *desirable*. As we pointed out, this idea comes hand in hand with an understanding of the *proper* way to perform assignments. The other two elements of the eminent trio exist in the same sense, if not as obvious. A mutual engagement, we wrote, is a feeling of togetherness. It does not exist just because community members have a common interest. In the sense of Wenger, two individuals (A and B) are mutually engaged if, and only if, A and B both think it *desirable* that they join forces and collaborate in the pursuit of some enterprise. As for a shared repertoire, in a legal context, as we explained, it takes essentially the form of a set of rhetorical tools: terminologies, concepts, methods, forms of argument, and so forth. What we should have spelled out is that a shared repertoire is more than just a set of rhetorical tools. In the sense of Wenger, there is a shared repertoire if, and only if, community members consider the use of these tools *appropriate*. Thinking that something (*p*) is desirable, proper or appropriate is to presuppose that *p should* be the case.

[76] See Section 2.1.
[77] Wenger, *Communities of Practice*, 72.

Having made these observations, we can start the actual search of a methodology that international lawyers can use to provide justification for their categorization of segments of the international legal system as communities of practice. This search raises a general question: how do you establish the existence of a normative presupposition of a person or a group of persons? As we believe, no normative presuppositions of the members of a community of practice can themselves be observed. What can be observed are the ways in which the normative presuppositions manifest themselves in the community practice. As Wenger was careful to stress, a mutual engagement, a joint enterprise, and a shared repertoire are not phenomena that exist in a vacuum. They develop in the course of a community practice as the result of a process of negotiation, much like the meanings that participants experience. This observation implicitly provides a response to our general question. If it is through the interactions of community members that their normative presuppositions form and develop, then it is through the medium of these same interactions that these presuppositions must be studied.

This does not make the study of the existence of a community of practice sociological in nature – not if this means that international lawyers and scholars are typically not equipped to perform it. The study is not significantly different from any inquiry into the proper way to do something from the point of view of international law. We will give two examples that very neatly illustrate this proposition.

Our first example calls attention to the work of international courts and arbitration tribunals. When two states bring a dispute before an international judiciary, sometimes, the nature of this dispute imposes on this body to engage in detail with the state of customary international law. Thus, in the *Anglo-Norwegian Fisheries Case*,[78] the International Court of Justice had to establish whether customary international law allowed the method of straight baselines that Norway had used when establishing its territorial sea. The existence of a rule of customary international law requires in all cases the presence of a certain general opinion among states: an *opinio juris*. The finer details of that opinion vary with the rule that you seek to establish. What the International Court had to establish in the *Anglo-Norwegian Fisheries Case* was the presence among states of the opinion that customary international law allowed Norway to use its method of straight baselines.

[78] *Anglo-Norwegian Fisheries Case (United Kingdom v. Norway)* [1951] I.C.J. Rep. 116.

Executing this task, the Court pointed to the relevance of the actions and omissions of all states involved. To cut the story short, it noted, first, that Norwegian authorities had applied their system of delimitation of the territorial sea consistently and uninterruptedly from 1869 until the time when the dispute arose. The three Royal Decrees that Norway had issued in 1869, 1889, and 1935 to delimit different parts of its territorial sea had all employed the same method.[79] Norwegian authorities had also taken measures to enforce this legislation: on several occasions, they had arrested and condemned British trawlers for violating it.[80] The Court noted, secondly, that neither the promulgation of the 1869 and 1889 Decrees, nor the measures that Norwegian authorities had taken to enforce them, had given rise to any opposition on the part of other states.[81] Up until the promulgation of the Decree of 1935, even the Government of the United Kingdom had not contested Norwegian law and legal practice.[82] The Court acknowledged, but did not accept, the argument of the counsel of the United Kingdom that the applicant had not known of the Norwegian system of delimitation of the territorial sea, and that the system therefore lacked the notoriety essential to provide the basis for an historic title enforceable against it.[83] The United Kingdom, the Court noted, is a coastal State on the North Sea, greatly interested in the fisheries in this area. It is a maritime power traditionally concerned particularly with defending the freedom of the seas. As such,

> [it] could not have been ignorant of the Decree of 1869 which had at once provoked a request for explanations by the French Government. Nor, knowing of it, could it have been under any misapprehension as to the significance of its terms, which clearly described it as constituting the application of a system. The same observation applies *a fortiori* to the Decree of 1889 relating to the delimitation of Romsdal and Nordmöre which must have appeared to the United Kingdom as a reiterated manifestation of the Norwegian practice.[84]

The attitude of governments, the Court concluded, bears witness to the fact that they did not consider the method of straight baselines employed by Norway to be contrary to international law.[85]

[79] Ibid., at 138.
[80] Ibid., at 124.
[81] Ibid., at 138.
[82] Ibid.
[83] Ibid., at 138–139.
[84] Ibid., at 139.
[85] Ibid.

Our second example shifts the focus from the inquiries made by international courts and tribunals to those typically conducted by legal researchers. For example, legal scholars have systematically investigated the rule of ordinary meaning laid down in Article 31, paragraph 1 of the 1969 Vienna Convention on the Law of Treaties.[86] This rule provides for the resort by interpreters to 'everyday language' – the conventions that all speakers of a language generally follow.[87] Many scholars contend that it provides also for the resort to technical languages, such as the language of banking and finance, aviation or international law.[88] Among those who maintain this position, some cite the judgement of the International Court in the *Case of Kasikili/Sedudu Island*.[89] The Special Agreement that Namibia and Botswana had concluded requested the Court to determine the status of an island located in the midst of the River Chobe.[90] It was to make this determination based on the Heligoland–Zanzibar Treaty concluded by the United Kingdom and Germany in 1890.[91] This treaty separated the spheres of influence of its two parties along a line that in English '[descended] the centre of the main channel' of the River Chobe, and in German 'sich dann im Thalweg des Hauptlaufes dieses Flusses [fortgesetzt]'.[92] Much emphasis was placed by the parties on the use of the German word '*Thalweg*', which is a technical term often found in treaties that establish boundaries along rivers. The International Court found that the ordinary meaning of this term was ambiguous: in boundary treaties at the time around 1890, states used it to mean sometimes the median line of a river, and sometimes its deepest sounding or most suitable channel for navigation.[93] Scholars cite

[86] See, for example, Richard Gardiner, *Treaty Interpretation*, 2nd edition (Oxford: Oxford University Press, 2008), 161–177.

[87] See Ulf Linderfalk, *On the Interpretation of Treaties* (Dordrecht: Springer, 2007), 62–63.

[88] See, for example, Oliver Dörr, 'Article 31', in Oliver Dörr and Kirsten Schmalenbach (eds.), *Vienna Convention on the Law of Treaties: A Commentary* (Heidelberg: Springer, 2012), 542.

[89] *Kasikili/Sedudu Island (Botswana/Namibia)*, [1999] I.C.J. Rep. 1045. Among those who cite the judgment, see, for example, Gardiner, *Treaty Interpretation*, 167; Dörr, 'Article 31', 542.

[90] Art. 1 of the Special Agreement. See *Kasikili/Sedudu Island*, 1049.

[91] Agreement between Great Britain and Germany, respecting Zanzibar, Heligoland, and the Spheres of Influence of the two Countries in Africa ('Heligoland-Zanzibar Treaty', or 'Anglo-German Treaty'), Berlin, 1 July 1890, in force 1 July 1890, 51 *Das Staatsarchiv, Sammlung der offiziellen Aktenstücke zur Geschichte der Gegenwart* (Verlag von Duncker and Humblot, 1891), 151.

[92] Ibid., at Art. 3(2).

[93] To confirm this point, the Court referred to the *Draft concerning the international regulation of fluvial navigation*, adopted by the Institute of International Law (IDI) in 1887. *Kasikili/Sedudu Island*, para. 25.

this finding because they see it as evidence of a presupposition. As they infer, in *Kasikili/Sedudu Island*, the Court considered the resort to technical languages to be consistent with the rule of ordinary meaning.

The two examples neatly illustrate the methodology that international lawyers typically use when they establish normative presuppositions. They think of them as implicit in certain action – depending on the nature of the inquiry, the action of states or international judiciaries. Importantly, these normative presuppositions can only be established based on certain assumptions. First, lawyers must assume that agents act rationally – that their action is warranted by a complete logical argument. Second, lawyers must assume that agents recognize the appropriateness of their own action.

In the *Anglo-Norwegian Fisheries Case*, the Court inquired into the practice and *opinio juris* of both Norway and the United Kingdom. It observed the legislation and legal practice of Norway. It similarly observed that the United Kingdom had made itself known for its great interest in North Sea fisheries; that it was fully aware of Norwegian legislation and legal practice; and that, under a period of more than 60 years – from 1869 to 1935 – it had not expressed any objection to them. The Court concluded

1. that Norway considered its method of straight baselines to be *consistent* with international law; and
2. that the United Kingdom considered the Norwegian method of straight baselines to be *consistent* with international law.

The observations of the Court do not themselves allow these conclusions. The Court had to add two further premises. It had to assume that, from the point of view of customary international law, (i) Norway considered its method of straight baselines *appropriate* and (ii) the United Kingdom considered objections to Norwegian legislation and legal practice *inappropriate*. These assumptions fill the logical gaps that would otherwise exist between the empirical observations and what the Court inferred from them.

When legal scholars scrutinize *Kasikili/Sedudu Island* to obtain a fuller understanding of the rule of ordinary meaning, logic similarly allows for either of three different conclusions:

(i) that the International Court considers the resort to technical languages to be consistent with the rule of ordinary meaning; or
(ii) that the International Court considers the resort to technical languages to be inconsistent with the rule of ordinary meaning; or again
(iii) that the International Court has no opinion on this matter.

Scholars opt for the first of the three conclusions. They cannot reach this conclusion based on the mere observation that in *Kasikili/Sedudu Island*, the International Court used technical language to determine the ordinary meaning of the terms of a treaty. They must also assume that the International Court acts rationally and that it recognizes the appropriateness of its own action.

These two examples highlight two general observations. The first observation is that traditionally framed legal inquiries often involve the task of establishing the existence of some or other normative presupposition. In our first example, the International Court had to establish whether Norway and the United Kingdom considered the Norwegian method of straight baselines to be consistent with international law. In our second example, international scholars had to establish whether the International Court considered the resort to technical languages to be consistent with the rule of ordinary meaning. The second observation is that international lawyers have already a method that helps them to carry out these tasks successfully. They establish the normative presuppositions of legal agents based on empirical observations of their actual conduct together with the twofold assumption that agents act rationally and that they recognize the appropriateness of the action that they are themselves taking.

This demonstrates our point: to establish the existence of a community of practice, international lawyers must not do anything that they are not already trained to do. To illustrate, consider the suggestion that international human rights law is a special regime distinct from other special regimes and from general international law. From the point of view of the idealist's conception of a special regime, this suggestion entails a twofold claim.

First, it entails the claim that international human rights specialists have a mutual engagement; that they think of themselves as engaged in a joint enterprise; and that they have a shared repertoire of rhetorical tools. This is to say that international human rights specialists think it desirable that they join forces and collaborate in the pursuit of some enterprise; that they have an idea of what desirable state of affairs they are pursuing; and that they have an idea of what rhetorical tools are appropriate to use for this pursuit. If and to the extent that these normative presuppositions do exist, they can be studied in much the same way as the *opinio juris* of Norway and the United Kingdom, or the understanding of the International Court of the rule of ordinary meaning. To spell it out, they can be studied as implicit in the actual conduct of international human rights specialists, based on the assumption that these specialists act rationally and that they recognize the appropriateness of their own action. If, for example, international human rights specialists arrange for the publication of journals or the organization of conferences confined to the consideration of the law and practice of international human rights law, this shows that they think it desirable that they join forces and collaborate in the pursuit of some enterprise. If international human rights specialists refer repeatedly to the respect for human dignity as an object and purpose of human rights treaties or as a criterion that serves to constrain the exercise of legal discretion, this shows that they have an idea of what desirable state of affairs they are pursuing. Again, if international human rights specialists develop a concept such as *absolute rights*, this shows that they have an idea of what rhetorical tools are appropriate to use in this pursuit.

Secondly, the suggestion that international human rights law is a special regime entails the claim that international human rights specialists are a community, which somehow distinguishes itself from other communities of international lawyers: that their engagement is different from that of other international lawyers; that they think of themselves as engaged in an enterprise, which is partly different from those which engage other international lawyers; and that they have a repertoire, which is partly different from that of other international lawyers. Thus, to justify the suggestion, the normative presuppositions of international human rights law specialists must be compared with those of other international lawyers. It must be shown, more precisely:

- that international human rights specialists think of themselves as engaged in the pursuit of an enterprise together with a more or less limited group of international lawyers;
- that international human rights specialists think of themselves as pursuing different states of affairs than that which other international lawyers pursue, and, consequently, that they have a different idea of the proper way to perform assignments;
- that international human rights specialists find different rhetorical tools appropriate than other international lawyers.

Once again, this task does not presuppose anything that international lawyers are not already trained to do. It requires, first, that we establish the normative presuppositions of some other community of international lawyers: either some other group of international law specialists or international lawyers generally. It requires, secondly, an element of comparison. Thus, international lawyers would have to provide an answer to the questions below:

- What is the engagement of this other community of lawyers? How does this engagement compare with that of international human rights law specialists?
- What desirable states of affairs are this other community of lawyers pursuing? How do these states of affairs compare with those pursued by international human rights law specialists?
- What rhetorical tools does this other community of lawyers consider appropriate? How do these rhetorical tools compare with those that are endorsed by international human rights law specialists?

In the three chapters to follow, it is around these questions that case studies will be designed.

3

A Mutual Engagement

3.1 Introduction

Assume that some particular segment of the international legal system is being categorized by some person or institution as a special regime. To facilitate further reference to this segment, we will call it 'X law'. From the point of view of the legal idealist's conception of a special regime, the categorization of X law as a special regime entails altogether three claims. One is the claim that there is among X law specialists a mutual engagement. A mutual engagement is a feeling of togetherness. Thus, if there is a mutual engagement among X law specialists, this is because X law specialists do what they do based on a very particular normative presupposition: they believe that it is desirable that they all join forces and collaborate in the pursuit of some particular enterprise.

In Chapter 2, we suggested a methodology that would help us to establish such normative presuppositions. This methodology presupposes the making of certain assumptions. Just like when we establish the existence of an *opinio juris* of states, we need to assume that X law specialists act rationally and that they recognize the appropriateness of their own action. Having made these assumptions, the existence of a mutual engagement among X law specialists can be inferred from the existence of two simple phenomena. Hence, mutual engagement can be understood to be implicit: (i) in the participation of X law specialists in a distinct legal discourse; and (ii) in the existence among X law specialists of different specializations and a distinct way of ascribing functions to judges, NGOs, scholars, international organizations, and other categories of legal agents.

In this chapter, we will conduct a number of case studies that will help to illustrate how this methodology translates into practical action. Section 3.2 will illustrate how a mutual engagement can be inferred from the participation of international law specialists in a distinct legal discourse. This section will ask:

> Relative to a selected segment of international law (X law), whose beliefs, attitudes and behaviour are X law specialists aiming to affect when they engage in legal discourse? How do these communicative patterns compare with those that can be observed among other communities of international lawyers?

Section 3.3 will illustrate how a mutual engagement can be inferred from the existence among X law specialists of different specializations and a distinct way of ascribing functions to judges, NGOs, scholars, international organizations and other categories of legal agents. This section will ask:

> Relative to a selected segment of international law (X law), do any further specializations exist among X law specialists? What are the functions that X law specialists ascribe to judges, NGOs, scholars, international organizations and other categories of legal agents? How do these functions compare with those that other communities of international lawyers ascribe to these same categories of agents?

3.2 A Distinct Legal Discourse

3.2.1 Specialized International Law Journal

The publication of journals in the broad field of public international law is a good example to investigate the existence or not of distinct legal discourses, as evidence of the mutual engagement of scholars in a particular field. The question not only requires looking at the distinct field of international law which a journal seeks to address and publish articles on, but the community a specific journal targets as readership also plays an important role.

It is not surprising that until a couple of decades ago, the international law journal market was mostly composed of and monopolized by generalist international law journals, whose coverage was public international law[1] as a whole, international law including private international law and

[1] See, for example, *Nordic Journal of International Law*, https://brill.com/view/journals/nord/nord-overview.xml (focusing on the publication of research on the 'different branches of international law'); *Leiden Journal of International Law*, www.cambridge.org/core/journals/leiden-journal-of-international-law (focusing on international law and in particular on 'international legal theory, international law and practice, international criminal law, as well as international courts and tribunals'); *European Journal of International Law*, www.ejil.org/; *Revue générale de droit international public (RGDIP)*, www.ridi.org/adi/rgdip/home.htm.

public international law,[2] or international and comparative law.[3] Over the past decades in particular, the international law journal market has become more diverse and specialized.[4] Journals such as the *Journal of International Dispute Settlement*, the *Journal on the Use of Force and International Law*, the *London Review of International Law*, the *Journal of International Criminal Justice* or the *Business and Human Rights Journal* are just a couple of examples to illustrate this point.

The interesting point, for our purposes, is not only the establishment of journals in specialized areas of international law per se. While the establishment of specialized law journals might be prompted by practical and pragmatic considerations such as broadening the outlet for scientific output, the interesting point here is the distinct discourse and hence mutual engagement in a certain area that specialized law journals consequently create. Specialized international law journals more than often have a specific focus and scope, which precisely tend to set itself apart from other fields. The *Journal on the Use of Force and International Law*, for example, explicitly aims at 'covering all aspects of the law governing the use of force (jus ad bellum), *as distinct from other areas of international law relating to security issues*, such as International Humanitarian Law or International Criminal Law'.[5]

The narrow scope compared to (public) international law in general, of course, aims to both attract submissions from and target readership from a community specialized in a particular area. The *Journal of International Criminal Justice (JICJ)*, for example, clearly indicates, despite its ambition to 'promote a profound collective reflection on the new problems facing international law', that it is intended for, among others, 'the hundreds of people working for international criminal courts'.[6] The *Journal of International Arbitration* likewise targets 'those involved in international

[2] See, for example, *Revue belge de droit international*, https://rbdi.bruylant.be; *American Journal of International Law*, www.cambridge.org/core/journals/american-journal-of-international-law ('addressing developments in public and private international law and foreign relations law'); *Journal du Droit International (Clunet)*, www.worldcat.org/title/journal-du-droit-international-clunet/oclc/231026790.

[3] See, for example, *International & Comparative Law Quarterly*, www.cambridge.org/core/journals/international-and-comparative-law-quarterly.

[4] See Carsten Stahn and Eric De Brabandere, 'The Future of International Legal Scholarship: Some Thoughts on "Practice," "Growth," and "Dissemination"' (2014) 27 *Leiden Journal of International Law* 1–10; Ignacio de la Rasilla, 'A Very Short History of International Law Journals (1869–2018)' (2018) 29 *European Journal of International Law* 137–168, 161.

[5] *Journal on the Use of Force and International Law*, www.tandfonline.com/action/journalInformation?show=aimsScope&journalCode=rjuf20 (emphasis added).

[6] *Journal of International Criminal Justice*.

arbitration',[7] the *Journal of International Dispute Settlement* is intended, aside from 'academics with an interest in international dispute settlement, international arbitration, private or public international law', also 'people working for international courts and tribunals and for international arbitration institutions',[8] and the *Criminal Law Forum* aims to serve 'the global community of criminal law scholars and practitioners'.[9] In the latter case moreover, the community addressed by the journal coincides with a formal association, in this case the Society for the Reform of Criminal Law of which it is the official journal.[10] The same goes, of course, for the general international law journals, which more often than not are also linked to a society or association, such as the *American Journal of International Law*, which is one of the 'primary publications' of the American Society of International Law.[11] Others in turn such as the *London Review of International Law* stress that 'the disciplinary affiliation of authors is not important',[12] but for all purposes has a narrower focus than generalist international law journals as it is aimed at research on 'international legal theory, international legal history and international socio-legal studies'.[13]

Occasionally, specialized international law journals claim to not only cater to a specialized community but also explicitly establish the common objective or endeavour of the community as represented by the journal. The *Business and Human Rights Journal* thus makes explicit that it seeks to 'promote concern for human rights in business practice'.[14] *Transnational Legal Theory* likewise makes clear that it welcomes submissions from 'academics, practitioners and legal activists in continuing and emerging debates in legal, post-colonial and social theory, commentary on governance trends and engagements with shifting boundaries between public and private law frameworks, alternative methodologies

[7] *Journal of International Arbitration*, https://kluwerlawonline.com/Journals/Journal+of+International+Arbitration/4.

[8] *Journal of International Dispute Settlement*, https://academic.oup.com/jids/pages/About.

[9] *Criminal Law Forum*, www.springer.com/journal/10609.

[10] Ibid.

[11] *American Society of International Law: Primary Publications*, www.asil.org/resources/primary-publications.

[12] *London Review of International Law*, https://academic.oup.com/lril/pages/About.

[13] Ibid.

[14] *Business & Human Rights Journal*, www.business-humanrights.org/en/latest-news/business-human-rights-journal.

and competing epistemologies, including those between the Global North and the Global South'.[15]

A similar trend as we have witnessed with journals, yet at a much lesser scale, can be detected in professional or learned societies through the creation of specialized societies, such as the Society of International Economic Law, which targets 'academics and academically-minded practitioners and officials in international economic law'.[16]

Here again, aside from the practical considerations that may prompt someone to choose one journal over another, such as rankings, time frame of publication, reputation or distribution, the establishment of specialized law journals most of all results in, and perhaps was the driving force behind the establishment of the journal itself, a belief that it is desirable that forces are joined to collaborate in the pursuit of some particular enterprise. This is of course most visible when the publication itself provides the particular enterprise that is being pursued, such as the *Business and Human Rights Journal* mentioned above.

Even with a more general or less explicit common objective, the mutual engagement is implicit in the participation of international law specialists in a distinct legal discourse by publishing in a given journal. This idea fits into the move or pressure within scholarship more generally to '*focus less on concrete applications of law, but needs to generate theories in the sense of models that express the patterns of data in the field under observation as parsimoniously and concisely as possible*'.[17] The implicit push towards taking positions and making choices for scholars,[18] as was noted by one of the authors of the present book,

> makes it partly more difficult to maintain the ideal of a generalist profile that characterized historical scholarship, or to retain expertise and a full picture of debate in multiple fields. The diffusion of knowledge and increasing competition provide an incentive for scholars to seek refuge in ever more specific niche areas, or to create new areas through legal scholarship. The prospects for discourse and interaction seem to be larger. But due to growing specificity, dialogue remains de facto often entrenched

[15] *Transnational Legal Theory*, www.tandfonline.com/action/journalInformation?show=aimsScope&journalCode=rtlt20.

[16] *Society of International Economic Law*, www.sielnet.org.

[17] Anne Peters, 'Realizing Utopia as a Scholarly Endeavour' (2013) 24 *European Journal of International Law* 533–552, 533.

[18] See also Isabel Feichtner, 'Realizing Utopia Through the Practice of International Law' (2012) 23 *European Journal of International Law* 1143–1157.

> in small discourse communities that engage with each other only occasionally. It is thus still partly open to question to what extent the discourse has become more open and interactive.[19]

The distinct legal discourse, which lies at the basis of the mutual engagement in specialized fields, as we argue here, hence is inextricably linked to the specialization in the outlet of scientific products. As well captured by de la Rasilla, 'the scientific and intellectual desire felt by specialists in every field *to address each other in terms that honour the depth and breadth of their expert knowledge* and *aim at contributing to the continuous progress of their respective areas of specialization and the embedded sub-disciplines within them* is broadly cherished'.[20]

3.2.2 *The Organization of Conferences and Workshops*

Examination of the way in which conferences and workshops are being organized may help to establish the mutual engagement of a group of international law specialists. This method places its focus on the topics that organizers of conferences and workshops wish them to address, but not only on it. It is also significant how organizers describe the intended audiences of these events.[21] To obtain an idea of the way in which conferences and workshops are being organized, we have searched all announcements posted on 'EJIL Talk!' from the beginning of January 2022 to the time of writing (1 December 2022). On this basis, we suggest that conferences and workshops be classified as belonging to either one of four different categories.

The first category comprises events with topics that do not make any distinction between different segments of the international legal system and with audiences that include more than just a narrowly defined group of specialists. Examples include:

- *The Rules of Change or Changing Rules Workshop*, organized by the TRICI-Law Project and the Department of Transboundary Legal Studies of the University of Groningen, on 30 September 2022.[22] The

[19] Stahn and De Brabandere, 'The Future of International Legal Scholarship', 7.

[20] de la Rasilla, 'A Very Short History of International Law Journals', 164 (emphasis added).

[21] The method is similar to that applied in the consideration of international law journals. See Section 2.1.

[22] See the announcement posted at EJIL Talk! on 25 September 2022 available at: www.ejiltalk.org/announcements-gandhi-research-seminar-series-conference-of-the-nova-centre-on-

organizers of this workshop describe themselves interested in elucidating the processes that drive change of rules of international law of all kinds.[23]

- *The International Law Weekend: The Next 100 years of International Law*, a conference organized by the American Branch of the International Law Association, on 20–22 October 2022.[24] The organizers anticipate 'nearly 2,000 registrants including practitioners, academics, diplomats, business leaders, federal and state government officials, NGO leaders, journalists, students, and interested citizens'; they plan to include 'a broad array of both public international law and private international law topics'.[25]
- The workshop organized on 10 June 2022 by the Oxford Law Faculty and the Old Souls College to mark the retirement of Judge Giorgio Gaja from the International Court of Justice.[26] The call for papers invited presentations on a wide variety of themes, including, 'the law of treaties, international institutional law, the protection of community interests, international responsibility, jurisdictional immunities, and international dispute settlement'.[27]

The second category comprises events, which have a somewhat limited topic and audience, but still does not make any distinction between different segments of the international legal system. Examples include:

- *The Deconstructing International Law Conference*, organized by the Maastricht Study Group for Critical Approaches to International Law, on 7 April 2022.[28] As described, the aim of this conference is 'to

business-human-rights-and-the-environment-cfp-cambridge-international-law-journal-cfp-the-aesthetics-of-international/.

23 Information about the event is available at: https://trici-law.com/2022/09/17/registration-for-september-30th-trici-law-workshop-now-open.

24 See the announcement posted at EJIL Talk! on 28 August 2022 available at: www.ejiltalk.org/announcements-colonialism-and-the-eu-legal-order-conference-echr-in-areas-of-conflict-conference-international-law-weekend-cfp-international-trade-and-business-law-review-cfs-student-rights-and-l/.

25 Information about this event is available at: www.ila-americanbranch.org/international-law-weekend.

26 See the announcement posted at EJIL Talk! on 22 March 2022 available at: www.ejiltalk.org/announcements-principle-of-normality-seminar-cfp-eycl-law-eu-labour-migration-summer-school-climate-security-workshop-international-law-and-human-rights-climate-confer/.

27 Information about the event is available at: www.law.ox.ac.uk/news/2022-02-22-international-law-workshop-call-abstracts.

28 See the announcement posted at EJIL Talk! on 13 March 2022 available at: www.ejiltalk.org/announcements-law-of-treaties-mini-series-transatlantic-data-flows-webinar-

identify the core, foundational myths of international law, and to break them down, critically analysing what international law is and making room to discuss what international law could be'.[29]

- *The Emerging Voices Workshop*, organized by the Women in International Law Network (WILNET), on 25–26 April 2022.[30] The call for papers encourages submissions 'that unsettle orthodox thinking(/s) about international law'; applicants are invited 'to propose new imaginaries and go beyond well-established beliefs, languages, assumptions, or ways of thinking in international law, or else to critically reflect upon this call to think beyond current imaginaries'.[31]
- *The Reality of International Legal Theory – The Reality in International Legal Theory*, a conference organized by the ESIL Interest Group on International Legal Theory and Philosophy together with iCourts in Copenhagen, on 19–20 May 2022.[32] The organizers describe this conference as a forum to explore '[v]arious shades of (international) legal realist argument,' as well as the 'empirical aspects and methods' that come with it.[33]

The third category comprises events with topics that make a clear distinction between different segments of the international legal system and with audiences limited to a narrowly defined group of specialists. Examples include:

- *Lighting the Shade: Effective Application of ECHR in Areas of Conflict in Europe*, a conference organized by the Irish Centre for Human Rights and the School of Law at the National University of Ireland, on

ukraine-seminar-deconstructing-international-law-conference-cfa-international-law-and-water-series-cfp-max-planck-yearb/.

29 Information about the event is available at: www.maastrichtuniversity.nl/events/deconstructing-international-law.

30 See the announcement posted at EJIL Talk! on 30 January 2022 available at: www.ejiltalk.org/announcements-human-rights-law-centre-lecture-cfe-wilnet-emerging-voices-workshop-cfp-decolonising-global-migration-law-sexual-violence-in-conflict-lecture-cfp-gyil-business-and-human-rights-c/.

31 Information about the event is available at: https://sites.manchester.ac.uk/wilnet/2022/01/19/wiwilnet-emerging-voices-workshop-2022.

32 See the announcement posted at EJIL Talk! on 23 January 2022 available at: www.ejiltalk.org/announcements-cfp-reality-of-international-legal-theory-cfp-ijlsa-from-sacred-trust-to-common-heritage-lecutre-celi-events-phd-summer-school-ila-american-branch-event-cfa-climate-change-confere/.

33 Information about the event is available at: https://jura.ku.dk/pdf/arrangementer/2022/The-Reality-of-International-Legal-Theory.pdf.

1 September 2022.[34] As described, this event 'will examine the practice of the Council of Europe's human rights system in European territories where CoE mechanisms cannot function freely and effectively from both normative and operational perspectives. Speakers will consider how the system might be better leveraged to improve the effectiveness of the European Convention on Human Rights throughout Europe'.[35]

- *The 4th Annual Law of Armed Conflict Conference*, organized by the Stockton Center for International Law, and co-sponsored by the Norwegian Defence University College and the Swedish Defence University, at the US Naval War College, on 13–15 December 2022.[36] As described in the announcement,

  > [t]his Conference will address a broad range of emerging dilemmas in international law, including deterrence, neutrality, civilians in full-spectrum conflict, littoral combat, sieges and blockades, grey-zone and hybrid warfare, and post-conflict remedies ... [It] will bring together international organizations, the global academic community, military and government attorneys, and experts in military operations from Europe, the United States, and allies and partners around the world.[37]

- *Persistent and Emerging Challenges in International Fisheries Law Conference*, organized by the University of the Faroe Islands and the Law of the Sea Institute of Iceland, in Tórshavn, Faroe Islands, 23–25 June 2022.[38] As described in the announcement, this Conference

  > will focus on challenges that emerge and those that persist in international fisheries law, including IUU fishing related matters, institutional mechanisms in RFMOs, jurisdictional aspects in regard to fisheries disputes, substantive aspects in regard to disputes on the conservation and man-

[34] See the announcement posted at EJIL Talk! on 28 August 2022 available at: www.ejiltalk.org/announcements-colonialism-and-the-eu-legal-order-conference-echr-in-areas-of-conflict-conference-international-law-weekend-cfp-international-trade-and-business-law-review-cfs-student-rights-and-l/.

[35] Information about the event is available at: www.eventbrite.ie/e/lighting-the-shade-application-of-echr-in-areas-of-conflict-online-only-tickets-405237364867.

[36] Information about the event is available at: https://usnwc.edu/News-and-Events/Events/4th-Annual-Stockton-Center-Law-of-Armed-Conflict-Conference-Russia-Ukraine.

[37] Ibid.

[38] See the announcement posted at EJIL Talk! on 22 March 2022 available at: www.ejiltalk.org/announcements-principle-of-normality-seminar-cfp-eycl-law-eu-labour-migration-summer-school-climate-security-workshop-international-law-and-human-rights-climate-confer/.

agement of transboundary and straddling fish stocks, trade related measures with respect to fisheries resources, and fisheries related matters concerning BBNJ.[39]

The fourth category comprises events organized to investigate the intersection, interaction or mutual influence of two or more segments of the international legal system. Examples include:

- *The Third Biennial Conference on Food Security and International Law*, organized by South Asia International Economic Law Network, on 19–20 December 2022.[40] As described in the call, this conference 'aims to provide a platform for experts, policymakers, lawyers, academics, economists, and civil society partners to exchange views on the multifaceted challenges of food security and offer innovative legal and policy solutions to address them'.[41] Among the theme topics covered are the coordination of international human rights law and international economic law in achieving food security; sustainable fishing practices and the preservation of fish stock for food security; and ensuring food security in future pandemics and international conflicts.[42]
- *Sanctions in the Light of Russia's Invasion of Ukraine: What's New in Law and Practice*, a workshop organized by the Law Department at the University of Luxembourg, on 4 July 2022.[43] This workshop explores 'the legality and implementation of, and possible challenges to, economic sanctions imposed by a number of international actors (including the EU, the US and the UK), as well as their potential impact on businesses and dispute resolution'. As described, panellists will talk over topics such as targeted sanctions and human rights; economic

[39] Information about the event is available at: www.faroeislandsfisherieslawconference2022.com.

[40] See the announcement posted at EJIL Talk! On 2 October 2022 available at: www.ejiltalk.org/announcements-un-audiovisual-library-of-international-law-knut-ipsen-lecture-series-cfa-saieln-conference-on-food-security-cfp-international-law-and-human-rights-postgrad-conference-evidentiary/.

[41] Information about the event is available at: https://ctil.org.in/cms/docs/EventDocs/SAILEN%20Biennial%20Conference%20on%20Food%20Security_-_Schedule.pdf.

[42] Ibid.

[43] See the announcement posted at EJIL Talk! on 5 June 2022 available at: www.ejiltalk.org/announcements-wilig-scholarship-prize-fossil-fuels-to-renewable-energy-webinar-i-hilt-e-lecture-series-russias-invasion-of-ukraine-sanctions-workshop-international-law-commission-lecture-disp/.

sanctions and international investment law; and the impact of sanctions on arbitration proceedings.[44]

- *International Law and Climate Change*, a conference organized by the British Branch of the International Law Association, on 28–29 April 2022.[45] As described in the conference programme, this conference 'will consider legal problems likely to emerge from ongoing changes resulting from climate change and its consequences, as set out in the 2021 IPCC report'; panel will be convened on the following themes: 'Impact of rising sea levels on migration and statehood; Climate change and international trade and investment law; Human rights and climate change; Litigating on climate change'.[46]

Not all of these events indicate the existence of a mutual engagement among international law specialists. The first and second category events do not, inasmuch as their topics do not make any distinction between different segments of the international legal system. The third category events do, for the exact opposite reason. The fourth category events constitute something of a hybrid of all others: while their topics do make a distinction between different segments of the international legal system, at the same time, their intended audiences include lawyers with different specializations, such as international economic law and human rights. If indications are that organizers arrange an event to develop ways of maintaining connections between different groups of international law specialists, these events manifest the existence of a mutual engagement among the members of each such group, much like third category events do.[47] If, on the other hand, organizers aim to create new connections across boundaries of different specializations, and enable coordination of work, they must be understood differently: as manifestations of a more wide-ranging engagement pointing to the emergence of a new special regime.[48]

[44] Information about the event is available at: www.eventbrite.fr/e/sanctions-in-the-light-of-russias-invasion-of-ukraine-tickets-355132469777?mc_cid=54bdab345b&mc_eid=f6bc482ad1.

[45] See the announcement posted at in the International Law Reporter available at: http://ilreports.blogspot.com/2022/03/conference-international-law.html.

[46] The program of the event is available at: https://mcusercontent.com/47624183ad52dd8428c97d3f6/files/34ee286b-f985-2950-5738-d48c7c8134a4/International_Law_Association_British_Branch_Spring_Conference_2022_Programme.pdf. A brief description of the aim the conference is available at: https://10times.com/e15z-xxh5-x0x3.

[47] Compare Etienne Wenger, *Communities of Practice: Learning, Meaning and Identity* (Cambridge: Cambridge University Press, 1998), 103.

[48] Compare ibid.

3.2.3 *The Creation of Intergovernmental Organizations*

Intergovernmental organizations are created for the purpose of promoting particular topics or areas. To a certain extent, it is somehow trite to observe or even argue that intergovernmental organizations are created for a specific purpose, as an international organization only exists to perform the function assigned to it by the States that have created it. Yet the purpose of the discussion here is to identify the distinct legal discourse associated with the work of certain international organizations.

The first example is the United Nations Commission on International Trade Law (UNCITRAL), a UN subsidiary organ established by the General Assembly in 1966.[49] UNCITRAL has as its objective 'the promotion of the progressive harmonization and unification of the law of international trade'.[50] More recently, in 2017, UNCITRAL has entrusted its Working Group III (WG III) 'to work on the possible reform of investor-State dispute settlement (ISDS)'.[51] UNCITRAL WG III has been established with a specific request to ensure that in discharging is mandate, the deliberations benefit from the widest possible breadth of available expertise from all stakeholders.[52] WG III is thus tasked with the specific mandate to work towards the reform of investor–state dispute settlement (ISDS) as a distinct objective.

Aside from being 'Government-led, with high-level input from all Governments',[53] an interesting feature of the working method of WG III is the close interaction and connection with the 'Academic Forum on ISDS', the purpose of which is 'for academics active in the field of ISDS to exchange views, explore issues and options, test ideas and solutions, and make a constructive contribution to the ongoing discussions on possible reform of ISDS, in particular the discussions in the context of UNCITRAL's Working Group III (WGIII)'.[54] The Academic Forum on ISDS is composed of academics, who, aside from the specialized nature of their expertise, are participating in the work of (mostly) WG III and hence in exploring the options for the reform of ISDS. This peculiar

49 Establishment of the United Nations Commission on International Trade Law, 17 December 1966, U.N. Doc. A/RES/2205 (XXI).

50 Ibid., at Art. I.

51 Report of the United Nations Commission on International Trade Law, Fiftieth Session, 3–21 July 2017, U.N. Doc. A/72/17, paras. 263–264.

52 Ibid., at para. 264.

53 Ibid.

54 *Academic Forum on ISDS*, www.jus.uio.no/pluricourts/english/projects/leginvest/academic-forum/.

feature shows a clear mutual engagement to participate in a specific legal discourse aimed at offering options for the reform of ISDS for States. That the intergovernmental organization in question, UNCITRAL, works towards a specific goal is rather straightforward in this example, having found early in its work that 'reform was desirable in light of the identified concerns'[55] and hence tailoring its work towards that end.

The second example is the United Nations Conference on Trade and Development (UNCTAD), an intergovernmental organization formally part of the UN Secretariat, which deals with trade, investment and development. UNCTAD has a rather peculiar history, which clearly shows the mutual engagement we seek to identify here.[56] In the midst of the Cold War, the General Assembly endorsed in 1962 a recommendation of the UN Economic and Social Council (ECOSOC) to organize an United Nations Conference on Trade and Development based on the conviction that 'the promotion of higher rates of economic growth throughout the world and the evolution of a new and more appropriate pattern of international trade will require the adaptation of the institutional framework for international co-operation in the field of trade'.[57] The initial one-off conference was later turned into a permanent UN agency after the 1964 Geneva Conference. The permanent institution of the UNCTAD was, in the minds of one of its architects, conceived to be 'an activist body which provided leadership and made its contributions through its studies, its analyses and its thoughts'.[58] The uneasy relationship between the neutrality of an international organization, and the specific mutual engagement and common endeavour pursued by the UNCTAD Secretariat – in line with the very founding purpose of the organization – was a point of tension from the start.[59] This specific feature of UNCTAD perhaps stands out from other international organizations:

> the question for researchers in the secretariat, and their superiors, was whether UNCTAD studies and analyses should always confirm and reinforce [the economic doctrine for developing countries], or whether they could be allowed to come up with findings that were inconsistent with

[55] Report of Working Group III (Investor-State Dispute Settlement Reform) on the work of its thirty-ninth session, Vienna, 5–9 October 2020, U.N. Doc. A/CN.9/1044, para. 3.

[56] See generally John Toye, UNCTAD at 50: A Short History (2014), U.N. Doc. UNCTAD/OSG/2014/1, https://unctad.org/system/files/official-document/osg2014d1_en.pdf.

[57] United Nations Conference on Trade and Development, 8 December 1962, U.N. Doc. A/RES/1785 (XVII), preamble.

[58] Toye, UNCTAD, 20.

[59] Ibid., at 21.

> it. This question was by no means unique to UNCTAD. It arises for all international (and national government) bodies that have a mission and also undertake to do research. Yet for an organization such as UNCTAD with usually strong activist ambitions, it had a special salience.[60]

The important point here, for our purposes, is that UNCTAD showcases precisely the belief that a joint collaborative effort is underlying not only the very existence of the organization, but more specifically the engagement of 'a team of exceptionally talented and dedicated officials and a worthy objective of advancing the development of poor countries'.[61]

3.2.4 The Work of NGOs

As intergovernmental organizations work towards a specific objective, so do NGOs work on particular areas such as human rights law, environmental law, international criminal justice and so forth. This also, as in the case for intergovernmental organizations, is perhaps somehow obvious. But the assumption that their own action is appropriate and rational is perhaps even more visible in the case of NGOs. NGOs have existed since long, but their effective and explicit participation in international legal discourse through various forms of participation is more recent. One can think of their increased participation as amicus curiae in the context of investment disputes, which we will cover in Chapter 4, or their increased (in)formal role in international law-making.[62] Indeed, the influence and informal involvement of non-state actors, such as NGOs, in various fields of international law and international relations is now beyond doubt.[63] The distinct legal discourse of NGOs then is relatively evident: 'the main reason for NGOs to exist is to do with the belief that they act for collective objectives'.[64]

[60] Ibid., at 22.

[61] Ibid., at 118.

[62] See generally Wybo Heere (ed.), *From Government to Governance: The Growing Impact of Non-State Actors on the International and European Legal System* (The Hague: T.M.C. Asser Press, 2004).

[63] For information in respect of NGO influence on treaty-making, see Alan Boyle and Christine Chinkin, *The Making of International Law* (Oxford: Oxford University Press, 2007), 62–77.

[64] Délber Andrade Lage and Leonardo Nemer Caldeira Brant, 'The Growing Influence of Non-Governmental Organizations: Chances and Risks' (2008) III-1 *Anuário Brasileiro de Direito Internacional* 79–93, 82.

NGOs and civil society actors or organizations more generally, are among others defined by reference to a precise goal or objective they seek to advocate for, and which constitutes the reason for their existence. The pursuance of an issue of 'public interest' at the domestic or global level,[65] or a 'non profit-making aim of international utility'[66] is therefore part of their (legal) discourse. The 'broader' interests represented by NGOs can either be general and related to human rights or environmental issues, or relatively specific or sectoral, such as the representation of the rights of a particular social group.

The legal discourse employed implies a specific focus, which often not only establishes a specific area of expertise, central to the NGOs' objective, but a clear and specific discourse associated with that expertise, reflecting the firm belief of and commitment to a joint enterprise and the appropriateness of the action pursued. Thus, Amnesty International has as its objective: 'through our detailed research and determined campaigning, we help fight abuses of human rights worldwide. We bring torturers to justice. Change oppressive laws. And free people jailed just for voicing their opinion'.[67] The Centre for International Environmental Law (CIEL) seeks to use 'the power of law to protect the environment, promote human rights, and ensure a just and sustainable society'.[68] These missions are then, in turn, channelled by joint enterprises pursued through various means as we will discuss below.

3.2.5 *The Specialized Research Profile of International Scholars and Description of Chairs*

Alongside the specialization we have discussed in relation to law journals and conferences or workshops, the specialized research profile of international scholars often is reflected in the description of chairs, a practice which by all means is not widespread but certain states, such as the Netherlands, have consistently developed this practice. Chairs, historically, were used to denote the general area of expertise of a scholar within

[65] See generally Louis Logister, 'Global Governance and Civil Society: Some Reflections on NGO Legitimacy' (2007) 3 *Journal of Global Ethics* 165–179.

[66] European Convention on the Recognition of the Legal Personality of International Non-Governmental Organizations, Strasbourg, 24 April 1986, in force 1 January 1991, European Treaty Series No. 124.

[67] Amnesty International, 'What We Do', www.amnesty.org/en/what-we-do/.

[68] Center for International Environmental Law, 'Our Mission', www.ciel.org/about-us/our-mission/.

science, and later on the law broadly speaking. While the first chair of law was established in the 1750s at Oxford, held by Professor William Blackstone,[69] chairs in international law only appeared in most States towards the end of the nineteenth and early twentieth century.[70] International law was then mostly taught by professors holding a chair in political economy.[71] Since then, international law has of course as is widely known established itself as a legal discipline of its own, and chairs in international law have become well established. For our purposes here, the important evolution relates more to the specialization of chairs *within* international law.

It is important to emphasize that in many states chairs still are generic chairs in law, international law, or, as is the case in Germany, chairs in multiple and broad fields of expertise, combining for example European and International Law or Public and International Law.[72] However, in many other states, we have seen an evolution towards specialization, which is reflected in the naming of chairs. The name of a chair is first and foremost an indication of expertise in a particular given field of international law. Professors can then hold a chair in international criminal law, international humanitarian law, international environmental law, the law of international organizations, international dispute settlement, the law of the sea, international legal theory and so forth. It is interesting to note that chairs tend to be labelled in accordance with relatively well-established or traditional sub-fields of international law. Moreover, aside from chairs in (public) international law, there are a few examples of specialized chairs of distinct areas of general international law, such as the law of state responsibility or the law of treaties.

In certain States, such as the Netherlands, chairs, aside from evidencing the specialization in a given field of international law, often have a more narrow or sub-specialized profile. Examples are chairs in War reparations,[73] or Interpretation and Dispute Settlement in International

[69] Matthew Parker, 'The Origin of LL.M. Programs: A Case Study of the University of Pennsylvania Law School' (2018) 39 *University of Pennsylvania Journal of International Law* 825, 832.

[70] Vincent Genin, *Le laboratoire belge du droit international* (Brussels: Académie royale de Belgique, 2018), 78.

[71] Ibid.

[72] Stahn and De Brabandere, 'The Future of International Legal Scholarship', 7.

[73] Prof. dr. L. (Liesbeth) Zegveld, https://acil.uva.nl/profile/z/e/l.zegveld/l.zegveld.html?origin=YU15UDmwSzGxsoxvNG1ACQ.

Law.[74] Specialized chairs tend be combined with a description of a certain 'mission' that may accompany the chair's generic title in a certain given field of expertise.[75]

3.3 Different Specializations and Distinct Ways of Ascribing Functions to Legal Agents

3.3.1 *Further Specialization*

Working as an international lawyer, you acquire skills and competencies that other people do not have. For example:

- You learn how to identify the information that you need to have to establish the existence of international norms.
- You learn how to understand and to interpret treaties and decisions issued by international organizations.
- You learn how to conceive of reality from the point of view of international law and to describe it in terms of legally relevant similarities and differences.
- You learn how to use previous legal decisions as a basis for conclusions about the state of international law generally.
- You learn to reflect on the role of international law in society and to speculate about the outcome of legal disputes and issues of legal policy.

[74] P. (Panos) Merkouris, Prof, www.rug.nl/staff/p.merkouris/cv?lang=en.

[75] See, for example, the Chair on International Law and Social justice, held by Professor Ingo Venzke at the University of Amsterdam. 'Ingo Venzke, professor of International Law and Social Justice', www.uva.nl/en/content/news/professor-appointments/2018/08/ingo-venzke-professor-of-international-law-and-social-justice.html. The specific 'mission' accompanying the chair is described as:

> research and teaching on the connection between International Law and social inequality (both between and within states). The question Venzke will now investigate is: How does international law relate to aspirations of social justice? Issues of economic distribution have traditionally been left to the discretion of states and have not typically been a concern for international lawyers. Wrongly so, Venzke argues, as international law has contributed to shaping the political economy, has distributed gains and losses within and between nations, and has influenced public policy space across levels of governance. Venzke places a particular emphasis on international law's role in the creation of past or present conditions of social (in) justice.

Ibid.

- You learn when to pick an argument and when to let things go unremarked.
- You learn how to argue and to convince audiences of the soundness or propriety of legal propositions.
- You learn what to expect from your interaction with other international lawyers in terms of attitudes, mindsets, ideals and aspirations.
- You learn how to express yourself and to behave more generally in your interaction with other international lawyers, depending on such things as the capacity in which they are acting, their age, rank and position.

These competencies help to distinguish the international lawyer from lawyers more generally. They are not distinguishing marks of any international law specialists, although, obviously, international lawyers possess them to different degrees.

What we wish to highlight is rather the separation of tasks and division of labour that come naturally with a prolonged engagement with some spheres of international legal regulation. International law governs different fields of activities. When we teach international law, it is often in terms of precisely these spheres of activities that we describe it. Thus, we talk about 'space law', 'the law of the sea', 'international investment law', 'the international law of environmental protection' and so forth. When the occupation of an international lawyer demands in-depth engagement with one such sphere of regulation, not only will this lawyer increase his or her knowledge of the law strictly speaking but will also develop a certain familiarity with the activities governed. This, however, typically takes considerable time, especially when activities are diverse and highly technical. This is why international lawyers, when preoccupied with the practice of a sphere of international regulation such as space law or the law of the sea, typically develop their different specializations. Thus, among law of the sea specialists, there are those who engage only with issues of international fisheries or off-shore drilling.[76] Among space law specialists, there are those who engage only with issues of arms control or exploitation of resources.[77] Among international environmental law

[76] See, for example, Said Mahmoudi, *The Law of Deep Sea-Bed Mining* (Stockholm: Almqvist & Wiksell International, 1987); Rosemary Rayfuse, *Non-Flag State Enforcement in High Seas Fisheries* (Leiden: Koninklijke Brill NV, 2004).

[77] See, for example, Cassandra Steer and Matthew Hersch (eds.), *War and Peace in Outer Space* (New York: Oxford University Press, 2021); Ricky Lee, 'Creating a Practical Legal Framework for the Commercial Exploitation of Mineral Resources in Outer Space', PhD thesis, Murdoch University (2009).

specialists, again, there are those who engage only with issues of water or biodiversity.[78] As Etienne Wenger would have it, this is proof of a mutual engagement.

3.3.2 *The Function Ascribed to the Judiciary: Judicial Activism*

The role of international judges and arbitrators is in theory relatively straightforward: they settle disputes in accordance with the law. As a matter of principle, courts and tribunals are thus limited in their mandate by the dispute brought before them and are based on the idea that a third party, the judge(s) or the arbitrator(s) objectively interprets and applies international law to that dispute.[79] From that orthodox perspective, the function ascribed to international courts and tribunals leaves little room for manoeuvre[80] and in fact stands in stark contrast to judicial activism. Judicial activism can be described as the situation where a judge or arbitrator 'deals with legal issues arising in the case other than those which could suffice to constitute the logical structure leading up to his ruling'.[81]

Judicial activism and the role of courts and tribunals in the development of international law are closely connected, and the dividing line may be 'fluid'.[82] We will however, in this book, analytically distinguish both; we will refer to judicial activism, discussed here, as the choice made by judges and arbitrators to deliver a reasoning or opinion that would in principle not be necessary for the settlement of the dispute before it or to exercise or establish jurisdiction in order to do so. More generally, we will look at judicial activism as 'a course of action that goes beyond the boundaries of what is deemed appropriate for the judiciary in a given context',[83] and it is precisely what is 'deemed appropriate for the

[78] See, for example, Stephen McCaffrey, *The Law of International Watercourses: Non-Navigational Uses* (Oxford: Oxford University Press, 2001); Alexander Gillespie, *Conservation, Biodiversity and International Law* (Cheltenham: Edward Elgar Publishing Limited, 2011).

[79] Except if the parties agree on a decision *ex aequo et bono* (equity).

[80] Fuad Zarbiyev, 'Judicial Activism in International Law – A Conceptual Framework for Analysis' (2012) 3 *Journal of International Dispute Settlement* 247–278, 251. See also Hugh Thirlway, 'Judicial Activism and the International Court of Justice', in Nisuke Ando, Edward McWhinney, Rüdiger Wolfrum, and Betsy Baker Röben (eds.), *Liber Amicorum Judge Shigeru Oda*, vol. 1 (The Hague: Kluwer Law International, 2002), 75–76.

[81] Thirlway, 'Judicial Activism', 75–76.

[82] Ibid., at 77.

[83] Zarbiyev, 'Judicial Activism in International Law', 251–252.

judiciary in a given context' that will vary when looking at several regimes showing a distinct legal discourse. The function of courts and tribunals in the development of the law on the other hand can then be viewed from the perspective of judges and arbitrators of their role as not only applying the law but also contributing to their development, or the practice of doing so – this will be discussed in the next section.

The ascription of different functions to judges and arbitrators is quite contrasting in the examples we will mention below, which show a clear different understanding of how various communities view the role of judges and arbitrators. This may not seem surprising, as it has been argued that 'the notion of judicial activism depend on the social conventions in effect within a given society about what is the appropriate role of the judiciary'.[84] But the interesting point here is that this 'appropriate role' of the judiciary in effect differs *within* the international law society to use the same terminology.

The traditional or orthodox function, as described above, can easily be detected in the case law and practice of the International Court of Justice, showing a reserved approach in line of the traditional discourse of general international law. The Court has on multiple occasions adopted an approach which in effect boils down to judicial restraint, i.e. the opposite of judicial activism.[85] This is notable from the Court's decisions in relation to mootness, for example. On several occasions, the ICJ has made clear that it cannot exercise its jurisdiction when the case no longer has a substantial object.[86] The concept of 'mootness' is linked to the fact that courts and tribunals settle disputes, and in doing so exercise a judicial or arbitral function, which is to pronounce on a dispute by applying international law. When the 'object of the dispute' no longer exists, a court or tribunal cannot exercise its function. An example is the *Nuclear Tests* case, which had been brought by Australia and New Zealand against France and related to the legality of atmospheric nuclear tests conducted by France in the South Pacific region.[87] After the initiation of the case, the French authorities had repeatedly stated that they would no longer conduct atmospheric nuclear tests and gave assurances

84 Ibid., at 252.

85 See generally Pieter Kooijmans, 'The ICJ in the 21st Century: Judicial Restraint, Judicial Activism, or Proactive Judicial Policy' (2007) 56 *The International and Comparative Law Quarterly* 741–753.

86 Hugh Thirlway, *The International Court of Justice* (Oxford: Oxford University Press, 2016), 57.

87 *Nuclear Tests (Australia v. France)* [1974] I.C.J. Rep. 253, para. 16.

that the tests would cease.[88] The ICJ held that it 'must not fail to take cognizance of a situation in which the dispute has disappeared because the object of the claim has been achieved by other means'.[89] As a consequence, the Court decided it could not exercise its functions: 'the object of the claim having clearly disappeared, there is nothing on which to give judgment'.[90] It is important to note that the ICJ linked this finding to the need for the Court to act 'in accordance with the proper interpretation of its judicial function'.[91]

The ICJ and its predecessor the Permanent Court of International Justice (PCIJ) have often repeated that absent consent to adjudicate the dispute before it, the Court cannot exercise its jurisdiction, thereby showcasing a discourse associated with the traditional position of international lawyers.[92] This, however, has been criticized by certain (former) ICJ Judges. Judges Kooijmans, Higgins, Simma and Owada, for example, have criticized the ICJ's position, arguing in a Separate Opinion in the *Armed Activities on the Territory of the Congo* case that precisely the discourse that 'it is still for States to choose whether they consent to the Court adjudicating claims that they have committed genocide' is outdated 'at the twenty-first century'.[93]

Judge Kooijmans also argued in a subsequent article that the requirement of consent as a 'precondition for the Court's functioning is a serious set-back'. He further sets off the generalist discourse applicable to the ICJ to the role of other courts and tribunals: 'it prevents the Court from playing a role comparable to that of the European Court of Justice in Luxembourg or the European Court of Human Rights, whose jurisdiction flows automatically from their basic treaties'.[94]

Judge Kooijmans' argument precisely reflects what we attempt to show here, namely that other courts and tribunals on the contrary are seen as having a different function. The European Court of Human Rights,

[88] Ibid., at paras. 32, 51, 55–56.
[89] Ibid., at para. 55.
[90] Ibid., at para. 59.
[91] Ibid., at para. 57.
[92] *Status of Eastern Carelia* [1923] P.C.I.J. (ser. B) No. 5, 27. See also in respect of the ICJ: *Armed Activities on the Territory of the Congo (New Application: 2002) (Democratic Republic of the Congo v. Rwanda)*, Jurisdiction of the Court and Admissibility of the Application, [2006] I.C.J. Rep. 6, para. 65.
[93] *Armed Activities on the Territory of the Congo (New Application: 2002) (Democratic Republic of Congo v. Rwanda)*, Joint Separate Opinion of Judges Higgins, Kooijmans, Elaraby, Owada, & Simma, [2006] I.C.J. Rep. 65, para. 25.
[94] Kooijmans, 'The ICJ in the 21st Century', 743.

which Kooijmans explicitly mentions, stated in its 1978 judgement in the *Ireland v. United Kingdom* case that its judgements 'serve not only to decide cases brought before the Court but, more generally, to elucidate, safeguard and develop the rules instituted by the Convention'.[95] At that time, the Rules of the Court explicitly stated that the Court could 'decide that, notwithstanding the notice of discontinuance, friendly settlement, arrangement or other fact referred to in the two preceding paragraphs, it should proceed with the consideration of the case'.[96] In the meantime, changes were made to the Rules of the Court, but it is still enshrined in Article 37 of the Convention that the Court 'shall continue the examination of the application if respect for human rights as defined in the Convention and the Protocols thereto so requires'.[97] Even after an application has been struck out, the Court 'may restore it to its list if it considers that exceptional circumstances so justify'.[98] In its 2016 decision in *Jeronovičs v. Latvia*, the European Court of Human Rights (ECtHR) noted that:

> the Court's rulings serve not only to decide those cases brought before it but, more generally, to elucidate, safeguard and develop the rules instituted by the Convention, thereby contributing to the observance by the States of the engagements undertaken by them as Contracting Parties.[99]

A second example relating to the ECtHR is its way of dealing with possible reservations to its jurisdiction, which, although dissimilar, is close to the previous one. In the *Loizidou* case,[100] the Respondent State had inter alia argued that the jurisdictional provisions of the original ECHR (Articles 25 and 46, the latter being modelled on the 'optional clause' provision in Article 36 of the ICJ Statute) permitted appending reservations *ratione loci* to the exercise by (at that time) the Commission and the Court. The ECtHR, however, opined that the provisions of the ECHR 'cannot be interpreted solely in accordance with the intentions of

[95] Case 5310/71, *Ireland v. United Kingdom*, [1978] ECHR 1, para. 154. See also, more recently, Case No. 44898/10, *Jeronovičs v. Latvia*, [2016] IHRL 3954, para. 109.

[96] Amendments to the Rules of Procedure of the European Court of Human Rights, (1974) 17 *Yearbook of the European Convention on Human Rights* 30, rule 47(3).

[97] Convention for the Protection of Human Rights and Fundamental Freedoms, as amended by Protocols Nos. 11 and 14, Rome, 4 November 1950, European Treaty Series No. 5, Art. 37(1).

[98] Rules of the Court, European Court of Human Rights, Strasbourg, 23 June 2023, www.echr.coe.int/documents/rules_court_eng.pdf, rule 43(5).

[99] *Jeronovičs v. Latvia*, para. 109.

[100] Case No. 15318/89, *Loizidou v. Turkey*, [1995] ECHR 10.

their authors as expressed more than forty years ago'.[101] The Court further argued, and in doing so emphasized the distinctive nature of both the European Convention and its role (opposing it – sometimes implicitly – to other international courts and tribunals, such as the International Court of Justice), that authorizing reservations 'would not only seriously weaken the role of the Commission and Court in the discharge of their functions but would also diminish the effectiveness of the Convention as a constitutional instrument of European public order (ordre public)'.[102] It further noted that:

> [the] context in which the International Court of Justice operates is quite distinct from that of the Convention institutions. The International Court is called on inter alia to examine any legal dispute between States that might occur in any part of the globe with reference to principles of international law. The subject-matter of a dispute may relate to any area of international law. In the second place, unlike the Convention institutions, the role of the International Court is not exclusively limited to direct supervisory functions in respect of a law-making treaty such as the Convention.[103]

The ECtHR thus in essence sees itself as 'a developer of legal doctrines on human rights [. . .] based on the object and purpose of the Convention' and in light of 'its special character as a treaty for the collective enforcement of human rights and fundamental freedoms'.[104] The European Court of Justice too is not merely seen as a dispute settlement body akin to the International Court of Justice and has even been described by the President of the Court, Koen Lenaerts, as 'the guarantor of the rule of law within the EU, whose role is, in effect, to act as both the Constitutional and Supreme Court of the European Union'.[105]

Another example we want to discuss here is the specific role of the WTO Appellate Body (WTO AB), which is defunct since 10 December 2019, and which has been, among others, criticized precisely for engaging

[101] Ibid., at para. 71.
[102] Ibid., at para. 75.
[103] Ibid., at para. 84.
[104] Jukka Viljanen, 'The Role of the European Court of Human Rights as a Developer of International Human Rights Law' (2008) 62/63 *Cuadernos constitutucionales de la Catedra Fadrique Furio Ceriol* 249–265, 249. See also Kanstantsin Dzehtsiarou, 'European Consensus and the Evolutive Interpretation of the European Convention on Human Rights' (2011) 12 *German Law Journal* 1730–1745.
[105] Koen Lenaerts, 'The European Court of Human Rights and the Court of Justice of the European Union: Creating Synergies in the Field of Fundamental Rights Protection', in *Solemn Hearing for the Opening of the Judicial Year* (26 January 2018), at 2.

in 'judicial activism'.[106] The particularity of the WTO AB's function resides in a couple of features specific to its functioning and mandate, which makes it stand out compared to other courts and tribunals and exactly shows the distinctiveness of the mutual engagement in this field and the different perceptions thereof depending on the engaged community. While the title of the Annex to the WTO Agreement governing dispute settlement – the Dispute Settlement Understanding (DSU)[107] – clearly indicates that the procedures set up are designed to settle international disputes, the institutions involved and their mandate differ from other international courts and tribunals. Moreover, while the question of whether a 'dispute' exists between parties is essential to establish and delimit the issues upon which a court of tribunal is empowered to pronounce itself, resulting in a final and binding decision, the WTO DSU does not limit settlement to 'disputes' but also extends to 'situations' and 'non-violation complaints' in case a benefit under a WTO Agreement is being nullified or impaired.[108] For present purposes, the important point is the different perceptions on the role of the WTO panels and AB. The dispute settlement mechanism, which is in essence quasi-judicial in nature[109] and as discussed is very peculiar in its set-up, functions with a different terminology than usually seen in other international courts and tribunals. Among many other features, the first tier of settlement is done by 'panels', not by 'tribunals'; both the panels and the AB issue 'reports', which become binding only upon adoption by the WTO Dispute Settlement Body, and the procedure followed is different from judicial or arbitral proceedings.[110] The dispute settlement system has therefore been described in rather opposite terms as both a genuine dispute settlement system whereby panel and AB reports are equated with 'judgements',[111] or, on the contrary, more as a 'complaints

[106] See Ambassador Robert E. Lighthizer, Office of the United States Trade Representative: Report on the Appellate Body of the World Trade Organization (February 2020), 50.

[107] Understanding on Rules and Procedures for the Settlement of Disputes, in Agreement Establishing the World Trade Organization, Marrakesh, 15 April 1994, 1869 U.N.T.S. 401, Annex 2.

[108] See ibid., at Art. 3(3); General Agreement on Tariffs and Trade, in Agreement Establishing the World Trade Organization, Marrakesh, 15 April 1994, 1867 U.N.T.S. 187, Annex 1A, Article XXIII.

[109] See 'WTO Bodies Involved in the Dispute Settlement Process', www.wto.org/english/tratop_e/dispu_e/disp_settlement_cbt_e/c3s3p1_e.htm.

[110] See Understanding on Rules and Procedures for the Settlement of Disputes, Art. 12.

[111] Peter Van den Bossche, 'The Demise of the WTO Appellate Body: Lessons for Governance of International Adjudication?' (28 October 2021) *World Trade Institute*,

process'.[112] This has resulted in a constant struggle between perceptions of the WTO dispute settlement mechanism (and more specifically the role of the AB therein) by various agents ranging from the members of the AB itself, the WTO Membership and scholars. The perceptions vary from seeing the AB as 'an independent, semi-autonomous judicial branch of the WTO system' or 'the ultimate guardian of the new WTO system and its neo-liberal values' thereby "constitutionalizing" the project of economic globalization'[113] and its mere role as a 'a safeguard against the occasional aberrant decisions made by the ad hoc panels'.[114] Contrary to the ascription of the role of other courts and tribunals such as the ECJ or the ECtHR discussed above, the WTO AB was considered by one of its former presidents to be not the place to 'broaden the scope of the WTO treaty' by extending the responsibilities of the WTO 'in the context of discrete disputes as a result of decisions by WTO jurists responding to innovate claims that are beyond the current scope of the WTO treaty'.[115] At the same time, it is quite surprising that the majority of the AB members have been selected for their expertise in general (international) law rather than their expertise in WTO law only.[116] This shows a discrepancy between the (perception of) the function (originally) ascribed to the WTO AB by (some of) the membership of the WTO compared to the Members of the AB and scholars.

3.3.3 *The Function Ascribed to the Judiciary: Developing the Law*

The function ascribed to judges and arbitrators in the development of the law constitutes, in line with and complementary to the question of judicial activism discussed above, is perceived differently through various communities. As Sir Gerald Fitzmaurice explained, aside from the approach to see a judge's task and duty 'to decide the case in hand, with

Working Paper No. 02/2021, www.wti.org/research/publications/1333/the-demise-of-the-wto-appellate-body-lessons-for-governance-of-international-adjudication/.

112 Michael Trebilcock and Joel Trachtman, *Advanced Introduction to International Trade Law* (Cheltenham: Edward Elgar Publishing Limited, 2020), 29.

113 Robert Howse, 'The World Trade Organization 20 Years On: Global Governance by Judiciary' (2016) 27 *European Journal of International Law* 9–77, 25.

114 Ibid.

115 James Bacchus, 'Not in Clinical Isolation', in Gabrielle Marceau (ed.), *A History of Law and Lawyers in the GATT/WTO: The Development of the Rule of Law in the Multilateral Trading System* (Cambridge: Cambridge University Press, 2015), 515–516.

116 Howse, 'The World Trade Organization 20 Years On', 27.

the minimum of verbiage necessary for this purpose', another approach conceives the function of the judge 'while duly deciding the case in hand, with the necessary supporting reasoning, and while not unduly straying outside the four comers of the case, to utilize those aspects of it which have a wider interest or connotation, in order to make general pronouncements of law and principle that may enrich and develop the law'.[117]

The inevitable by-product of dispute settlement is, one would agree, the development of international law, as the interpretation of norms often coincides with the 'making' of international law.[118] The role played by and influence of courts and tribunals in shaping international law, in many fields, both of a general and of a specific nature, is unquestionable.[119] The different ways in which this occurs, or for the present purposes, the different functions that various communities and legal agents ascribe to courts and tribunals in the development of the law however is noticeable – ranging from restraint (or an acceptance of the inevitability of (indirect) contribution) to a clear acceptance or even obligation to do so. Interestingly, as the examples below show, there often is no unanimity in the precise function ascribed to courts and tribunals *within* a specialization – the distinct perspectives within an area of specialization perhaps show precisely the tension between the level of mutual engagement expected by the various actors involved.

A good example to start with is the contrast between the WTO AB, and other courts and tribunals. An important aspect of the DSU is the mandate of the institutions involved, including the WTO AB. Article 2 DSU mentions that 'the dispute settlement system of the WTO is a central element in providing security and predictability to the multilateral trading system'. The same article adds that the mechanisms are there

> to preserve the rights and obligations of Members under the covered agreements, and to clarify the existing provisions of those agreements in accordance with customary rules of interpretation of public international law. Recommendations and rulings of the DSB cannot add to or diminish the rights and obligations provided in the covered agreements.

[117] Gerald Fitzmaurice, 'Hersch Lauterpacht – The Scholar as Judge' (1961) 37 *British Yearbook of International Law* 1, 14–15.

[118] See Ingo Venzke, *How Interpretation Makes International Law: On Semantic Change and Normative Twists* (Oxford: Oxford University Press, 2012).

[119] Zarbiyev, 'Judicial Activism in International Law', 247–278.

Under Article IX:2 of the WTO Agreement, the Ministerial Conference and the General Council have the exclusive authority to adopt interpretations of the WTO Agreement and of the Multilateral Trade Agreements. The mandate of the WTO AB, as a consequence, is more restricted or at least more specific than, say the ICJ, which has no mandate to only 'clarify' the existing norms in settling disputes.

Without engaging in a discussion of the rather thin and perhaps semantic distinction between clarification of norms and their interpretation, a former AB member and president noted that it is precisely in light of this specific mandate that the AB has given 'primary importance to the wording actual used' as such interpretative processes 'are more easily accepted by the parties to the treaty than the often "surprising" results of interpretative approaches that, for example, give more importance to the object and purpose of the treaty'.[120] However, it is precisely (amongst others) on these points that the United States has criticized the WTO AB resulting in the AB's dysfunction – thereby showing a clear discrepancy between how various agents – Member States and the AB members and even the community of scholars – see the very function of the AB. The United States indeed claims that the AB 'has not functioned according to the rules agreed by the United States and other WTO Members'.[121] In particular, the United States claims that panels or the AB cannot 'provide interpretations in the abstract or on issues not necessary to resolve the particular dispute' and that 'any "clarification" resulting from the system cannot take the form of judicial activism by panels or the Appellate body'.[122]

The ICJ, in turn, has been known for exercising judicial restraint and a lack of inclination to deal with issues not 'essential to the chain of reasoning leading to its decision'.[123] At the same time, the ICJ has also not shied away from doing precisely the opposite in certain cases. A good example is the ICJ's decision in the *Oil Platforms* case.[124] The case related to the question whether the United States had breached international law (and more specifically the 1955 Treaty of Amity between Iran and the United States) by the attacks on and destruction of Iranian oil platforms.

120 Van den Bossche, 'The Demise of the WTO Appellate Body'.
121 Ibid., at 1 (introduction).
122 Report on the Appellate Body of the World Trade Organization.
123 Thirlway, 'Judicial Activism', 88.
124 *Oil Platforms (Islamic Republic of Iran v. United States of America)*, [2003] I.C.J. Rep. 161.

The Court in that case, and contrary to its decision in the *Nicaragua* case, decided to first examine the existence of a justification for the acts complained of (under Article XX of the Treaty), before even turning to the question of whether at all there was a breach of Article X of the Treaty as alleged by Iran. The Court even added in the *dispositif* that the United States' claim on self-defence was not justified although it had found that there was in fact no breach of the Treaty itself.[125] The Court cited its 'freedom to choose the grounds for its decision',[126] but at the same time seems to have endorsed the position of the United States that 'The self-defense issues presented in this case raise matters of the highest importance to all members of the international community.'[127] This course of action, was seemingly justified by the ICJ's intention to 'say something' on preventive self-defence on which at that time there was much controversy and hence legal uncertainty,[128] has been criticized both by certain ICJ Judges themselves[129] and scholars,[130] which have explained that 'the judgment exposes the Court to arguments that it was not acting as an impartial decision-maker, but was set on lecturing the United States at a time when use of military force in Iraq in 2003 was being harshly criticized'.[131]

If we look at investment arbitration, we see that investment tribunals struggle with the precise role they should assume or the role they have been ascribed in the development of international investment law. The debate of course is influenced by the fact that the case law in the field has only boomed since a couple of decades, and that, in the de-centralized system of adjudication that investment arbitration is characterized by

[125] Ibid., at para. 125.

[126] Ibid., at para. 37.

[127] Ibid., at para. 38.

[128] See *Oil Platforms (Islamic Republic of Iran v. United States of America)*, Separate Opinion of Judge Simma, in which he explains that it is 'of utmost importance, and a matter of principle, for the Court to pronounce itself on questions of the threat or use of force in international relations whenever it is given the opportunity to do so' [2003] I.C.J. Rep. 324, para. 5.

[129] See, for example, *Oil Platforms (Islamic Republic of Iran v. United States of America)*, Separate Opinions of Judge Higgins, [2003] I.C.J. Rep. 225; *Oil Platforms (Islamic Republic of Iran v. United States of America)*, Separate Opinions of Judge Kooijmans, [2003] I.C.J. Rep. 246.

[130] Sean Murphy, 'The United States and the International Court of Justice: Coping with Antinomies', in Cesare Romano (ed.), *The Sword and the Scales: The United States and International Courts and Tribunals* (Cambridge: Cambridge University Press, 2009), 82.

[131] David Small, 'The Oil Platforms Case: Jurisdiction Through the – Closed – Eye of the Needle' (2004) 3 *The Law and Practice of International Courts and Tribunals* 113–124.

arbitral tribunals operating independently and requiring to interpret and apply mostly bilateral investment treaties, decisions tend to be not necessarily consistent. Here too, in its core, arbitral tribunals should in principle settle a dispute and in doing so apply and interpret the law as defined by parties in line with the general perception of the role of investor–state arbitral tribunals as operating within general international law.[132] However, some arbitrators (and arbitral tribunals as a whole) see a more specific role for investor–state arbitral tribunals. which evidences a level of engagement specific to the perceived specialized field of international investment law. Some tribunals thus have argued that tribunals have a duty to contribute to the harmonization of international investment law. The idea is that the development of a *jurisprudence constante* is necessary 'to foster consistency', especially in those areas of the law that are not yet well developed.[133] In *Saipem v. Bangladesh* for example, the tribunal, although adhering to the principle that 'it is not bound by previous decisions'[134] noted that 'it has a duty to seek to contribute to the harmonious development of investment law and thereby to meet the legitimate expectations of the community of States and investors towards certainty of the rule of law'.[135]

From within the arbitration community, however, there has been criticism of this role. While the tribunal in *Burlington v. Ecuador*[136] adhered to the need for tribunals to contribute to the development of international investment law, the award on this point was not supported by all three arbitrators: 'Arbitrator Stern does not analyze the arbitrator's role in the same manner, as she considers it her duty to decide each case on its own merits, independently of any apparent jurisprudential trend.'[137]

[132] See Eric De Brabandere, *Investment Treaty Arbitration as Public International Law: Procedural Aspects and Implications* (Cambridge: Cambridge University Press, 2014).

[133] Gabrielle Kaufmann-Kohler, 'Arbitral Precedent: Dream, Necessity or Excuse?' (2007) 23 *Arbitration International* 357–378, 377.

[134] *Saipem v. People's Republic of Bangladesh*, ICSID Case No. ARB/05/7, Award, 30 June 2009, para. 90.

[135] Ibid., at para. 90. See also *M.C.I. Power Group L.C. and New Turbine Inc. v. Republic of Ecuador*, ICSID Case No. ARB/03/6, Decision on Annulment, 19 October 2009, para. 25; *Víctor Pey Casado and President Allende Foundation v. Republic of Chile*, ICSID Case No. ARB/98/2, Award, 8 May 2008, para. 119, for other examples of similar language. See for similar, but perhaps more nuanced understanding of *jurisprudence constante*, *Electrabel S.A. v. Republic of Hungary*, ICSID Case No. ARB/07/19, Decision on Jurisdiction, Applicable Law and Liability, 30 November 2012, para. 4.15.

[136] *Burlington Resources v. Republic of Ecuador and Empresa Estatal Petróleos del Ecuador*, ICSID Case No. ARB/08/5, Decision on Jurisdiction, 2 June 2010, para. 100.

[137] Ibid.

Certain scholars too have described the absence of binding precedent in international investment law as a problem that undermines the consistency within the field,[138] and have in turn emphasized the need for legal predictability in international business transactions,[139] thereby ascribing to arbitrators the function to (contribute to) the development of a *jurisprudence constante*. Others in turn have analysed the role and function of arbitral tribunals in international investment law as requiring a more strict adherence to the principle that their main objective is to settle investment disputes.[140]

3.3.4 Scholars Are Unequally Prone to Argumentative Legal Research

International legal scholars do a whole lot of things. A considerable part of their activities can be captured by the use of a grammatical verb.[141] Thus, international legal scholars:

1. *Describe*: for example, a scholar may engage in the description of an arbitration award in which the abuse of rights doctrine is applied to the facts of a particular dispute.
2. *Interpret and understand*: for example, a scholar may engage in the study of an arbitration award in order to understand whether a reference by the arbitrators to the conduct of an investor as an 'abuse of process' means something other than an 'abuse of rights'.
3. *Systemize*: for example, a scholar may engage in the study of a vast series of arbitration awards seeking to establish a pattern that can help to come to grips with the abuse of rights doctrine in the context of investor–state arbitration disputes.
4. *Analyse*: for example, a scholar may engage in the study of arbitration awards in order to understand whether the occasional reference by arbitrators to the abuse of rights doctrine as an aspect of the principle

[138] Ian Laird and Rebecca Askew, 'Finality Versus Consistency: Does Investor-State Arbitration Need an Appellate System' (2005) 7 *Journal of Appellate Practice and Process* 285–302.

[139] Frank Spoorenberg and Jorge Viñuales, 'Conflicting Decisions in International Arbitration' (2009) 8 *The Law and Practice of International Courts and Tribunals* 91–113, 92.

[140] See Eric De Brabandere, 'Arbitral Decisions as a Source of International Investment Law', in Tarcisio Gazzini and Eric De Brabandere, *International Investment Law* (Leiden: Koninklijke Brill NV, 2012), 245–288.

[141] Although analytically distinct, in the actual conduct of legal research, these activities tend to overlap and are often difficult to distinguish.

of good faith sheds further light on the precise relationship between these two legal phenomena.

5. *Conceptualize and define*: for example, a scholar may investigate what it is precisely that defines the conduct of investors as an abuse of rights.
6. *Critically reflect*: for example, a scholar may demonstrate a lack of coherence between the abuse of rights doctrine and the theory according to the definition of the precise terms of application of an investment treaty is a matter exclusively for the treaty parties.
7. *Theorize*: for example, a scholar may draw up a theory that explains the relationship between the abuse of rights doctrine and the principle of good faith.
8. *Speculate*: for example, a scholar may ruminate on the future assessment by arbitrators of certain kinds of conduct on the part of investors.
9. *Solicit*: for example, a scholar may propose that the abuse of rights doctrine be applied differently in investor–state arbitration disputes or not at all.

In carrying out this work, international legal scholars make an important contribution to international legal discourse. A legal discourse, as we understand this rarely defined concept, is a collection of verbal exchanges of legal propositions. In this book, consequently, 'international legal discourse' refers to the sum of all utterances in oral or written form, expressing a proposition about international law. Understood in this sense, international legal discourse extends over a great number of different activities. They include, but are certainly not limited to, the negotiation and adoption of international agreements, the issuing of public statements and decisions, the pleading on behalf of a disputing party before an international court, the holding of conference presentations and the publication of reports, academic articles and monographs.

International legal scholars contribute to international legal discourse in two fundamentally different ways.[142] First, scholars contribute by developing an understanding of phenomena or issues, which were earlier either not clearly defined or insufficiently studied. In the earlier list of scholarly activities, the ones that tend to leave such contributions are the first seven. In line with common practice, we will refer to these activities

[142] See Ulf Linderfalk, 'Rational Reconstruction and International Legal Reasoning' (13 December 2022) *SSRN*, Working Paper, at 13.

as 'exploratory research'. Secondly, scholars contribute by predicting the consequences of phenomena or issues and by proposing conduct relative to these, such as discontinuing earlier practices, enacting new legislation or negotiating a new treaty. In the earlier list of scholarly activities, the ones that tend to leave such contributions are the last two. We will refer to these as 'argumentative legal research'.

If argumentative legal research is properly conducted, it uses information obtained by exploratory research to support its proposals. Hence, we should not think of the relationship between exploratory and argumentative research as in any way antagonistic but rather as complementary. Stated more precisely, we should think of exploratory research as subservient to argumentative legal research and other normative contributions to international legal discourse.[143] Still, it remains a fact that in different communities of international lawyers, scholars place different emphasis on the different kinds of legal research. To put it simply, sometimes, the specialization of scholars would seem to make them unequally prone to argumentative legal research.

Compare, for example, the way that case notes are typically framed, depending on whether they are written by an international law generalist or a human rights specialist. Human rights specialists *describe*: for example, a scholar may provide an outline of the factual and legal context of a case brought before the European Court of Human Rights, and give an account of the response of this court to the arguments of the applicant and respondent.[144] They *interpret*: for example, a scholar may provide her opinion on what might have been perceived by the European Court as a factor in its assessment of the proportionality of a measure restricting the exercise of a human right.[145] They *systemize*: for example, a scholar may refer to the pattern of practice of the European Court to establish that a certain kind of conduct could amount to an inference with a

143 Ibid.

144 See, for example, Fiona de Londras and Kanstantsin Dzehtsiarou, 'Grand Chamber of the European Court of Human Rights, A, B & C v. Ireland, Decision of 17 December 2010' (2013) 62 *International and Comparative Law Quarterly* 250–262, 257; Julie Maher, 'Eweida and Others: A New Era for Article 9?' (2014) 63 *International and Comparative Law Quarterly* 213–233, 224–225; Tatyana Eatwell, 'Selling the Pass: Habeas Corpus, Diplomatic Relations and the Protection of Liberty and Security of Persons Detained Abroad' (2013) 62 *International and Comparative Law Quarterly* 727–739, 734.

145 See, for example, de Londras and Dzehtsiarou, 'Grand Chamber of the European Court of Human Rights', 257.

certain right.[146] They *analyse*: for example, a scholar may find that concerns raised by dissenters have little bearing on a case.[147] They *conceptualize*: for example, a scholar may distinguish the case at hand from one or several earlier human rights cases brought before the European Court under the same provision of the European Convention.[148] They *critically reflect*: for example, a scholar may remark that the response of the European Court to arguments probably took many by surprise.[149] They *theorize*: for example, a scholar may infer that, generally speaking, a European consensus has been applied by the European Court in order to establish an expanded scope of protection for the European Convention in areas not expressly mentioned within it or contemplated at the time of its drafting.[150] They *speculate*: for example, a scholar may warn about the risk that a certain judicial approach poses to the continuing development of 'a rights-based, constitutionalist public order' throughout Europe.[151] They *solicit*: for example, a scholar may advise a government not to rely on the non-binding nature of MoUs to escape the scrutiny of courts with regard to its efforts to ensure their enforcement.[152] Overall, generalists do much the same things, but to different degrees. It is only on rare occasions that you find them speculating and soliciting.[153]

If it is our assumption that international legal scholars recognize the appropriateness of their own action, these differences can be understood to reflect some very different ideas of the function of legal scholarship.

[146] See, for example, Maher, 'Eweida and Others', 224–225.
[147] See, for example, Eatwell, 'Selling the Pass', 734.
[148] Ibid., at 738.
[149] See, for example, Maher, 'Eweida and Others', 220.
[150] See, for example, de Londras and Dzehtsiarou, 'Grand Chamber of the European Court of Human Rights', 251.
[151] Ibid., at 258.
[152] See, for example, Eatwell, 'Selling the Pass', 739.
[153] See, for example, J. Craig Barker, 'International Court of Justice: 'Jurisdictional Immunities of the State (Germany v. Italy)', Judgment of 3 February 2012' (2013) 62 *International and Comparative Law Quarterly* 741–752, 753; Filippo Fontanelli and Eirik Björge, 'International Court of Justice, "Application of the Interim Accord of 13 September 1995 (the Former Yugoslav Republic of Macedonia v. Greece)" Judgment of 5 December 2011' (2012) 61 *International and Comparative Law Quarterly* 775–784, 775. This is not to say that speculating and soliciting is equally rare in other kinds of texts. Still, we do believe that whatever kind of text we are studying, we will find human rights specialist more prone to argumentative legal research than the generalists.

All scholars look upon themselves as engaged in an enterprise that seeks to affect the behaviour of legal and political decision-makers. Whereas generalists admit that their role is largely limited to providing the groundwork for practical argument, human rights specialists believe that they are themselves acting to affect directly the behaviour of those decision-makers, much like any other participant in international human rights discourse. This is proof of a mutual engagement among human rights lawyers that does not exist among the generalists.

3.3.5 *Scholars Are Providers of Legal Knowledge in Different Senses*

A considerable part of the work of the international legal scholar is concerned with the development of knowledge about international law, in one way or another. As we have argued extensively elsewhere, there can be no knowledge about international law without an idea of how single legal propositions should be fitted together.[154] Thus, the work of international legal scholars presupposes a conception of the international legal system. There are different ways of conceiving this system. To simplify matters, we will distinguish between a legal positivist's, a legal idealist's and a legal realist's conception.

By 'legal positivism', we mean exclusive and not inclusive legal positivism. The latter branch of legal positivism takes a markedly more flexible stance to questions concerning moral constraints on the concept of law.[155] Identifying legal positivism with the 'harder' of its several different versions would seem to be justified, while it helps to divide between different conceptions of an international legal system into sharper relief. For legal positivism, the constitutive elements of a legal system are its legal norms, and its legal norms only.[156] A legal norm is a reason for action and a basis for justification of legal decisions.[157] In a legal system, legal norms are organized along chains of authority – according to the way in which they confer authority upon each other.[158]

[154] See Ulf Linderfalk, *The International Legal System as a System of Knowledge* (Cheltenham: Edward Elgar Publishing Limited, 2022), 1–18.

[155] On the distinction between exclusive and inclusive legal positivism, see, for example, Kenneth Himma, 'Legal Positivism', in *Internet Encyclopedia of Philosophy*, https://iep.utm.edu/legalpos.

[156] See Section 1.2.

[157] See Section 1.2.

[158] See Section 1.2.

Since, in such chains of authority, a 'superior' norm provides only a reason of validity but does not itself provide the contents of the norm or norms that are 'inferior' to it, the relation between norms is purely formal. It is conditioned only by the pedigree of norms and their logical form.[159] Ultimately, then, a legal system is nothing but a logical framework.[160] It remains to be furnished with substantial contents drawn from social facts, such as the conclusion of an agreement creating an international organization, or the adoption of a resolution by an organ of this organization.

Whereas legal positivists see law as a form of social order valuable in its own right, legal idealists do not.[161] For legal idealists, no law can be self-justifying. If law exists, then this is because of the presence of some or other idea, either of what law should be like, or what the legal project should achieve.[162] To have an idea of what law should be like, or what law should achieve, is to set an ideal for the legal project.[163] Although legal idealists are divided over the issue of what precisely are the ideals set for the legal enterprise,[164] in the final analysis, they have a common conception of an international legal system. For legal idealists, the constitutive elements of a legal system are its legal norms and the one or several ideals set for the legal project.[165] A legal norm is a reason for action and a basis for justification of legal decisions. Since ideals lack this prescriptive dimension, the logical form of a norm cannot explain the relationship between a legal norm and an ideal. This relationship can only be a matter of the efficacy of the norm relative to the ideal.[166] Interestingly, legal idealists conceive similarly of the relationship between the legal norms among themselves. The one conclusive issue that determines this relationship is the degree to which norms help to bring about the ideal or ideals set for the legal project.[167]

159 See Section 1.2.

160 See Section 1.2.

161 See Section 1.2.

162 See Section 1.2.

163 See Section 1.2.

164 For a brief survey, see Ulf Linderfalk, *Understanding* Jus Cogens *in International Law and International Legal Discourse* (Cheltenham: Edward Elgar Publishing Limited, 2020), 53–59.

165 See Linderfalk, *The International Legal System*, 30–32.

166 See Section 1.2.

167 See Section 1.2.

By 'legal realism', we mean American legal realism in its classical version.[168] We do not mean Scandinavian legal realism,[169] which is a school with few followers among international legal researchers, in contrast to American legal realism. For legal realists, the constitutive elements of law are everything that figures in a prediction of how legal decision-makers in a jurisdiction would *generally* decide.[170] This includes legal culture. It includes all social facts, which legal culture urges the legal decision-makers to consider and which, thus, have a predictable influence on adjudicators and legal decision-making. Examples range from international agreements, state practice and decisions and recommendations issued by international organizations, to non-binding international agreements and declarations. Some of these facts are such that also legal positivists would include in *their* conception of law, but for different reasons. For legal realists, the function of law is to influence legal decision-makers.[171] To *influence* is to cause someone to change a behaviour, belief or opinion or to cause something to be changed.[172] Hence, for legal realists, the constituent elements of law connect as cause and effect. If we can ever think about international law as a system, then this is because, in the light of legal culture, some social facts are the predictable cause of future legal decisions.[173] It is no mere coincidence that prominent realists, such as Myres McDougal and Rosalyn Higgins, refer to the international legal system as a 'process'.[174] If the constituent elements of international law connect as cause and effect, the international legal system will remain in a constant flux, and we cannot possibly tie its existence to a single point in time. This distinguishes the realists' conception of an international legal system

[168] Prominent legal realists in this sense are Karl Llewelyn, Jerome Frank, Felix Cohen and Herman Oliphant. For an introduction to American legal realism, see, for example, Michael Green, 'Legal Realism as a Theory of Law' (2005) 46 *William and Mary Law Review* 1915–2000; Brian Leiter, 'Rethinking Legal Realism: Towards a Naturalized Jurisprudence' (1997) 76 *Texas Law Review* 267–315.

[169] On the difference between American and Scandinavian legal realism, see Torben Spaak, 'Realism About the Nature of Law' (2017) 30 *Ratio Juris* 75–104.

[170] See Green, 'Legal Realism as a Theory of Law', 1934.

[171] See Linderfalk, *The International Legal System*, 34–35.

[172] See *Cambridge English Dictionary*, https://dictionary.cambridge.org/us/dictionary/english.

[173] See Chapter 1.2.

[174] See, for example, Rosalyn Higgins, *Problems and Process: International Law and How We Use It* (Oxford: Oxford University Press, 1994); Myres McDougal, 'Law as a Process of Decision: A Policy-Oriented Approach to Legal Study' (1956) *Natural Law Forum*, Paper 6.

from those of the legal positivists and legal idealists, which, because they build upon elements that are abstractions of reality, have a time-bound existence.[175]

Interestingly, these different conceptions of an international legal system are not equally endorsed among international legal scholars. The legal idealist's conception of an international legal system, for example, seems to be endorsed less among international law generalists than among some groups of specialists, such as human rights or international criminal law scholars. We will illustrate this proposition by the discussion that scholars have entertained over the last twenty-five or so years on the immunity of states and state officials for the violations of *jus cogens* obligations.[176] To simplify presentation, we will confine ourselves to the facts and legal context of the famous *Pinochet (No 3) Case*.[177]

This case raised an important general question concerning the legal effects of the *jus cogens* status of the prohibition of torture: does the *jus cogens* status of the prohibition of torture imply that charges for the perpetration of torture can be brought in domestic courts against the former Head of State of another country, *irrespective of the immunity enjoyed by that person under rules of international law*? To answer this question, discussants had to engage with the rule, which affords priority to rules of *jus cogens* over rules of ordinary international law. This rule applies on the condition of the existence of a normative conflict. If a

175 See Linderfalk, *The International Legal System*, 38.

176 See, for example, Andrea Bianchi, 'Gazing at the Crystal Ball (again): State Immunity and *Jus Cogens* beyond Germany v. Italy' (2013) 4 *Journal of International Dispute Settlement* 1–19; François Boudreault, 'Identifying Conflicts of Norms: The ICJ Approach in the Case of the "Jurisdictional Immunities of the State (Germany v. Italy: Greece Intervening"' (2012) 25 *Leiden Journal of International Law* 1003–1012; Carlos Espósito, '*Jus Cogens* and Jurisdictional Immunities of States at the International Court of Justice: A Conflict Does Exist' (2011) 21 *Italian Yearbook of International Law* 161–174; Ulf Linderfalk, 'The Principle of Rational Decision-Making: As Applied to the Identification of Normative Conflicts in International Law' (2013) 73 *Zeitschrift für ausländisches öffentliches Recht und Völkerrecht* 591–614; Alexander Orakhelashvili, 'The Classification of International Legal Rules: A Reply to Stefan Talmon' (2013) 26 *Leiden Journal of International Law* 89–103; Stefan Talmon, '*Jus Cogens* after Germany v. Italy: Substantive and Procedural Rules Distinguished' (2012) 25 *Leiden Journal of International Law* 979–1002; Jure Vidmar, 'Rethinking *Jus Cogens* After Germany v. Italy: Back to Article 53?' (2013) 60 *Netherlands International Law Review* 1–25; Thomas Weatherall, '*Jus Cogens* and Sovereign Immunity: Reconciling Divergence in Contemporary Jurisprudence' (2014–2015) 46 *Georgetown Journal of International Law* 1151–1212.

177 *R v. Bow Street Metropolitan Stipendiary Magistrate, ex parte Pinochet Ugarte (No 3)*, [1999] 199 I.L.R. 261.

conflict between a rule of *jus cogens* and a rule of ordinary international law had not existed, priority had not been an issue in the first place.

On the face of it, the proper application of the *jus cogens* priority rule would seem to require consideration of two obligations. First, there is the obligation of states not to allow charges for the perpetration of torture to be brought in domestic courts against the former Head of State of another country. Secondly, there is the obligation of states and individuals not to perpetrate torture. General opinion confers on the former obligation the status of ordinary international law; it confers on the latter obligation the status of *jus cogens*.[178] These two obligations, however, do not relate to the same conduct, which is a condition for the existence of a normative conflict, irrespective of one's preferred definition of this tricky concept.[179] Understandably, over time, the focus of the debate has gradually shifted – from the obligation of states not to allow charges for the perpetration of torture to be brought in domestic courts against the former Head of State of another country, to the obligation of states not to absolve perpetrators of torture of criminal responsibility.

To reach the conclusion that this third obligation exists, and that the obligation should be afforded priority over the rule of immunity for foreign Heads of State, scholars have to find some argument, which suggests that it derives from a *jus cogens* norm. The argument that human rights specialists often use reads something along the following lines: The obligation of states not to absolve perpetrators of torture of criminal responsibility derives from the same norm as the obligation of states and individuals not to perpetrate torture. If the latter of these two obligations has the status of *jus cogens*, then consequently, the former obligation has that status, too.[180]

[178] See, for example, *Questions Relating to the Obligation to Prosecute or Extradite (Belgium v. Senegal)* [2012] I.C.J. Rep. 99, para. 99.

[179] See, for example, Linderfalk, *The International Legal System*, 94–108.

[180] See, for example, Kerstin Bartsch and Björn Elberling, '*Jus Cogens* vs. Immunity, Round Two: The Decision of the European Court of Human Rights in the Kalogeropoulou et al. v. Greece and Germany Decision' (2003) 4 *German Law Journal* 477–491, 483–484; Carlos Espósito, 'Of Plumbers and Social Architects: Elements and Problems of the Judgment of the International Court of Justice in the Jurisdictional Immunities of the State' (2013) 4 *Journal of International Dispute Settlement* 439–456, 453; Andrew Mitchell, 'Leave Your Hat On: Head of State Immunity and Pinochet' (1999) 25 *Monash University Law Review* 225–256, 235; Jodi Horowitz, 'Regina v. Bartle and the Commissioner of Police for the Metropolis and Others Ex Parte Pinochet: Universal Jurisdiction and Sovereign Immunity for Jus Cogens Violations' (1999) 23 *Fordham*

This argument entails a structural claim. More precisely, it entails a claim of how lawyers should individuate international norms and separate them from other individual norms belonging to the same legal system.[181] Interestingly, international law generalists typically use a different argument. This argument entails a different structural claim: The obligation of states not to absolve perpetrators of torture of criminal responsibility cannot possibly derive from the same norm as the obligation of states and individuals not to perpetrate torture. Hence, the *jus cogens* status of the one obligation does not tell anything about either the status of the other obligation, or even its existence.[182]

These widely diverging structural claims can be explained by the proposition that generalists and human rights specialists endorse different conceptions of an international legal system.[183] From the point of view of a legal positivist's conception of an international legal system, criteria of individuation help to understand norms as separate units in a system, which recognizes only the logical form of norms and their function as sources of authority of yet other norms. According to this way of thinking, the obligation of states not to absolve perpetrators of torture of criminal responsibility cannot possibly derive from the same norm as the obligation of states and individuals not to perpetrate torture. The two obligations have two entirely different logical functions. Whereas the one imposes on states an obligation not to perpetrate torture, the other is concerned with the enforcement of this same obligation. For legal positivists, these different functions of obligations presuppose the existence of two different norms.[184]

From the point of view of a legal idealist's conception of an international legal system, criteria of individuation help to understand norms as means for the realization of a presupposed legal ideal. According to

International Law Journal 489–527, 511, 523–524; Roger Taylor, '*Pinochet*, Confusion, and Justice: The Denial of Immunity in U.S. Courts to Alleged Torturers Who Are Former Heads of State' (2001) 24 *Thomas Jefferson Law Review* 101–120, 114.

181 See Ulf Linderfalk, 'The Legal Consequences of *Jus Cogens* and the Individuation of Norms' (2020) 33 *Leiden Journal of International Law* 893–909.

182 See, for example, Hazel Fox, *The Law of State Immunity* (Oxford: Oxford University Press, 2002), 525; Talmon, '*Jus Cogens* after Germany v. Italy', 979–1002; Vidmar, 'Rethinking *Jus Cogens* After Germany v. Italy', 1–25; Andreas Zimmermann, 'Sovereign Immunity and Violations of International *Jus Cogens*' (1995) 16 *Michigan Journal of International Law* 433–440, 438.

183 Linderfalk, 'The Legal Consequences of *Jus Cogens*', 893–909.

184 Ibid., at 901–902.

this way of thinking, the obligation of states not to absolve perpetrators of torture of criminal responsibility derives from the same norm as the obligation of states and individuals not to perpetrate torture. Considered as means for the realization of whatever ideal idealists presuppose have been set for the legal enterprise, the two obligations cannot be distinguished. They both serve to eradicate the perpetration of torture. This similarity of functions of obligations tells legal idealists that they derive from the same norm.[185]

If it is our assumption that international legal scholars recognize the appropriateness of their own actions, these differences can be understood to reflect some very different ideas of the function of legal scholarship. International legal scholars are providers of legal knowledge, but, apparently, different scholars understand this function differently. Whereas international law generalists tend to think of legal knowledge in the sense of propositions fitting the legal positivist's conception of an international legal system, human rights specialists tend to think of it from the point of view of the legal idealist's conception. This difference can be explained by the widespread idea of human rights specialists that they are engaged in the pursuit of some desired state of affairs – we will return to this issue in subsequent Chapter 4. It can also be seen as proof of a mutual engagement among human rights specialists that does not exist among the generalists.

[185] Ibid., at 902–904. This is why legal idealists tend to confer a *jus cogens* status on obligations concerned with the enforcement of *jus cogens* norms more generally. Examples include: the obligation to exercise jurisdiction over *jus cogens* crimes; the obligation to enact domestic law prohibiting *jus cogens* offences; and the obligation not to absolve perpetrators of such offences of criminal responsibility. See, in turn, Third report on peremptory norms of general international law (*jus cogens*) by Dire Tladi, Special Rapporteur, 29 May 2018, U.N. Doc. A/CN.4/714/Corr.1, 68; *YATAMA v. Nicaragua* [2005] Inter-. Am. Ct. H.R. (ser. C) No. 127, para. 185; *Prosecutor v. Furundžija*, Trial Chamber, Judgment Case No. IT-95-17/1-T, 10 December 1998, paras. 155–157.

4

A Joint Enterprise

4.1 Introduction

We began Chapter 3 by assuming that some particular segment of the international legal system, called 'X law', was being categorized by some person or institution as a special regime. We pointed out that, from the point of view of the legal idealist's conception of a special regime, this categorization entails altogether three claims, all of which require justification. First, there is the claim that X law specialists have a mutual engagement. Second, there is the claim that X law specialists are engaged in a joint enterprise. Third, there is the claim that X law specialists have a shared repertoire.

In Chapter 3, we occupied ourselves with the issue of how to establish the first of these claims. This claim expresses the existence among X law specialists of a normative presupposition. Maintaining that X law specialists have a mutual engagement is to say that these specialists believe that it is desirable that they join forces and collaborate in the pursuit of some particular enterprise. We suggested the use of a methodology that would regard such normative presuppositions as implicit in the actual conduct of X law specialists and ascertainable based on the assumption that these specialists act rationally and that they recognize the appropriateness of their own action.

Our proposal is that the second claim be approached in much the same way. To say that X law specialists are engaged in a joint enterprise is to assume the existence of a normative presupposition. It is to assert that X law specialists do what they do based on the idea that some certain state of affairs is desirable. If, once again, we assume that X law specialists act rationally and that they recognize the appropriateness of their own action, the existence of such a presupposition can be established based on actual conduct. More specifically, as Chapter 2 indicated, it can be inferred from: (i) the pursuit of X law specialists of a distinct state of affairs; and (ii) the way in which X law specialists perform assignments.

The case studies that we will highlight in this chapter will help to illustrate the practical implications of this suggestion. Section 4.2 will illustrate how the engagement of international law specialists in a joint enterprise can be inferred from their pursuance of a distinct state of affairs. This section will ask:

> Relative to a selected segment of international law (X law), what desirable state of affairs are X law specialists pursuing? How does this state of affairs compare with those pursued by other communities of international lawyers?

Section 3 will illustrate how the engagement of international law specialists in a joint enterprise can be inferred from the way in which they perform assignments. This section will ask:

> Relative to a selected segment of international law (X law), how do X law specialists perform assignments? How does their approach compare with the approach of other communities of international lawyers to similar assignments?

4.2 The Pursuit of a Distinct State of Affairs

4.2.1 The Exercise of Discretion

The exercise of discretion is a central feature of legal decision-making. 'Discretion' refers to a power that a lawmaker vests in a legal decision-maker.[1] This power is conferred under a legal norm, either explicitly or implicitly. It enables a person or an institution to make decisions in conformity with a legal norm, while giving him/her or it the possibility to choose between diverse courses of action. A legal decision-maker exercises discretion when it avails itself of a decision-making power so framed. That said, there is no such thing as an absolute legal discretion in the sense of a power to act at will. In all cases, international law makes the exercise of discretion subject to pre-established criteria. We will refer to these as 'constraining criteria'.[2]

[1] On the concept of discretion, see Ulf Linderfalk, 'The Exercise of Discretion in International Law – Why Constraining Criteria Have a Proper Place in the Analysis of Legal Decision-Making' (2019) 62 *German Yearbook of International Law* 407–430.

[2] Ibid.

In exercising discretion, legal decision-makers tend to be influenced by different constraining criteria, depending on the law that they are applying. In many cases, decision-makers refer to the principle of good faith and the object and purpose of the treaty that they are considering.[3] Consider, for example, the judgement of the ICJ in the case concerning the *Application of the Interim Accord of 13 September 1995*.[4] The Government of Greece had contended that the Applicant had breached the obligation imposed by Article 5, paragraph 1 of the Interim Accord of 13 September 1995 between the Former Yugoslav Republic of Macedonia (FYROM) and Greece, which reads:

> The Parties agree to continue negotiations under the auspices of the Secretary-General of the United Nations pursuant to Security Council resolution 845 (1993) with a view to reaching agreement on the difference described in that resolution and in Security Council resolution 817 (1993).[5]

This provision, although it clearly imposed on the Greek and FYROM governments an obligation to 'continue negotiations', conferred on them the discretion to decide precisely how negotiations were to be conducted and when.

In response to the claim of a breach of Article 5, paragraph 1, the Court stressed that it is a requirement following implicitly from this provision that the parties must negotiate in good faith.[6] As the Court noted, the parties to the Accord have an obligation 'not only to enter into negotiations, but also to pursue them as far as possible, with a view to concluding agreements'.[7] No doubt, so understood, Article 5, paragraph 1 did not impose on the parties the obligation to reach an agreement; nor did it require that lengthy negotiations be pursued of necessity. As the Court seemed keen to convey, the provision entailed an obligation of conduct. In exercising the discretion conferred under Article 5, paragraph 1, the parties would have to conduct themselves so as not to

[3] See Ulf Linderfalk, 'What Are the Functions of the General Principles? Good Faith and International Legal Pragmatics' (2018) 78 *Zeitschrift für ausländisches öffentliches Recht und Völkerrecht* 1–32.

[4] *Application of the Interim Accord of 13 September 1995 (The Former Republic of Macedonia v. Greece)*, [2011] I.C.J. Rep. 644.

[5] Interim Accord between Greece and the Former Yugoslav Republic of Macedonia, New York, 13 September 1995, in force 13 October 1995, 1891 U.N.T.S. 7.

[6] *Application of the Interim Accord of 13 September 1995*, para. 131.

[7] Ibid., at para. 132. Quotes are from the PCIJ in *Railway Traffic between Lithuania and Poland*, [1931] P.C.I.J. (ser. A/B) No. 42.

frustrate the object and purpose of the provision – the creation of conditions favourable to reaching an agreement. As the Court explained:

> States must conduct themselves so that the 'negotiations are meaningful'. This requirement is not satisfied, for example, where either of the parties 'insists upon its own position without contemplating any modification of it' or where they obstruct negotiations, for example, by interrupting communications or causing delays in an unjustified manner or disregarding the procedures agreed upon. Negotiations with a view to reaching an agreement also imply that the parties should pay reasonable regard to the interests of the other.[8]

The principle of good faith, in the sense in which the International Court applied it in this case, suggests a deference to the intention of treaty parties. In the terminology of the Court, the 'object and purpose' of Article 5, paragraph 1 is merely shorthand for the state of affairs that the government of Greece and FYROM sought to obtain by including this provision in the Interim Accord. In other cases, when international legal decision-makers exercise discretion conferred under a treaty provision, they are influenced by constraining criteria that cannot as easily be explained in terms of a deference to party intention. Take, for example, the judgement of the International Court in the *Pulp Mills on the River of Uruguay* case.[9]

To cut the story short, Uruguay had authorized the construction of a pulp mill in the River Uruguay. This had prompted the Government of Argentina to bring before the International Court a number of claims of violations of provisions of the 1975 Statute of the River Uruguay, among them Article 27:

> The rights of each Party to use the waters of the river, within its jurisdiction, for domestic, sanitary, industrial and agricultural purposes shall be exercised without prejudice to the application of the procedure laid down in articles 7 to 12 when the use is liable to affect the régime of the river or the quality of its waters.[10]

Article 27 recognizes the power of the parties to authorize activities such as the construction and operation of a pulp mill. As the Court noted, this power is not unlimited: due regard must be had to the interests of the other riparian state in the shared resource and to its environmental

[8] Ibid. References to earlier case-law have been omitted.

[9] *Case Concerning Pulp Mills on the River Uruguay (Argentina v. Uruguay)*, [2010] I.C.J. Rep. 14, para. 177.

[10] Statute of the River Uruguay, Salto, 26 February 1975, in force 18 September 1976, 1295 U.N.T.S. 331.

protection.[11] Article 27, the Court explained, embodies the idea of sustainable development and the balance between economic development and environmental protection that is its essence.[12] Readers should recall the short history of the principle of sustainable development. It did not appear in a legally binding international instrument until the conclusion of the 1992 Climate Change Convention.[13] This being the case, it is indeed very difficult to explain this finding of the Court in terms of any intention of the parties to the 1975 Statute. The finding would seem to flow instead from a more recent idea of the function of international environmental law, which now transcends the understanding of this entire sphere of regulation.

As Etienne Wenger would have it, the judgement of the ICJ in *Pulp Mills* is proof of the construction of international environmental law as a joint enterprise and a special regime. The ICJ is often characterized by international lawyers as one of the few 'general international courts'.[14] The better description is that the ICJ is a court, which adjudicates disputes involving all parts of international law. In *Pulp Mills*, it was certainly not approaching the 1975 Statute in a way that characterizes an international law generalist, seeking guidance in the principle of good faith and the intention of the treaty parties. It was approaching the 1975 Statute in a way typical of the international environmental law specialist.

4.2.2 *Predictability and Legal Certainty*

Legal certainty is part of the broader notion of the 'rule of law' and is also related to concepts such as (in)determinacy, coherence and consistency. In general, legal certainty has been defined as 'the idea that the law must be sufficiently clear to provide those subject to legal norms with the means to regulate their own conduct and to protect against the arbitrary exercise of public power'.[15] The European Court of Human Rights, in

[11] *Case Concerning Pulp Mills on the River Uruguay*, para. 177.

[12] Ibid.

[13] See, for example, Ulrich Beyerlin and Thilo Marauhn, *International Environmental Law* (Oxford: Hart Publishing Ltd, 2011), 74.

[14] See, for example, Gabriele Gagliani, 'The International Court of Justice and Cultural Heritage: International Cultural Heritage Law Through the Lens of World Court Jurisprudence?', in Anne-Marie Carstens and Elizabeth Varner (eds.), *Intersections in International Cultural Heritage Law* (Oxford: Oxford University Press, 2020), 223.

[15] Mark Fenwick and Stefan Wrbka, 'The Shifting Meaning of Legal Certainty' in Mark Fenwick and Stefan Wrbka (eds.), *Legal Certainty in a Contemporary Context* (Singapore: Springer, 2016), 1.

turn, has argued in the context of deprivation of property that the 'general principle of legal certainty' requires that 'the law itself be foreseeable in its application, so that it meets the standard of "lawfulness" set by the Convention, a standard which requires that all law be sufficiently precise to allow the person – if need be, with appropriate advice – to foresee, to a degree that is reasonable in the circumstances, the consequences which a given action may entail'.[16] Others have defined it more generally a requiring that 'rules of law be known, clear, precise, stable, certain and predictable'.[17]

The broad implications of the principle of legal certainty in international law, however, are still unclear, as legal certainty as a general principle is not recognized,[18] and its precise implications on the international legal level unclear.[19] In fact, as we will show here, there are indeed different states of affairs that international lawyers seek to pursue depending on the precise regime in which they operate, and it is precisely the specific and distinct nature of a given regime that is invoked or underlies the differentiation.

A first example is the fragmented legal framework of international investment law. The regime is noticeable for its variety of mostly bilateral international investment agreements (IIAs), which contain similar generic provisions, but which at the same time are often formulated (very) differently. Because of that, arbitral tribunals dealing with investment disputes have on occasion attempted to provide 'legal certainty', that is, by providing interpretations of provisions in investment treaties which match the interpretations of similar provisions by arbitral tribunals in other disputes. One can easily understand why certain consistency in the outcome of arbitral decisions would be beneficial to the development of international investment law, and in the long run, references to and reliance on previous awards can indeed enhance legal certainty within

16 Case No. 75039/01, *Korchuganova v. Russia*, [2006] ECHR 602, para. 47.

17 Jérémie Van Meerbeeck, 'The Principle of Legal Certainty in the Case Law of the European Court of Justice: From Certainty to Trust' (2016) 41 *European Law Review* 275–288, 275.

18 James Maxeiner, 'Legal Certainty and Legal Methods: A European Alternative to American Legal Indeterminacy?' (2007) 15 *Tulane Journal of International & Comparative Law* 541–607. See also Isabel Lifante-Vidaln, 'Is Legal Certainty a Formal Value?' (2020) 11 *Jurisprudence* 456–467.

19 Rosalyn Higgins, '"The Rule of Law: Some Sceptical Thoughts" Lecture Given at the British Institute for International and Comparative Law 16 October 2007', in Rosalyn Higgins, *Themes and Theories*, vol. II (Oxford: Oxford University Press, 2009), 1330.

the regime of international investment law. This idea has been reflected in certain arbitral decisions, such as the decision of the Tribunal in *ADC v. Hungary*, which noted that 'cautious reliance on certain principles developed in a number of those cases, as persuasive authority, may advance the body of law, which in turn may serve predictability in the interest of both investors and host States'.[20] While the existence of inconsistencies does not run counter the idea that a certain field of law can be a regime of itself or part of a broader international legal system, the avoidance (or absence) of inconsistent decisions undoubtedly has certain value, because it does increase legal certainty. It has indeed been noted on occasion that consistent decisions are a fundamental aspect of the rule of law, at least when one confines the inconsistencies to the understanding of situations where the rules are identical and the facts similar or identical. Kurtz has argued that even 'the thinnest conception of rule of law in any legal system' would militate in favour of like cases to be treated alike.[21]

In the context of the UNCITRAL Working Group III discussions on the reform of investment arbitration, the need for certainty and predictability has also been highlighted.[22] This need has moreover been considered important in relation to States in order 'to understand whether their actions, such as possible future legislative or regulatory activities, might breach their obligations', but also in relation to foreign investors to allow them 'to assess whether certain treatment was in accordance with treaty obligations'.[23]

This pursuance of a joint enterprise within international investment law, though it can be criticized in several respects,[24] is obvious and interestingly is a state of affairs pursued by certain actors (such as arbitral tribunals) but only within a given regime (international investment law) and based on their own interpretation of the desirability of such a state of affairs.

20 *ADC Affiliate Limited and ADC & ADMC Management Limited v. Republic of Hungary*, ICSID Case No. ARB/03/16, Award, 2 October 2006, para. 293.

21 Ibid., at 271.

22 See in general Possible reform of investor-State dispute settlement (ISDS): Consistency and related matters, Note by the Secretariat, 28 August 2018, U.N. Doc. A/CN.9/WG.III/WP.150.

23 Ibid., at para. 28.

24 See Eric De Brabandere, 'Coherence, Consistency, and the Reform of Investment Treaty Arbitration', in Daniel Franchini, Russell Buchan and Nicholas Tsagourias, *The Changing Character of International Dispute Settlement* (Cambridge: Cambridge Academic, 2023).

The case law of the European Court of Human Rights similarly has often referred to 'legal certainty' as an overarching interest that should guide the Court. In *Chapman* for instance, the ECtHR noted that

> while it is not formally bound to follow any of its previous judgements, it is in the interests of legal certainty, foreseeability and equality before the law that it should not depart, without good reason, from precedents laid down in previous cases.[25]

The Court, however, then added that

> Since the Convention is first and foremost a system for the protection of human rights, the Court must, however, have regard to the changing conditions in Contracting States and respond, for example, to any emerging consensus as to the standards to be achieved.[26]

While the first citation might well align with more general perspectives on the need for international courts and tribunals to not depart from a tribunal or court's own case law, the ECtHR has in the second citation shown to nonetheless pursue a different approach, which it has moreover, as cited, explicitly linked to the 'human rights' nature of the system in which it operates. The ECtHR in doing so has 'contributed to establishing more legitimacy at the universal level for evolutive approaches to interpretation'.[27] This specific state of affairs that the ECtHR is pursuing clearly stands apart from, for example, the practice of arbitral tribunals in international investment law. The ECtHR's perspective on 'legal certainty' is tailored to the state of affairs it is pursuing as a human rights court, which implies that 'legal certainty' should warrant the reliance on the Court's previous cases but only to the extent that this does not go against 'any emerging consensus as to the standards to be achieved', to use the words of the Court.[28]

[25] Case No. 27238/95, *Chapman v. United Kingdom*, (2001) 33 EHRR 399, para. 70.

[26] Ibid.

[27] Georg Nolte, 'The European Court of Human Rights and the Sources of International Law', 23 September 2020, https://rm.coe.int/the-european-court-of-human-rights-and-the-sources-of-international-la/1680a05733, 3.

[28] For an expression of caution on this practice, see ibid. The author has argued that evolutive approaches to treaty interpretation need to be pursued with caution. They should, as far as possible, be undertaken on the basis of a broad supportive practice of the parties to a treaty so as to ensure the necessary degree of legal certainty and legitimacy. Report of the International Law Commission, Seventieth Session, 30 April–1 June and 2 July–10 August 2018, U.N. Doc. A/73/10, Chapter IV, Commentary to conclusion 8, at para. 10; see also ibid., Chapter IV, Commentary to conclusion 7, at para. 37.

4.2.3 The Effect of Invalid Declarations and Reservations

Consider the *Case of Loizidou v. Turkey (Preliminary Objections)*.[29] This case was referred to the European Court of Human Rights by the Government of Cyprus in 1993. It originated in an application against Turkey submitted to the European Commission of Human Rights by a Cypriot national, Mrs Titina Loizidou, pursuant to Article 25 of the European Convention then in force. Article 25 empowered the European Commission to receive petitions from any person claiming to be the victim of a violation by one of the High Contracting Parties of the rights set forth in the Convention, 'provided the High Contracting Party against which the complaint has been lodged had declared that it recognises the competence of the Commission to receive such petitions'. The new application referred to Article 48(b) of the Convention. According to this provision, cases could be brought before the European Court by a High Contracting Party when one of its nationals was alleged to be a victim of a violation by another High Contracting Party. But, like in Article 25, this right of petition was subject to the proviso that both Contracting Parties had recognized the compulsory jurisdiction of the Court. As envisaged by Article 46 of the Convention, recognition would normally be given by way of the deposition of a declaration with the Secretary-General of the Council of Europe.

By its application, the Government of Cyprus sought a decision on whether the rights of Mrs Loizidou had been affected as a result of the occupation and control of the northern part of Cyprus by Turkish armed forces. What raises our interest in the judgement is the territorial restrictions that the Government of Turkey had appended to its Articles 25 and 46 declarations. It had limited its acceptance of the competence of the European Commission to 'acts and omissions of public authorities in Turkey performed within the boundaries of the territory to which the Constitution of the Republic of Turkey is applicable'.[30] In a similar vein, it had recognized the jurisdiction of the European Court only to the extent of 'matters concerning the interpretation and application of the Convention which relate to the exercise of jurisdiction within the

[29] Case No. 15318/89, *Loizidou v. Turkey*, [1995] ECHR 10.

[30] Ibid., at para. 25. In 1990, some six months after the lodging by Mrs Loizidou of her application with the European Commission, the Government of Turkey revised this to read 'acts and omissions of public authorities in Turkey performed within the boundaries of the national territory of the Republic of Turkey'.

meaning of Article 1 (art. 1) of the Convention, performed within the boundaries of the national territory of the Republic of Turkey'.[31]

As expected, the Respondent asked the Court to take these restrictions into account. They were legally valid, it said, and they are binding on the Convention institutions. As the Respondent expressed it, 'the system set up under Articles 25 and 46 (art. 25, art. 46) is an optional one into which Contracting States may, or may not, "contract-in"'.[32] To corroborate this understanding, the Respondent referred to the established practice of the ICJ of permitting territorial restrictions to the optional recognition of its jurisdiction. The Respondent pointed to the wording of Article 36, paragraph 3 of the Statute of the ICJ, which was, 'in all material respects', the same as that of Articles 25 and 46 of the European Convention. This was no mere coincidence, it maintained, since Article 46 had actually been modelled on Article 36.[33] Consequently, if the Statute permitted territorial restrictions, Articles 25 and 46 should be understood to do this, too.

In addressing these claims, the Court recalled the emphasis that it had many times before placed on the dynamic character of the European Convention. The Convention was a living instrument, the Court explained, which had to be interpreted, at all times, in the light of present-day conditions. This had to be the approach whether interpretation concerned the substantive provisions of the Convention or the provisions that governed the operation of the Convention's enforcement machinery.[34] As the Court inferred, Articles 25 and 46 could not be interpreted solely in accordance with the intentions of their authors as expressed more than forty years ago, contrary to what the Respondent Government had suggested.[35] More importantly, the Court would have to consider the ordinary meaning to be given to the terms of these provisions in their context and in the light of their object and purpose.[36]

In this spirit, the Court noted the absence of any express provision permitting explicitly territorial restrictions on their acceptance of the competence of the Commission and Court similar to those that the Government of Turkey had added to its declarations.[37] The Court

[31] Ibid., at para. 27.
[32] Ibid., at para. 67.
[33] Ibid.
[34] Ibid., at para. 71.
[35] Ibid.
[36] Ibid., at para. 73
[37] Ibid., at para. 75.

pointed to the far-reaching consequences that such provisions would have entailed:

> If, as contended by the respondent Government, substantive or territorial restrictions were permissible under these provisions, Contracting Parties would be free to subscribe to separate regimes of enforcement of Convention obligations depending on the scope of their acceptances. Such a system, which would enable States to qualify their consent under the optional clauses, would not only seriously weaken the role of the Commission and Court in the discharge of their functions but would also diminish the effectiveness of the Convention as a constitutional instrument of European public order (ordre public).[38]

The Court further noted that Article 64 restricted the power of states to make reservations to the European Convention. According to this article, reservations could be made by a state at the time of its signature or ratification of the Convention in respect of particular provisions, but only to the extent that its domestic law then in force was not in conformity with those provisions; reservations of a general nature were altogether prohibited. As the Court inferred:

> the existence of such a restrictive clause governing reservations suggests that States could not qualify their acceptance of the optional clauses thereby effectively excluding areas of their law and practice within their 'jurisdiction' from supervision by the Convention institutions. The inequality between Contracting States which the permissibility of such qualified acceptances might create would, moreover, run counter to the aim, as expressed in the Preamble to the Convention, to achieve greater unity in the maintenance and further realisation of human rights.[39]

Prompted by the submissions of the Respondent, the Court considered the argument that the wording of Articles 25 and 46 of the European Convention should be interpreted in much the same way as Article 36 of the Statute of the ICJ. For reasons connected with the 'fundamental difference in the role and purpose of the respective tribunals',[40] this argument did not persuade it:

> In the first place, the context within which the International Court of Justice operates is quite distinct from that of the Convention institutions. The International Court is called on inter alia to examine any legal dispute between States that might occur in any part of the globe with reference to

[38] Ibid.
[39] Ibid., at para. 77.
[40] Ibid., at para. 85.

> principles of international law. The subject matter of a dispute may relate to any area of international law. In the second place, unlike the Convention institutions, the role of the International Court is not exclusively limited to direct supervisory functions in respect of a law-making treaty such as the Convention.[41]

As the Court finally concluded, the territorial restrictions that the Turkish Government had appended to its Articles 25 and 46 declarations were invalid.[42]

Having come to this conclusion, the Court had to engage with yet another tricky issue. It was necessary for it to establish the effect of its decision on the validity of the Turkish declarations as such.[43] Should the declarations be considered null and void in their entirety, as the Government of Turkey contended, or should they be applied without concern for the restrictions, as if they had never been made? This question is comparable to the much-debated issue of the effect of invalid reservations to a treaty. Interestingly, the European Court addressed it consistent with how it had earlier dealt with invalid reservations to the European Convention in the *Belilos v. Switzerland* and *Weber v. Switzerland* cases.[44] The Turkish declarations, it insisted, contained valid acceptances of the competence of the Commission and the Court.[45] The Court explained this decision in terms that were fairly brief, considering the fundamental importance of the issue. It recalled its earlier finding in the *Belilos v. Switzerland* judgement.[46] It noted once again 'the special character of the [European] Convention as an instrument of European public order',[47] which, as it insisted, militated 'in favour of the severance of the impugned clauses since it is by this technique that the rights and freedoms set out in the Convention may be ensured in all areas falling within Turkey's "jurisdiction" within the meaning of Article 1 (art. 1) of the Convention'.[48]

[41] Ibid., at para. 84
[42] Ibid., at para. 89.
[43] Ibid., at paras. 90–98.
[44] Case No. 10328/83, *Belilos v. Switzerland*, [1988] ECHR 4, paras. 50–60; Case No. 11034/84, *Weber v. Switzerland*, [1990] ECHR 13, paras. 36–38. For later case-law confirming earlier decisions, see for example, Case No. 18640/10, *Grande Stevens v. Italy* [2014] ECHR 4, paras. 204–211.
[45] *Loizidou v. Turkey*, para. 98.
[46] Ibid., at para. 94.
[47] Ibid., at para. 93.
[48] Ibid., at para. 96.

The *Loizidou* judgement showcases the distinctive normative presuppositions of the European Court of Human Rights. The ICJ has always permitted territorial restrictions to declarations submitted by states recognizing its jurisdiction in legal disputes.[49] In explaining this practice, the Court has referred to the consensual nature of the system established by Article 36, paragraph 2 of the ICJ Statute:

> Declarations of acceptance of the compulsory jurisdiction of the Court are facultative, unilateral engagements, that States are absolutely free to make or not to make. In making the declaration a State is equally free either to do so unconditionally and without limit of time for its duration, or to qualify it with conditions or reservations.[50]

The European Court, for its part, does *not* permit territorial restrictions to declarations submitted by states parties to the European Convention recognizing the competence of the European Commission and European Court. The *Loizidou* judgement helps to clarify the reason on which the Court bases this particular approach. If territorial restrictions were permissible under Articles 25 and 46 of the European Convention, that would diminish the effectiveness of the Convention as a constitutional instrument of a European public order. It would run counter to an overarching purpose of the Convention, which is to achieve greater unity in the maintenance and further realization of human rights.

As the *Loizidou* judgement reveals, the idea of this overarching purpose is what also motivates the Court to consider states bound by the Convention notwithstanding the invalidity of their reservations. With few exceptions, general international lawyers conceive differently of the effect of invalid reservations. They would say that if a reservation to a treaty is invalid, then no consensual bond has been created between the reserving state and the other states parties to the treaty.[51] Consequently, the reserving state cannot be bound by the treaty.[52] Before the *Loizidou* case, it was not very clear why the European Court thought this solution

[49] See, for example, *Military and Paramilitary Activities in and against Nicaragua (Nicaragua v. United States of America)*, Jurisdiction and Admissibility, [1984] I.C.J. Rep. 392, para. 59.

[50] Ibid.

[51] See, for example, Alain Pellet, 'Article 19: Formulation of a Reservation', in Olivier Corten and Pierre Klein (eds.), *The Vienna Conventions on the Law of Treaties: A Commentary*, vol. 1 (Oxford: Oxford University Press, 2011), 442.

[52] Ibid.

inappropriate in the particular case of the European Convention.[53] The analogy that the Court draws between the issue of invalid reservations and that of invalid declarations recognizing the competence of the Court and Commission provides this explanation. The European Court has a very clear idea of what desirable state of affairs they are pursuing, and this idea affects its decision-making. The ICJ has no similar idea, but merely defers to the idea of the crucial importance of state consent.

4.2.4 *The Principle of Sustainable Development*

The concept of sustainable development has since several decades been recognized as an important principle in international law and international affairs.[54] Its precise nature as a norm and its components, however, remain open to much debate. Among others, the question of how it is or can be applied in international economic law and international investment arbitration has revealed different perspectives. Sustainable development, in its core, 'is development that meets the needs of the present without compromising the ability of future generations to meet their own needs'.[55] Some argue that the concept of sustainable development is still not entirely sub-devisable into clear legal norms, although it has 'developed at the international, regional, and national level into a crucial political precept that governs virtually every sphere of activity aimed at embracing and balancing ecology and economy, conservation, and utilization'.[56] Other international lawyers specialized in international environmental law readily recognize that the concept in fact is 'a "norm" and, more specifically, a norm of international law', and that 'the legal content of such a norm can be sufficiently ascertained'.[57] The same specialists in international

[53] A careful study of *Belilos* and *Weber* cases cannot provide much of an answer to this fundamental question. The Court refers merely to the intention of the Respondent as inferred from its conduct: 'it is beyond doubt that Switzerland is, and regards itself as, bound by the Convention irrespective of the validity of the declaration'. *Belilos v. Switzerland*, para. 60.

[54] See Jorge Viñuales, 'Sustainable Development in International Law', in Lavanya Rajamani and Jacqueline Peel (eds.), *The Oxford Handbook of International Environmental Law*, 2nd edition (Oxford: Oxford University Press, 2019).

[55] World Commission on Environment and Development, *Our Common Future* (Oxford: Oxford University Press, 1987), 43.

[56] Ulrich Beyerlin, 'Sustainable Development', in Rüdiger Wolfrum (ed.), *The Max Planck Encyclopedia of Public International Law* (Oxford University Press, 2013), para. 1.

[57] Viñuales, 'Sustainable Development in International Law', 288.

environmental law and international sustainable development law also recognize that the content of sustainable development 'must be determined by reference to the evolving treaty and customary law of environmental protection'.[58]

However, its evolution from a concept to a principle has not been univocally transposed into special regimes, chiefly international investment law. The overarching and conceptual nature of sustainable development in itself might explain the different states of affairs that are pursued in special regimes in international law, as its malleability and scope have precisely made it easy to adapt to the specific needs and practices of special regimes. Aside from the fact that in general international law too, different states of affairs in connection to the principle of sustainable development exist, as is visible from the absence of any firm confirmation by the ICJ that sustainable development is more than a 'concept',[59] international investment law and perhaps more broadly international economic law is a good example for our point here.

The linkages between international economic law and sustainable development are at first sight obvious as one would expect both to be aligned.[60] The very *raison d'être* of organizations such as the United Nations Conference on Trade and Development (UNCTAD) as discussed in the previous chapter, is the connection between trade and development, and the International Centre for Settlement of Investment Disputes (ICSID) Convention was established under the auspices of the International Bank for Reconstruction and *Development* (emphasis added) and was notably based on several successful interventions of the Bank in investment disputes in the early 1960s.[61] However, while initially the linkage between investment and (sustainable) development was quite visible in the debates concerning the international regulation of foreign investment and the arbitration of disputes relating

[58] Ibid., at 291.

[59] See generally Tim Stephens, 'International Courts and Sustainable Development: Using Old Tools to Shape a New Discourse', in Brad Jessup and Kim Rubenstein (eds.), *Environmental Discourses in Public and International Law* (Cambridge: Cambridge University Press, 2012), 195–217.

[60] Anne van Aaken and Tobias Lehman, 'Sustainable Development and International Investment Law: A Harmonious View from Economics', in Roberto Echandi and Pierre Sauvé (eds.), *Prospects in International Investment Law and Policy* (Cambridge: Cambridge University Press, 2013), 317.

[61] See Taylor St John, *The Rise of Investor-State Arbitration: Politics, Law and Unintended Consequences* (Oxford: Oxford University Press, 2018), 127.

thereto, especially with the creation of ICSID,[62] the move from multilateralism to bilateralism, which has found its apex in the period following the Cold War, has resulted in a de-coupling of the law of foreign investment from the broader (multilateral) initiatives to other related themes such as permanent sovereignty over natural resources, and (sustainable) development. Investment treaties have for many years focused on only one specific goal: the promotion and protection of foreign investment.[63]

The distinctiveness of the state of affairs pursued by States at the (essentially) bilateral level stands in sharp contrast to previous attempts to precisely pursue an agenda based on the connection and need for joint regulation of both the promotion and protection of foreign investment and broader questions such as sustainable development. However, multilateralism has in recent years resurged and resulted in, among others, a return to (attempting) to regulate the law of foreign investment in a broader context, which includes sustainable development among others[64] and recently international investment treaties themselves, which function as a showcase of states' policies in this respect, have (re-)united foreign investment and sustainable development. The 2019 revised 'Model Investment Agreement' of the Netherlands (hereafter '2019 Dutch Model BIT')[65] is a good example, as it contains several innovative features, and stands out compared to the previous Dutch Model bilateral investment treaty (BIT) for including provisions on sustainable development and human rights, among others. The Draft Model BIT has been heralded as a pioneering text aiming at a 'sustainable investment policy'.[66] The importance the 2019 Dutch Model BIT attaches to sustainable development is also recognized in the Model's preamble, which reaffirms the states' 'commitment to sustainable development and to

[62] The conventional account is that there was a general sense that the 'availability of a stable facility for dispute settlement, presided over by an institution with both prestige and money, might reduce some of the disincentives to foreign direct investment and thereby contribute to the Bank's mission of furthering economic development'. Andreas Lowenfeld, 'The ICSID Convention: Origins and Transformation' (2009) 38 *Georgia Journal of International and Comparative Law* 47–61, 49–50.

[63] See generally Eric De Brabandere, '(Re)Calibration, Standard-Setting and the Shaping of Investment Law and Arbitration' (2018) 59 *Boston College Law Review* 2607–2634.

[64] See generally ibid.

[65] 'Netherlands model Investment Agreement', 22 March 2019, https://investmentpolicy.unctad.org/international-investment-agreements/treaty-files/5832/download.

[66] Bart-Jaap Verbeek, 'Organisaties lanceren platform voor kritische inspraak op blauwdruk Nederlandse investeringsverdragen', 31 May 2018, www.somo.nl/nl/organisaties-lanceren-platform-kritische-inspraak-op-blauwdruk-nederlandse-investeringsverdragen.

enhancing the contribution of international trade and investment to sustainable development'. Article 6 ('Sustainable development') contains a commitment of states 'to promote the development of international investment in such a way as to contribute to the objective of sustainable development', and an obligation on states to ensure that their investment law and policies provide for 'high levels of environmental and labor protection'. Article 6(5) also obliges the parties not to adopt legislation in relation to sustainable development, which would constitute an 'unjustifiable discrimination or a disguised restriction on trade and investment'.

Aside from these recent initiatives, overall, the presence of sustainable development objectives in IIAs is generally considered to be low,[67] and is limited to 'appear to limit its role mainly to exceptions, recommendations and political commitments rather than imposing binding obligations on states or investors to contribute to sustainable development'.[68] The practical relevance, in terms of decisions of international arbitral tribunals, which have in effect applied the concept or principle of sustainable development has moreover remained relatively limited. The limited practical effect of the application of the concept or principle of sustainable development in decisions, however, does not imply that sustainable development is a mere overarching objective that is taken into account in investment law. Notably, the inclusion of sustainable development in the 2019 Dutch Model BIT shows that sustainable development, indeed is, at least in that recent practice, considered a principle that carries normative implications.

4.2.5 *Amicus Curiae Briefs*

The practice of 'opening up' international judicial or arbitral proceedings to third parties provides an interesting entry point to showcase the distinct state of affairs pursued by actors involved in different international law regimes. Participation as a 'friend of the court' or *amicus curiae* (or third-party interventions) implies that the intervening party is not actually a party to the dispute but is nevertheless allowed to submit a written

[67] Markus Gehring and Avidan Kent, 'International Investment Agreements and the Emerging Green Economy: Rising to the Challenge', in Freya Baetens (ed.), *Investment Law within International Law: Integrationist Perspectives* (Cambridge: Cambridge University Press, 2013), 201.

[68] Right to development in international investment law: Overview of the ongoing study by the Expert Mechanism on the Right to Development, 1 March 2022, U.N. Doc. A/HRC/EMRTD/5/CRP.2, para. 21.

statement during the proceedings and, less commonly, is permitted to be heard by the court or tribunal. The practice of allowing an *amicus curiae* to participate in proceedings is in essence and in its core relatively neutral, in that it merely is a procedural device, which is alien to any presupposition in terms of the substance of the dispute in question. However, this neutrality has resulted in very different practices in the different international courts and tribunals. While some have remained very closed to *amici*, others in turn have embraced this development based on various considerations such as transparency. The principled neutrality of this procedural device, contrasted to the different engagement of international courts and tribunals with accepting *amicus curiae* participation and submissions, reveals distinct approaches notwithstanding the fact that, as we will show, the courts and tribunals discussed operate under the same broad umbrella of international law.

The European Court of Human Rights has since many years been open to a wide variety of third-party interventions. Under Article 36 of the European Convention on Human Rights, a 'a High Contracting Party one of whose nationals is an applicant', has the 'right to submit written comments and to take part in hearings' (para. 1), but the President of the Court may also invite 'any High Contracting Party which is not a party to the proceedings or any person concerned who is not the applicant' to submit written comments or to take part in the hearings 'in the interest of the proper administration of justice' (para. 2). While the ECHR originally did not provide for any third-party interventions, the Court's practice has since 1981 accepted third-party interventions by actors other than states, and enshrined this practice in its Procedural Rules in 1983.[69] In 1998, the Convention itself was modified to include a new Article 36(2), which explicitly allows third-party interventions.

The interesting point here is the reasoning behind the practice and the subsequent modifications in the Procedural Rules and Convention and the categorization of the intervening *amici*. In terms of rationale, the access of third parties to the ECtHR can be explained by various considerations, such as providing legitimacy to the Court's activity and judgement,[70] but above all in fact relate to the broader public interest present in disputes before the Court. This public interest resides either in the broader interest of the work and the decisions of the Court, beyond the

[69] See generally Ludovic Hennebel, 'Le rôle des Amici Curiae Devant la Cour Européenne des Droits de L'Homme' (2007) *Revue Trimestrielle des Droits de l'Homme* 641–668.

[70] See Laura Van den Eynde, 'Amicus Curiae: European Court of Human Rights (ECtHR)', in Hélène Fabri (ed.), *The Max Planck Encyclopedia of International Procedural Law* (Oxford: Oxford University Press, 2019), para. 36.

mere parties to the dispute, or to the interest of other parties than only those before the Court. This point, in fact, connects well with the rationale of *amicus curiae* interventions by looking at the identity of the *amici*. Leaving aside the intervention by third states or the Council of Europe Commissioner for Human Rights, the practice demonstrates that the intervening parties are either *amici curiae* in the true sense, or, in fact, have a direct interest in the case or the underlying dispute.[71] In the first category, one finds NGOs, (academic) societies or organizations and companies who seek to present (legal) arguments to the Court in order to influence the Court's decision. In case of a direct interest, one finds mostly the parties who were the opposing parties to the dispute on the domestic level.[72] The distinction between both types of *amici*, but also of the types of interests involved, has also been explained by the different functions of the Court: the *jus dicere* function of the European Court, as opposed, or as a complement to its 'doing justice' function.[73] The former's interest indeed is generating a public interest and gives the Court a mission that exceeds the mere parties to the disputes. But the latter can also justify the presence of third parties as their *direct* interests are at stake. The distinction made in light of the interest involved, the identity of the *amici* and the perspective from the function of the Court is interesting to contrast the practice with other international courts and tribunals, such as the ICJ.

The ICJ has remained, on the contrary, very closed to *amicus curiae* submissions. As far as contentious cases are concerned, the Statute allows the Court to request a 'public international organization' to furnish information relevant to a case before the Court.[74] The Statute also allows such organizations to furnish, on their own initiative, information relevant to a case before the Court.[75] To avoid any ambiguity, the last paragraph of that article clarifies that a 'public international organization' is an international organization of states,[76] thus explicitly excluding NGOs.[77]

71 Hennebel, 'Le rôle des amici curiae', 653.

72 Ibid., at 654.

73 Frédéric Krenc, '"Dire le droit", "rendre la justice". Quelle Cour européenne des droits de l'homme?' (2018) 2 *Revue trimestrielle des droits de l'homme* 311–346, 320.

74 Statute of the International Court of Justice, San Francisco, 26 June 1945, in force 24 October 1945, XV U.N.C.I.O. 355, Art. 69(1).

75 Ibid., at Art. 69(2).

76 Ibid., at Art. 69(4).

77 See also *Asylum Case (Colombia v. Peru)*, Oral proceedings-Documents-Correspondence, Part IV: Correspondence, [1950] I.C.J. Rep. 202, 228, in which a request to intervene from an NGO was refused.

In Advisory Proceedings, the Statute provides that the Court may invite any 'international organization' considered by the Court as likely to be able to furnish information on the question to submit written statements or hear oral statements relating to the question.[78] The use here of the term 'international organization' as opposed to 'public international organisation' in the rules relating to contentious cases has been interpreted as opening the door for *amicus curiae* participation.[79] However, except on one occasion, which was not followed by the actual submission of a written statement,[80] the Court has never officially requested any written submission by an NGO.[81] In recent requests for advisory opinions, the ICJ typically limits those entities likely to furnish information on the question submitted to the Court to the United Nations and its Member States.[82] In practice, the Court has received spontaneously many *amicus* submissions in advisory opinions proceedings, but the Court treats these merely as factual information placed at the disposal of the Judges without officially considering them as *amicus curiae* briefs and thus part of the record in those cases.[83] This practice has since then been enshrined in the ICJ's practice directions.[84]

The closed nature of the proceedings, and the clear unwillingness of the ICJ to adopt an approach similar to that of, for example, the ECtHR, can probably be explained by various facts, but, in fact, are simply the result of very different perceptions of the state of affairs that Judges seek to pursue. The ICJ could, in fact, rely on the same considerations which we have discussed in relation to the ECtHR, such as the broader public interest involved in its cases (aside from the participation of those involved in the dispute, which gives rise to the one before the ICJ, which only exceptionally would be relevant), or also the benefit of other

[78] Art. 66(2) of the Statute of the International Court of Justice.

[79] Dinah Shelton, 'The Participation of Nongovernmental Organizations in International Judicial Proceedings' (1994) 88 *American Journal of International Law* 611–642.

[80] *International Status of South-West Africa, Advisory Opinion*, [1950] I.C.J. Rep. 130.

[81] Eduardo Valencia-Ospina, 'Non-Governmental Organizations and the International Court of Justice', in Tulio Treves, Alessandro Fodella, Attila Tanzi, Marco Frigessi di Rattalma, *Civil Society, International Courts and Compliance Bodies* (The Hague: T.M.C. Asser Press, 2005), 230.

[82] See, for example, *Accordance with International Law of the Unilateral Declaration of Independence by the Provisional Institutions of Self-Government of Kosovo*, Order, [2008] I.C.J. Rep. 409, para. 1.

[83] See for an overview Valencia-Ospina, 'Non-Governmental Organizations and the International Court of Justice', 231.

[84] International Court of Justice, Practice Direction XII, *Acts and Documents No. 7*, 169.

perspectives in the ICJ's exercise of its *jus dicere* function (mostly visible of course in the context of advisory proceedings). But the Court remains indeed open only to States, and international organizations, and even more so in advisory proceedings than in contentious cases.

4.2.6 *Interpretation in International Law*

When international courts and tribunals engage in the interpretation of international instruments, typically, they place great emphasis on the rules of interpretation laid down in common Articles 31–33 of the two Vienna Conventions on the Law of Treaties. At all stages of the interpretation process, references to Articles 31–33 tend to be accompanied by remarks stressing the significance of the intention of treaty parties or other authors.[85] This practice reflects the common understanding of Articles 31–33 as throughout designed to help determining the 'utterance meaning' of treaties, that is to say, the meaning which the parties to each treaty intended it to communicate.[86] It is emblematic of the normal configuration of the interpretation process, which features assumptions such as all of the below:

- The parties expressed themselves so that the treaty conforms to the lexicon, grammar and pragmatic rules of the language used for every authenticated version of it.[87]
- The parties expressed themselves so that a consistent meaning can be conferred on all words and lexicalized phrases used in the interpreted treaty.[88]
- The parties expressed themselves so that no norm expressed in the treaty logically contradicts any other.[89]

[85] See, for example, *Maritime Delimitation in the Indian Ocean (Somalia v. Kenya)*, Preliminary Objections, [2017] I.C.J. Rep. 3, para. 85: '[T]he singular and plural versions of the term are used interchangeably elsewhere in the text, even in the same paragraph, such as the fourth paragraph, which provides that Somalia's submission of preliminary information "may include the *area* under dispute" and that Kenya has no objection to "the inclusion of the *areas* under dispute" in that submission (emphasis added). This suggests that no differentiation in meaning was intended by the use of the plural form "areas" in the MOU'.

[86] On the concept of utterance meaning, see, for example, Dianne Blakemore, *Understanding Utterances: Introduction to Pragmatics* (Wiley, 1992).

[87] See, for example, *Kasikili/Sedudu Island (Botswana/Namibia)*, [1999] I.C.J. Rep. 1045, para. 25.

[88] See, for example, *Navigational and Related Rights (Costa Rica v. Nicaragua)*, [2009] I.C.J. Rep. 213, para. 54.

[89] See, for example, Case No. 14038/88, *Soering v. United Kingdom*, [1989] ECHR 14, paras 102 and 103.

- The parties expressed themselves so that no part of the treaty comes out as redundant.[90]
- The parties expressed themselves so that the application of the treaty helps to obtain its object and purpose.[91]
- The parties expressed themselves so that the treaty does not derogate from any other international legal norm applicable in the relationship between them.[92]

What is interesting about interpretation in international law is that, occasionally, international courts and tribunals use arguments, which cannot be explained easily based on common Articles 31–33 of the two Vienna Conventions and the idea that interpretation is a method for the determination of utterance meaning. A very neat example of this is the judgement of the Trial Chamber of the International Criminal Tribunal for the Former Yugoslavia (ICTY) in *Furundžija*.[93]

The indictment charged the accused with counts of violations of the laws or customs of war, in the sense of Article 5 of the Statute of the Tribunal, including the prohibition of rape.[94] In considering especially whether forced oral penetration should be classified as *rape*, the Trial Chamber noted the lack of a precise definition of this concept in international law.[95] It acknowledged that in domestic law, forced oral penetration was characterized differently: it was regarded in some countries as rape, and in others as sexual assault.[96] To find a way out of this legal predicament, the Chamber turned its attention to the 'principle of respect for human dignity', which it insisted is 'the basic underpinning and indeed the very raison d'être of international humanitarian law and human rights'.[97] It inferred from this principle that in international humanitarian law (IHL), forced penetration of the mouth by the male

[90] See, for example, *Application of the International Convention on the Elimination of All Forms of Racial Discrimination (Georgia v. Russian Federation)*, Preliminary Objections, [2011] I.C.J. Rep. 70, paras. 133–134.

[91] See, for example, *Kasikili/Sedudu Island*, para. 43.

[92] See, for example, *Award in the Arbitration regarding the Iron Rhine ('Ijzeren Rijn') Railway between the Kingdom of Belgium and the Kingdom of the Netherlands*, [2005] 27 U.N.R.I.A.A. 35, para. 79.

[93] *Prosecutor v. Furundžija*, Trial Chamber, Judgment Case No. IT-95-17/1-T, 10 December 1998.

[94] Ibid., at para. 2.

[95] Ibid., at para. 175.

[96] Ibid., at paras. 180–182.

[97] Ibid., at para. 183.

sexual organ should be classified as rape, similar to forced penetration of the vagina or anus.[98]

In cases both before and after the *Furundžija* judgement, the ICTY has used the rules laid down in Articles 31–33 of the two Vienna Conventions as guidance in the interpretation of the Statute of the Tribunal. It has done so, although the Statute is not a treaty.[99] Still, it is very difficult to explain the reasoning of the Chamber in *Furundžija* as a case of a straightforward application of these rules. The principle of human dignity is not a general principle of international law, in the sense of Article 31, paragraph 3(c) of the two Vienna Conventions. Some would perhaps argue that respect for human dignity is an object and purpose of the ICTY Statute. But in international law, the object and purpose of a legal instrument is not determined by any exigencies of human life, as understood by the interpreter, but by the intentions of its authors. Thus, 'the object and purpose' of a treaty, in the sense of common Article 31, paragraph 1 of the two Vienna Conventions, means simply the state of affairs that the treaty parties thought would be obtained by applying it. Importantly, there is no mention of respect for human dignity in the preamble to UN Security Council resolution 827. It describes the establishment of the ICTY as a measure that would put an end to widespread and flagrant violations of IHL occurring within the territory of the former Yugoslavia; one that would bring to justice the persons who are responsible for them and contribute to the restoration and maintenance of international peace and security.[100]

The better explanation of the *Furundžija* judgement is that the Trial Chamber acted based on the idea that, irrespective of what Articles 31–33 tells it to do, there can be no way of understanding the Statute that compromises the pursuit of human dignity. For those international criminal law specialists who accept this way of reasoning, the judgement is proof of the existence of a joint enterprise.

[98] 'The Trial Chamber finds that the following may be accepted as the objective elements of rape: (i) the sexual penetration, however slight: (a) of the vagina or anus of the victim by the penis of the perpetrator or any other object used by the perpetrator; or (b) of the mouth of the victim by the penis of the perpetrator; (ii) by coercion or force or threat of force against the victim or a third person.' Ibid., at para. 185.

[99] This practice was confirmed by the Appeals Chamber in *Prosecutor v. Slobodan Milošević*. Case Nos. IT-99-37-AR73, IT-01-50-AR73, IT-01-51-AR73, Reasons for Decision on Refusal to Order Joinder, 18 April 2002, para. 16.

[100] See Security Council Resolution 827, 25 May 1993, U.N. Doc. S/RES/827, preambular paras. 5–6.

4.3 A Distinct Way to Perform Assignments

4.3.1 *Jura Novit Curia*

The principle of *jura novit curia*, namely that the Court of the arbitral tribunal knows the law and that it must apply the law ex officio, a principle related to the maxim *da mihi factum dabo tibi jus* ('give me the facts and I shall give you the law'), is one of the basic principles of judicial procedure. It implies that the contents of the applicable law need not be proven by the parties as factual elements need to be proven. Yet the use of the principle in the practice of international courts and tribunals is not consistent and, in fact, shows different perspectives on how courts and tribunals perform their function. While the ICJ has recognized and applied the principle consistently, the application in the context of investment arbitration is different and less consistent, as is the case of the European Court of Human Rights.

Jura novit cura implies several elements: 'first, the duty of the Court to determine what the law is; second, the non-binding nature of the Parties' claims; and third, the practical application of law to settle disputes'.[101] The application of the principle *jura novit curia* has since long been recognized by the ICJ in respect of international judicial proceedings. In the 1974 *Fisheries Jurisdiction* case, the ICJ described in general terms the application of the principle:

> The Court however, as an international judicial organ, is deemed to take judicial notice of international law, and is therefore required in a case falling under Article 53 of the Statute, as in any other case, to consider on its own initiative all rules of international law which may be relevant to the settlement of the dispute. It being the duty of the Court itself to ascertain and apply the relevant law in the given circumstances of the case, the burden of establishing or proving rules of international law cannot be imposed upon any of the parties, for the law lies within the judicial knowledge of the Court.[102]

In the *Nicaragua* case, the ICJ also made clear that, while concordant views of the parties to a dispute as to the law applicable to the dispute are

[101] Takane Sugihara, 'The Principle of Jura Novit Curia in the International Court of Justice: With Reference to Recent Decisions' (2012) 55 *Japanese Yearbook of International Law* 77–109, 80.

[102] *Fisheries Jurisdiction (United Kingdom v. Zealand)*, [1974] I.C.J. Rep. 3, para. 17. See also *Fisheries Jurisdiction (United Kingdom v. Zealand)*, Separate Opinion of Judge de Castro, [1974] I.C.J. Rep. 79.

important,[103] it does not 'dispense the Court from having itself to ascertain what rules of customary international law are applicable'.[104] The Court's use of the principle can be explained by several elements. First of all, Article 38 of the ICJ Statute in fact contains some reference to the obligation of the Court to decide cases based on international law, as it provides: 'the Court, whose function is to decide in accordance with international law such disputes as are submitted to it [. . .]'. Secondly, as Sugihara has pointed out, the ICJ's position within the UN system and its institutional nature warrant the application of the principle: 'its status as a judicial organ means that it settles disputes generally by application of the law; it also means that it is not subordinate to any other authority. In this manner, if one were to view the ICJ as the judicial organ applying international law, naturally it must be considered to know international law'.[105]

The practice of arbitral tribunals in investment treaty arbitration shows a clear departure from the practice of international commercial arbitration where the application of *jura novit curia* is much more contested and seems to align itself with the practice of international courts and tribunals. But this alignment is not constant, as some arbitral tribunals seem to oscillate between adhering to the commercial arbitration practice and the public international law approach evidenced by the ICJ. The application of the principle *jura novit curia* has been confirmed by annulment decisions rendered under the ICSID Convention in which Ad Hoc Committees have refrained from annulling awards based on other arguments than those presented by the parties.[106] In one of the very first annulment proceedings under the ICSID Convention, in *Klöckner v. Cameroon*, the Ad Hoc Committee summarized the application of the principle as follows:

> As for the Tribunal itself, when in the course of its deliberations it reached the provisional conclusion that the true legal basis for its decision could well be different from either of the parties' respective arguments, it was not, subject to what will be said below, in principle prohibited from choosing its own argument. [. . .] Within the dispute's "legal framework",

[103] *Military and Paramilitary Activities in and Against Nicaragua*, para. 29.
[104] Ibid., at para. 184.
[105] Sugihara, 'The Principle of Jura Novit Curia in the International Court of Justice', 82.
[106] Christoph Schreuer, 'Three Generations of ICSID Annulment Proceedings', in Emmanuel Gaillard and Yas Banifatemi (eds.), *Annulment of ICSID Awards* (New York: Juris Publishing, 2004), 30.

> arbitrators must be free to rely on arguments which strike them as the best ones, even if those arguments were not developed by the parties (although they could have been). Even if it is generally desirable for arbitrators to avoid basing their decision on an argument that has not been discussed by the parties, it obviously does not follow that they therefore commit a 'serious departure from a fundamental rule of procedure'.[107]

Outside the formal ICSID context, the application of the maxim *jura novit curia* in investment treaty arbitration is slightly more contested, as perhaps non-ICSID arbitrations are more prone to the fluctuation between the public international law and the commercial arbitration rules and practices. Being broadly based on the procedural rules applicable to international commercial arbitration, the application of the principle *jura novit curia* has not uniformly been accepted in non-ICSID arbitrations, essentially because of the emphasis on the principle of party autonomy in international commercial arbitration.[108] However, several tribunals in non-ICSID arbitration have also upheld the inherent power of investment tribunals to apply legal arguments that have not been advanced by the parties, which may prove that in treaty-based investment arbitration, even outside the ICSID framework, the principle should be applied. Referring to 'ICSID practice', the Tribunal in *Bogdanov v. Moldova* conducted under the SCC Arbitration Rules,[109] considered that

> [. . .] the Arbitral Tribunal is not limited to the arguments made by the parties. As long as the Arbitral Tribunal limits its evaluation to the facts as presented by the parties, it remains free, within the borders of the applicable law (particularly, as long as it remains within the frame of the legal sources mentioned in the proceeding), to give the legal qualifications and determine the legal consequences that it deems appropriate, even if they were not pleaded by the parties. [. . .] In the present proceedings, even though the Claimant did not invoke any specific article of the

[107] *Klöckner Industrie-Anlagen GmbH v. United Republic of Cameroon and Société Camerounaise des Engrais*, ICSID Case No. ARB/81/2, Decision of the *ad hoc* Committee, 3 May 1985. See also *Wena Hotels Ltd. v. Arab Republic of Egypt*, ICSID Case No. ARB/98/4, Decision on Annulment, 5 February 2002, para. 70.

[108] Giuditta Cordero Moss, 'Tribunal's Powers versus Party Autonomy', in Peter Muchlinski, Frederico Ortino and Christoph Schreuer (eds.), *The Oxford Handbook of International Investment Law* (Oxford: Oxford University Press, 2009), 1210–1211.

[109] *Iurii Bogdanov, Agurdino-Invest Ltd. and Agurdino-Chimia JSC v. Republic of Moldova*, SCC Case No. 93/2004, Arbitral Award, 22 September 2005, para. 2.2.1.

> BIT, the BIT constitutes the legal basis of the arbitral proceedings, as the Claimant has initiated the present proceedings under the BIT, and has listed the BIT as one of the legal sources to be applied in the decision. Therefore, consideration of the BIT may not be deemed as a surprise to any of the parties. [. . .][110]

In its 1979 award in the case *BP Exploration Co (Libya) Ltd. v. The Government of the Libyan Arab Republic*, the Tribunal composed of a sole arbitrator found that tribunals are not only entitled, but also 'compelled to undertake an independent examination of the legal issues deemed relevant by it, and to engage in considerable legal research going beyond the confines of the materials relied upon by the Claimant. The conclusions in the Award therefore are based on a broader consideration of the issues than that permitted by the format of the Claimant's arguments in support of its claim'.[111]

The reasons behind the general acceptance of the application of the *jura novit curia* principle in investment treaty arbitration, at least as far as ICSID Arbitration is concerned, evidently lies in the public international law character of investment disputes and the application of public international law to the dispute as a matter of applicable law. The only reasonable and logical explanation, which warrants the application of the principle of *jura novit curia* in investment treaty arbitration, is the application of public international law as part of the applicable law. Referring to the ICJ's opinion in the *Fisheries Jurisdiction* case cited above, Paulsson argues that the public international law character of international investment disputes justifies an application of the *jura novit curia* principle to international investment tribunals. Paulsson argues that 'a tribunal in an investment dispute cannot content itself with inept pleadings, and simply uphold the least implausible of the two'.[112]

The European Court of Human Rights has since several years increased its reliance on *jura novit curia*. While it has been argued that the European Court of Human Rights made little use of the principle

[110] Ibid., at para. 4.2.2.

[111] *BP Exploration Co (Libya) Ltd. v. The Government of the Libyan Arab Republic*, [1979] 53 I.L.R. 297, 313.

[112] Jan Paulsson, *International Arbitration and the Generation of Legal Norms: Treaty Arbitration and International Law* (Alphen aan den Rijn: Kluwer Law International, 2007), 888–889.

before 2013,[113] recent evidence suggests an increased reliance on *jura novit curia* by the European Court of Human Rights.[114]

One of the first and explicit mentions of the principle can be found in *Guerra v. Italy*, where the ECtHR stated

> since the Court is master of the characterisation to be given in law to the facts of the case, it does not consider itself bound by the characterisation given by an applicant, a government or the Commission. By virtue of the *jura novit curia* principle, it has, for example, considered of its own motion complaints under Articles or paragraphs not relied on by those appearing before it and even under a provision in respect of which the Commission had declared the complaint to be inadmissible while declaring it admissible under a different one. A complaint is characterised by the facts alleged in it and not merely by the legal grounds or arguments relied on.[115]

The interesting point is that the increased use of the principle by the ECtHR can be explained by various considerations that are very specific to the ECtHR's exercise and performance of its mandate. Not only is the ECtHR compared to the ICJ or even investment tribunals, tasked with the application and interpretation of one specific convention, but importantly also, it decides cases based (mostly) on applications from private parties. The first specific element explains the recurrent use by the ECtHR of the fact that 'the Court is master of the characterisation to be given in law to the facts of the case' as mentioned in the citation above.[116] As indeed the Court is the main 'interpreter' of the Convention, it seeks to establish its authority as the ultimate authority on the interpretation of the Convention. The fact that the Court is tasked with deciding cases based on applications from private parties has been used by some to explain the specific and increased reliance in the past decade by the Court of the principle of *jura novit curia*, notably to re-characterize claims made by the applicants and the choice it then makes to focus on one violation only, and refusing to analyse other claims, in

[113] Dinah Shelton, '*Jura Novit Curia* in International Human Rights Tribunals', in Nerina Boschiero, Tullio Scovazzi, Cesare Pitea and Chiara Ragni (eds.), *International Courts and the Development of International Law* (The Hague: T.M.C. Asser Press, 2013), 189–211.

[114] Mathias Möschel, 'Jura Novit Curia and the European Court of Human Rights' (2022) 33 *European Journal of International Law* 631–650.

[115] Case No. 14967/89, *Guerra and Others v. Italy* [1998] ECHR 7, para. 44.

[116] For other examples, see Möschel, 'Jura Novit Curia and the European Court of Human Rights', 631–650.

order to reduce its docket.[117] This view has even explicitly been introduced by the ECtHR in its 'Practical Guide on Admissibility Criteria', where it is stated that

> By virtue of the jura novit curia principle the Court is not bound by the legal grounds adduced by the applicant under the Convention and the Protocols thereto and has the power to decide on the characterisation to be given in law to the facts of a complaint by examining it under Articles or provisions of the Convention that are different from those relied upon by the applicant (*Navalnyy v. Russia* [GC], §§ 62–66, where the Court observed that the factual elements of the complaints under Article 18 were present in all the initial applications although the applicant had only relied on this provision in two of them, and therefore dismissed the Government's objection that parts of these complaints had been introduced out of time, that is to say, during the Grand Chamber proceedings).[118]

This stands in contrast to the practice of the ICJ discussed above and investment tribunals, as the use by the European Court of the principle of *jura novit curia* not only corresponds to different concerns, but also in actual fact operates differently than the more traditional reliance on the same principle by the ICJ, which aligns more with the traditional understanding of *jura novit curia* as a principle leaving a court or tribunal to not be confined to the arguments put forward by the parties but also to the absence of any requirement of proof of the law by the parties to the disputes.

4.3.2 *Incidental Jurisdiction*

The jurisdiction of international courts and tribunals, and of international arbitral tribunals, is based on the consent of the parties to the dispute. No state is, without consenting, under an obligation to agree on a particular means of settlement of disputes – consent is a necessary prerequisite for the settlement of international disputes. A court or tribunal can only exercise jurisdiction once it is established that the parties have consented to submitting a given dispute to that court or tribunal, and when expressing consent in advance of a dispute, the definition of the conditions under which such consent is given further delineate the jurisdictional conditions under which disputes may be settled.

[117] Ibid., at 647–649.

[118] European Court of Human Rights, 'Practical Guide on Admissibility Criteria', 28 February 2023, www.echr.coe.int/documents/admissibility_guide_eng.pdf, para. 157.

Incidental jurisdiction technically covers two distinct questions: the mandate and jurisdiction of courts and tribunals over incidental proceedings such as provisional or interim measures, and the mandate and jurisdiction of courts and tribunals over questions, which are in essence outside of the jurisdiction of a court or tribunal, as being not covered by the consent of the parties to the dispute but which are nonetheless necessary to be determined for a court or tribunal to exercise jurisdiction.[119] This section will cover the second understanding of 'incidental jurisdiction'.

If and to what extent an international court or tribunal can effectively decide an 'incidental' question, however, is in actual effect very dependent on how courts and tribunals perform their duties. This, in turn, will showcase a different approach and the pursuance of a distinct state of affairs by the various courts and tribunals that operate in special regimes. These cases indeed show variations on the application by those courts and tribunals of the principle of consent and jurisdiction, which can be tied to different perceptions on how their specific mandate should or can be exercised.

A good example is the recent series of disputes between Russia and Ukraine stemming from the annexation by Russia of Crimea in 2014, as it has been brought before many different courts and tribunals operating in different special regimes: the ICJ, the European Court of Human Rights, an arbitral tribunal established under Annex VII of the UNCLOS, and investor–state arbitral tribunals. In these cases, the question arose whether or not the court or tribunal could or should settle the territorial and sovereignty dispute and the lawfulness of the Russian annexation of Crimea, in order to exercise their jurisdiction as an 'ancillary' question.

The case before the ICJ, aside from the more recent one concerning the allegations of violations of the Genocide Convention, relates to the application of the International Convention for the Suppression of the Financing of Terrorism and of the International Convention on the Elimination of All Forms of Racial Discrimination. The case is still pending at the time of writing, and aside from a decision on preliminary objections, the question of sovereignty over Crimea has not (yet) been addressed.[120]

[119] See Peter Tzeng, 'Incidental Jurisdiction', in Hélène Fabri (ed.), *The Max Planck Encyclopedia of International Procedural Law* (Oxford: Oxford University Press, 2022), para. 1.

[120] *Application of the International Convention for the Suppression of the Financing of Terrorism and of the International Convention on the Elimination of All Forms of Racial Discrimination (Ukraine v. Russian Federation)*, Preliminary Objections, [2019] I.C.J. Rep. 558.

The arbitral tribunal established under Annex VII of the UNCLOS, however, has decided that it could not engage in the question of sovereignty over Crimea. The *Dispute Concerning Coastal State Rights in the Black Sea, Sea of Azov, and Kerch Strait (Ukraine v. the Russian Federation)* arbitration[121] concerns the question of coastal state rights of both states in the Black Sea, Sea of Azov, and Kerch Strait. The Tribunal established that a sovereignty dispute existed and then engaged in the question of whether deciding that part of the dispute fell within its jurisdiction. The tribunal concluded that the dispute regarding sovereignty over Crimea 'is not a minor issue ancillary to the dispute concerning the interpretation or application of the Convention'.[122] The Tribunal as a consequence concluded that it had no jurisdiction over Ukraine's claims, to the extent that a ruling of the tribunal would necessarily require it to decide, directly or implicitly, on the sovereignty of either Party over Crimea.

This decision can be contrasted with the decisions of the European Court of Human Rights and of several arbitral tribunals established to settle investment disputes between Ukrainian investors in Crimea, who have initiated proceedings against Russia on the basis of the Russia–Ukraine BIT.

This practice, specific perhaps to courts and tribunals, which have been established or derive their jurisdiction from the UNCLOS,[123] can be contrasted with other courts and tribunals that have conversely interpreted their mandate differently. Interesting cases to compare the UNCLOS cases to are the decisions of the European Court of Human Rights and of several arbitral tribunals established to settle investment disputes between Ukrainian investors in Crimea who have initiated proceedings against Russia on the basis of the Russia–Ukraine BIT. The comparison is interesting and relevant as the latter series of cases are also concerned with territorial questions as in the *Black Sea, Sea of Azov, and Kerch Strait (Ukraine v. the Russian Federation)* arbitration.

In its decision of 16 December 2020,[124] the European Court of Human Rights issued its decision on an application filed by Ukraine against Russia alleging violation of the European Convention on Human Rights in Crimea following the annexation by Russia of the peninsula

[121] *Dispute Concerning Coastal State Rights in the Black Sea, Sea of Azov, and Kerch Strait (Ukraine v. the Russian Federation)*, PCA Case No. 2017-06, Award on Preliminary Objections, 21 February 2020.

[122] Ibid., at para. 195.

[123] Tzeng, 'Incidental Jurisdiction', para. 10.

[124] Case Nos. 20958/14 and 38334/18, *Ukraine v. Russia (Re Crimea)*, Admissibility, [2020] ECHR 12.

in 2014. Ukraine argued that since then, Crimea was under the 'effective control' of Russia, which the Court accepted.[125] A threshold question which the Court had to decide in this case was whether it could in effect decide the case since it would, in doing so, pronounce on the sovereignty over Crimea. Russia indeed argued that asserting jurisdiction based on 'effective control' 'would be inappropriate' because it 'would take the Court into questions concerning sovereignty between States that are outside its jurisdiction'.[126]

The Court, when discussing the 'object of the case' before it, had already considered that

> it is not called upon to decide in the abstract on the 'legality' of the Russian Federation's purported 'invasion' and 'occupation' of Crimea other than by reference to the rules contained in the Convention. Nor are the applicant Government seeking a ruling from the Court on the legality per se under international law of the 'annexation of Crimea' and, accordingly, of its consequent legal status thereafter. These matters were not referred to the Court and do not therefore constitute the subject matter of the dispute before it. Accordingly, they are outside the scope of the case and will not be directly considered by the Court.[127]

The Court had, in doing so, referred to the decision of the ICJ in the case *Application of the International Convention for the Suppression of the Financing of Terrorism and of the International Convention on the Elimination of All Forms of Racial Discrimination (Ukraine v. the Russian Federation)*[128] and the discussed Award of 21 February 2020 of the Arbitral Tribunal in the case Coastal State Rights in the Black Sea, Sea of Azov, and Kerch Strait between Ukraine and the Russian Federation.

The Court further explained that 'the respondent State's jurisdiction under Article 1 of the Convention is a necessary prerequisite for the Court's exercise of its competence'.[129] It then explained that, as it has been decided in several other cases by the Court, that the notion of 'jurisdiction' under the ECHR is understood to mean both 'territorial jurisdiction' and 'in the form or nature of "effective control over an area"

[125] Ibid., at para. 315.
[126] Ibid., at para. 338.
[127] Ibid., at para. 244.
[128] *Application of the International Convention for the Suppression of the Financing of Terrorism and of the International Convention on the Elimination of All Forms of Racial Discrimination (Ukraine v. the Russian Federation).*
[129] Ibid., at para. 340.

rather than in the form or nature of territorial jurisdiction'.[130] The Court's exercise of its competence (under Article 19, which is to 'ensure the observance of the engagements undertaken by the High Contracting Parties in the Convention and the Protocols thereto' is thus intrinsically linked to the nature of the jurisdiction exercised by a respondent State over a given territory.[131]

The interesting point here is that the European Court, in its decision, in fact did not discuss the question of sovereignty over Crimea as an 'ancillary question', and hence whether it could exercise incidental jurisdiction over the question. In fact, as others have pointed out, human rights courts and bodies do not in principle rely on the very concept of incidental jurisdiction.[132] The ECtHR being an international court, which has jurisdiction based on the consent expressed by States to that effect, can as a consequence and as a matter of principle rely on the doctrine of incidental jurisdiction. There is, as Lea Raible has pointed out, 'nothing unique about the institutional set up of human rights courts and human rights bodies in international law that might explain the absence of incidental jurisdiction'.[133] If the ECtHR had, in fact, followed the decision of the Arbitral Tribunal in the *Black Sea* Arbitration, which it in fact cited on several occasions, then one might have expected the Court to decline the exercise of jurisdiction as it would then have to pronounce on the legality of the annexation of Crimea, which according to the Arbitral Tribunal in the *Black Sea* Arbitration was not a mere ancillary question which would fall under the Tribunal's incidental jurisdiction. The ECtHR, however, has decided (admittedly, in accordance with its previous case law on the interpretation of the Convention) that what matters indeed is not the interpretation of the contours of its jurisdiction, but rather the scope of application of the Convention itself, which it has interpreted as going beyond 'territorial jurisdiction' as discussed. As a consequence, dealing with disputes concerning the extraterritorial application of the Convention are within the Court's jurisdiction, as per its own interpretation of the Convention, and are not an 'ancillary question', which the Court can decide based on the doctrine of incidental jurisdiction.

[130] Ibid., at para. 345.

[131] Ibid., at para. 341.

[132] Lea Raible, 'Incidental Jurisdiction in Human Rights Litigation: Surprising Absence and Rival Techniques' (2022) 116 *AJIL Unbound* 176–180, 176.

[133] Ibid.

While there are several plausible explanations to this practice,[134] this approach can in fact only be evidence of a distinct way that the Court performs its duties as an international court. The focus of the Court indeed clearly lies on the interpretation of the Convention in such a way as to bypass the application of the doctrine of incidental jurisdiction instead of relying on the Convention and its jurisdictional limits, which would in principle circumscribe the scope of the Court's jurisdiction, and then deal with ancillary questions through the application of the doctrine of incidental jurisdiction.[135] It is moreover interesting to point out that, as the Court itself has acknowledged in its decision in the *Ukraine v. Russia* case, several arbitral tribunals in the context of investment disputes brought by Ukrainian investors in Crimea against Russia have adopted an approach that is similar to the Court's approach.[136]

4.3.3 *Proportionality Assessment*

Proportionality assessments are conducted by legal decision-makers in the course of the application of many norms of international law.[137] They concern the relationship between a measure taken by a legal agent pursuant to an international norm and the injury that this measure entails. The relationship is examined in the light of a presupposed legal objective. Thus, simply put, proportionality assessments are conducted to ensure that a measure is not incommensurate with the injury suffered, considering the legal objective for the sake of which the measure is being taken.[138] In the application of law, as in other spheres of human activity, the end does not always justify the means. This fixation on the presupposed legal objectives makes proportionality assessments a perfect candidate for a study of the legal idealist's conception of a special regime. By identifying the objectives involved in the proportionality calculi, we

[134] Ibid., at 176–180.

[135] Ibid., at 176–180, 179.

[136] See, for example, *Everest Estate LLC v. Russian Federation*, PCA Case No. 2015-36, Award, 2 May 2018; *Public Joint Stock Company 'State Savings Bank of Ukraine' (JSC Oschadbank) v. the Russian Federation*, PCA Case No. 2016-14, Award, 26 November 2018, as cited by the European Court of Human Rights in Case Nos. 20958/14 and 38334/18, *Ukraine v. Russia (Re Crimea)*, Decision on Admissibility, 16 December 2020, para. 341.

[137] See Ulf Linderfalk, 'Proportionality and International Legal Pragmatics' (2020) 89 *Nordic Journal of International Law* 422–437.

[138] Ibid.

can gain a fuller understanding of the different normative presuppositions of international lawyers and especially the different state of affairs that they find desirable. We will conduct our study as a comparison of the way in which proportionality assessments are being conducted in international responsibility law and the law of the European Convention on Human Rights.

As provided by international responsibility law, the proportionality of a countermeasure is a condition for its legality. Thus, according to the Articles on the Responsibility of States for Internationally Wrongful Acts, '[c]ountermeasures must be commensurate with the injury suffered, taking into account the gravity of the internationally wrongful act and the rights in question'.[139] The Draft Articles on the Responsibility of International Organizations, adopted by the ILC in 2011, include an identically worded provision.[140] Interestingly, neither of these provisions include any information on the objective that they seek to protect. International lawyers have reacted differently to this absence.

Some express the proportionality test in terms that would allow those who take countermeasures considerable flexibility, as when they suggest that countermeasures should serve goals 'which are consistent with the expressed desire of the international community'.[141] Some believe that the proportionality rule is based on a very specific objective, while still not agreeing on what that particular objective might be. Thus, according to one commentator, the proportionality of a measure 'is tested by what appears reasonably necessary to induce the wrongdoer to cease its course of action'.[142] As other commentators express it, it is the objective of the proportionality rule to ensure that countermeasures do not lead to inequitable results.[143] The great majority of commentators, however,

[139] Articles on the Responsibility of States for Internationally Wrongful Acts, 28 January 2002, U.N. Doc. A/RES/56/83, Art. 51. On 12 December 2001, the UN General Assembly adopted resolution 56/83, recognising the work of the ILC and the adoption of the ILC Articles. From then on, the ILC Articles are officially referred to as the *Articles on Responsibility of States for Internationally Wrongful Acts*. See ibid., at Art. 51.

[140] Draft Articles on the Responsibility of International Organizations with Commentaries, Report of the International Law Commission on the work of its Sixty-third session, (2001) II-2 *Yearbook of the International Law Commission* 39, Art. 54.

[141] Rosemary Rayfuse, 'Countermeasures and High Seas Fisheries Enforcement' (2004) 51 *Netherlands International Law Review* 41–76, 71.

[142] Enzo Cannizzaro, 'The Role of Proportionality in the Law of International Countermeasures' (2001) 12 *European Journal of International Law* 889–916, 910.

[143] Draft Articles on Responsibility of States for Internationally Wrongful Acts with Commentaries, Report of the International Law Commission on the work of its Fifty-

use language that altogether avoids recognizing the relevance of any objective. Lawyers may warn, for example, that since recourse to countermeasures involves the great risk of causing an escalation of conflict, countermeasures should be 'a wager on the wisdom, not on the weakness of the other party'.[144] This survey of the discourse on international responsibility law gives a very clear impression: overall, lawyers do not seem to have a very clear idea of what desirable state of affairs that they are pursuing.

This observation is in stark contrast with the jurisprudence of the European Court of Human Rights. In the application of the European Convention and its additional protocols, the European Court uses 'the principle of proportionality' in various situations.[145] Often, it uses it to establish the necessity of measures restricting the enjoyment of fundamental freedoms.[146] In these situations, the Court would typically start by pinning down that 'a fair balance has to be struck between the demands of the general interest and the requirements of the protection of the individual's fundamental rights'.[147] This standard implies consideration of an objective that can help to determine when a fair balance has been struck and when it has not. It is not often that the Court articulates this objective explicitly, but it would seem to have done so in *Refah Partisi* and *United Communist Party of Turkey*, both of which concerned complaints of the dissolution of a political party by the Turkish Constitutional Court.

In commenting upon the possibility of imposing restrictions on the enjoyment of the right to freedom of association, the Court affirmed: 'the Convention was designed to maintain and promote the ideals and values of a democratic society'.[148] As it insisted, 'no one must be authorised to

third Session, (2001) II-2 *Yearbook of the International Law Commission* 1, 135. See also Fourth Report on State Responsibility, by Mr Gaetano Arangio-Ruiz, Special Rapporteur, Report of the International Law Commission on the work of its Forty-fourth Session, (1992) II-1 *Yearbook of the International Law Commission* 1, at 23.

144 *Air Services Agreement*, [1978] 18 R.I.A.A. 417, para. 91.

145 See, for example, Jonas Christoffersen, *Fair Balance: Proportionality, Subsidiarity and Primarity in the European Convention on Human Rights* (Leiden: Martinus Nijhoff Publishers, 2009), 31.

146 Sometimes, the Court uses the principle to establish the very substance of human rights, such as the right to life, the right to property, and the right not to be subjected to inhuman or degrading treatment or punishment.

147 Case No. 24768/06, *Perdigão v. Portugal*, IHRL 1822 (ECHR 2010), para. 63.

148 Case No. 19392/92, *United Communist Party of Turkey v. Turkey*, [1998] ECHR 1, para. 45.

rely on the Convention's provisions in order to weaken or destroy the ideals and values of a democratic society'.[149] This same objective explains why the Court refers to measures as disproportionate when they are the result of an arbitrary or discriminatory application of a rule of law[150]; when they are not 'accompanied by specific reasoning'[151]; when they thwart 'the free expression of the people in the choice of the legislature'[152]; when public authorities have failed to act with 'diligence' or within a 'sufficiently prompt' time-frame[153]; when the decision-making process resulting in the adoption of a measure does not involve a judiciary[154]; when measures are contrary to 'the demands of that pluralism, tolerance, and broad-mindedness, without which there is no democratic society'[155]; when there is no access to a court or possibility of appeal[156]; and so forth. Overall, the European Court seems to have a very clear idea of what desirable state of affairs it is pursuing when applying the proportionality test. For those European human rights specialists who accept its jurisprudence, it can be considered proof of the existence of a joint enterprise.

4.3.4 *Teleological Reasoning in Treaty Interpretation*

In a legal setting, 'teleological reasoning' means the drawing of inferences or conclusions based on the purpose of a legal act, a norm or a treaty (sometimes referred to as its *telos*). Such arguments occur in the consideration of many different issues, such as claims of an abuse of rights,[157] the validity of reservations to a treaty,[158] the validity of resolutions

149 Case Nos. 41340/98, 41342/98, 41343/98, 41344/98, *Refah Partisi (The Welfare Party) v. Turkey*, [2003] ECHR 87, para. 99.

150 Case No. 6339/05, *Evans v. United Kingdom*, [2007] ECHR 264, para. 89; Case No. 48876/08, *Animal Defenders International v. United Kingdom*, [2013] ECHR 362, para. 122.

151 Case No. 20201/04, *Frodl v. Austria*, [2010] ECHR 508, para. 35.

152 Case No. 126/05, *Scoppola v. Italy (No 3)*, [2012] ECHR 23, para. 84.

153 Case No. 25/7/13, *Rousk v. Sweden*, [2013] ECHR 746, paras. 122, 124.

154 *Scoppola v. Italy (No 3)*, para. 98.

155 Case No. 13470/87, *Otto-Preminger Institut v. Austria*, [1994] 19 EHHR 34, para. 49.

156 Case Nos. 22083/93, 22095/93, *Stubbings v. United Kingdom*, [1996] ECHR 44, paras. 65–66.

157 See, for example, Ulf Linderfalk, 'Philip Morris Asia Ltd. v. Australia: Abuse of Rights in Investor-State Arbitration' (2017) 86 *Nordic Journal of International Law* 403–419.

158 See Vienna Convention on the Law of Treaties, Vienna, 23 May 1969, in force 27 January 1980, 1155 U.N.T.S. 331, Art. 19(c).

adopted by an organ of an international organization,[159] the necessity of measures restricting the enjoyment of human rights,[160] and the ascription of obligations prior to the entry into force of a treaty.[161] In the context of this chapter, they attract an interest especially in situations of choice – when the practice of a legal decision-maker demonstrates a clear preference for teleological reasoning, although from a legal point of view, other forms of argument would be equally possible.

Consider the interpretative practices of the European Court of Human Rights. In the application of Article 31 of the 1969 Vienna Convention on the Law of Treaties (VCLT), the European Court occasionally finds that it has to make a choice between different rules of interpretation, since different rules provide justification of different ways of understanding the European Convention and Protocols. A commonly occurring conflict is that between Rule No. 1 in the below list and either of Rule Nos. 2–8:

Rule No. 1 If one of the two possible ordinary meanings of a treaty provision helps to obtain the object and purpose of the treaty, whereas the other ordinary meaning does not, then the former meaning shall be adopted.[162]

Rule No. 2 If one of the two possible ordinary meanings of a treaty provision makes a part of the treaty redundant, whereas the other ordinary meaning does not, then the latter meaning shall be adopted.[163]

Rule No. 3 If one of the two possible ordinary meanings of a treaty provision makes the treaty appear logically consistent, whereas the other ordinary meaning does not, then the former meaning shall be adopted.[164]

Rule No. 4 If one of the two possible ordinary meanings of a treaty provision involves a logical tautology, whereas the other

159 See, for example, Daniëlla Dam-de Jong, 'Who Is Targeted by the Council's Sanctions? The UN Security Council and the Principle of Proportionality' (2020) 89 *Nordic Journal of International Law* 383–398.

160 See any of the decisions of the European Court of Human Rights cited in Section 4.3.3.

161 See Art. 18 of the 1969 Vienna Convention on the Law of Treaties.

162 See, for example, *Kasikili/Sedudu Island*, para. 43.

163 See, for example, *Application of the International Convention on the Elimination of All Forms of Racial Discrimination (Georgia v. Russian Federation)*, paras. 133–134.

164 See, for example, *Soering v. United Kingdom*, paras. 101 and 103.

ordinary meaning does not, then the latter meaning shall be adopted.[165]

Rule No. 5 If one of two possible ordinary meanings of a treaty implies that a word or lexical phrase is given a consistent meaning throughout the treaty, whereas the other ordinary meaning does not, then the former meaning shall be adopted.[166]

Rule No. 6 If one of two possible ordinary meanings of a treaty implies that different terms or lexical phrases belonging to the same lexical field is given a different meaning, whereas the other ordinary meaning does not, then the former meaning shall be adopted.[167]

Rule No. 7 If one of two possible ordinary meanings of a treaty is consistent with a subsequent practice developed in the application of the treaty, whereas the other ordinary meaning is not, then the former meaning shall be adopted.[168]

Rule No. 8 If one of two possible ordinary meanings of a treaty implies a derogation from a rule of international law applicable in the relations between the parties, whereas the other ordinary meaning does not, then the latter meaning shall be adopted.[169]

Rule No. 1 serves as a support for a conclusion based on an assumed relationship between the treaty and its object and purpose. It provides arguments that seek to make a treaty an efficient means for the realization of its *telos*. Rule Nos. 2–8 all serve as support for a conclusion based on an assumed relationship between the interpreted treaty provision and its context. They provide arguments that seek to make a treaty provision appear logically and linguistically coherent with its context. There is nothing in the law laid down in Articles 31–33 of the VCLT that helps resolve a conflict between rules of interpretation belonging to these different categories. The VCLT leaves it to be resolved at the discretion of legal decision-makers.

[165] See, for example, *Border and Transborder Armed Action (Nicaragua v. Honduras)*, Jurisdiction and Admissibility, [1988] I.C.J. Rep. 69, para. 45.

[166] See, for example, *Navigational and Related Rights*, para. 54.

[167] See, for example, Case Nos. 1120984, 1123484, 1126684, 1138685, *Brogan and Others v. United Kingdom*, [1989] 11 EHRR 117, para. 59.

[168] See, for example, Case No. 16130/90, *Sigurjónson v. Iceland*, [1993] ECHR 264, paras. 33–35.

[169] See, for example, *Award in the Arbitration regarding the Iron Rhine*, para. 79.

In the exercise of this discretion, the European Court has always favoured Rule No. 1: it has consistently favoured teleological efficiency over logical and linguistic coherence.[170] In *Engel and Others v. The Netherlands*,[171] for example, the Court considered the meaning of the term 'a criminal charge', in the sense of Article 6, paragraph 1 of the European Convention. It noted the practice of the Contracting States, which all 'make a distinction of long standing, albeit in different forms and degrees, between disciplinary proceedings and criminal proceedings'.[172] (Compare Rule No. 7 in the above list.) On the other hand, the Court was reluctant to ascribe to Article 6 a meaning that would make the practice of states itself decisive:

> If the Contracting States were able at their discretion to classify an offence as disciplinary instead of criminal, or to prosecute the author of a 'mixed' offence on the disciplinary rather than on the criminal plane, the operation of the fundamental clauses of Articles 6 and 7 (art. 6, art. 7) would be subordinated to their sovereign will. A latitude extending thus far might lead to results incompatible with the purpose and object of the Convention.[173]

In *Mamatkulov and Askarov v. Turkey*,[174] the Court acknowledged that 'Contracting States have the right, as a matter of well-established international law … to control the entry, residence and expulsion of aliens'.[175] (Compare Rule No. 8 in the above list.) Nevertheless, the Court added, the extradition of an alien by a Contracting State may engage the responsibility of that State under the Convention, depending on the conditions in the requesting country:

[170] See, for example, Case No. 5100/71, *Engel v. The Netherlands*, [1976] ECHR 3, para. 81; Case No. 28957/95, *Goodwin v. United Kingdom*, [2002] ECHR 588, paras. 71–75; Case No. 6232/73 (A/27), *König v. Germany*, IHRL 18 (ECHR 1978), para. 88; Case No. 39652/98, *Maaouia v. France*, [2000] ECHR 455, para. 34; Case No. 5029/71 (A/28), *Klass and Others v. Germany*, [1979–1980] 2 EHRR 214, paras. 33–34; Case No. 5095/71 (A/23), *Kjeldsen v. Denmark*, [1976] ECHR 6, paras. 53–54; Case No. 46827/99, *Mamatkulov and Askarov v. Turkey*, [2005] ECHR 64, paras. 66–68; Case No. 23459/03, *Bayatyan v. Armenia*, IHRL 169 (ECHR 2011), paras. 72, 92–109; Case No. 10249/03, *Scoppola v. Italy (No 2)*, [2010] 51 EHRR 12, paras. 92–109; Case No. 25965/04, *Rantsev v. Cyprus and Russia*, IHRL 3632 (ECHR 2010), paras. 272–282.

[171] *Engel v. The Netherlands*.

[172] Ibid., at para. 80.

[173] Ibid., at para. 81.

[174] *Mamatkulov and Askarov v. Turkey*.

[175] Ibid., at para. 66.

> It would hardly be compatible with the 'common heritage of political traditions, ideals, freedom and the rule of law' to which the Preamble refers, were a Contracting State knowingly to surrender a person to another State where there were substantial grounds for believing that he would be in danger of being subjected to torture or inhuman or degrading treatment or punishment [. . .].[176]

In *Bayatyan v. Armenia,*[177] the Court considered whether the conviction of the applicant for refusal to serve in the army constituted a violation of Article 9 of the European Convention. It revisited the case law of the European Commission, which had stressed the relationship of Article 9 with Article 4, paragraph 3(b) of the Convention and left the choice of recognizing conscientious objectors to each Contracting Party.[178] (Compare Rule No. 3 in the above list.) At the same time, as it declared, it was not convinced that this interpretation reflected 'the true purpose' of the Convention.[179] The Court reiterated that the European Convention 'is a living instrument which must be interpreted in the light of present-day conditions and of the ideas prevailing in democratic States today'.[180] It noted the trend among European countries to recognize the right to conscientious objection: at the time of the alleged inference with the applicant's rights, only four member states of the CoE, in addition to Armenia, did not provide in their laws for the possibility of claiming conscientious objector status.[181] In the light of this observation, the Court found that it was unable to confirm the case law established by the European Commission. As it concluded, Article 9 should no longer be read in conjunction with Article 4, paragraph 3(b).[182]

As is evident, the European Court has an unmistakable idea of what desirable state of affairs it is pursuing: the task that it has been assigned is not primarily to ensure coherence between the provisions of the European Convention and their logical and linguistic context, but to make the Convention an efficient means for the realization of its *telos* or *telê* (in the plural). For those European human rights specialists who accept this jurisprudence, it can be considered as proof of the existence of a joint enterprise.

176 Ibid., at para. 68.
177 *Bayatyan v. Armenia.*
178 Ibid., at paras. 93–96.
179 Ibid., at para. 100.
180 Ibid., at para. 102.
181 Ibid., at para. 103.
182 Ibid., at para. 109.

5

A Shared Repertoire

5.1 Introduction

To facilitate a general consideration of the concept of a special regime, we earlier introduced the term 'X law', which in our view stands for any randomly selected segment of the international legal system. As a point of departure from the case studies that we conducted in Chapters 3 and 4, we assumed that some person or institution had categorized X law as a special regime. We pointed out that, from the point of view of the legal idealist's conception of a special regime, this categorization entails altogether three claims. Thus, to say that X law is a special regime is in effect to say: (1) that X law specialists have a mutual engagement; (2) that X law specialists are engaged in a joint enterprise; and (3) that X law specialists have a shared repertoire.

In Chapters 3 and 4, we occupied ourselves with the issue of how to establish the first and second of these three claims. Justification is complicated by the fact that these are essentially claims about the existence of normative presuppositions, which are not, as such, susceptible to direct empirical studies. We suggested the use of a methodology that would regard these normative presuppositions as implicit in the actual conduct of X law specialists and ascertainable based on the assumption that these specialists act rationally and that they recognize the appropriateness of their own action.

We propose that the third claim be approached in much the same way. To say that X law specialists have a shared repertoire is to say that X law specialists consider the use of a set of rhetorical tools appropriate. If, once again, we assume that X law specialists act rationally and that they recognize the appropriateness of their own actions, the existence of such a presupposition can be established based on actual conduct. More specifically, as Chapter 2 indicated, it can be inferred from the use of a distinct set of: (i) terminologies; (ii) concepts; (iii) methods; (iv) forms of argument; and (v) theories, principles and doctrines.

The several case studies that we will conduct in this chapter will help to illustrate this methodology. Sections 5.2–5.6 will illustrate how the existence of a shared repertoire can be inferred from the use of, in turn, a distinct terminology, a distinct concept, a distinct method, a distinct form of argument, and a distinct theory, principle or doctrine. These sections will ask:

> Relative to a selected segment of international law (X law), what concepts are X law specialists using? How do these concepts compare with those used by other communities of international lawyers? (Section 5.2)
> Relative to a selected segment of international law (X law), what terminologies are X law specialists using? How does this terminology compare with that used by other communities of international lawyers? (Section 5.3)
> Relative to a selected segment of international law (X law), what methods are X law specialists using? How do these methods compare with those used by other communities of international lawyers? (Section 5.4)
> Relative to a selected segment of international law (X law), what forms of argument are X law specialists using? How do these forms of argument compare with those used by other communities of international lawyers? (Section 5.5)
> Relative to a selected segment of international law (X law), what theories, principles and doctrines are X law specialists using? How do these theories, principles and doctrines compare with those used by other communities of international lawyers? (Section 5.6)

5.2 The Use of a Distinct Set of Concepts

5.2.1 The Concept of a Jus Cogens Norm

For purposes of the present book, a concept is a mental representation.[1] It is the generalized idea of an empirical or normative phenomenon or state of affairs (e.g. *the Government of Sweden, the Quran, the occupation by Russia of Crimea,* or *the diplomatic relations of Sweden with Turkey*) or a class of such phenomena or states of affairs (e.g. *BMW motor cars, international waters, diplomatic immunities,* or *foreign armed occupation*).[2] As implied by the word 'generalized', concepts are formed through

[1] On the ontology of concept, see, for example, Eric Margolis and Stephen Laurence, 'The Ontology of Concepts: Abstract Objects or Mental Representations?' (2007) 41 *Noûs* 561–593.

[2] Compare Birger Hjørland, 'Concept Theory' (2009) 60 *Journal of the American Society for Information Science and Technology* 1519–1536.

a process of abstraction. They are the result of the ability of the human brain to perceive of particular qualities or properties of phenomena or states of affairs as common characteristics – irrespective of the many particular qualities or properties that those same phenomena or states of affairs do not have in common.[3]

The organization of this book builds on a distinction between a set of concepts and a terminology. Thus, the use by international law specialists of a distinct set of concepts is the topic of this section, whereas the use by specialists of a distinct terminology is the topic of the subsequent Section 5.3. To understand this distinction, it is important that readers acknowledge the difference between a concept and a *conceptual term*. A concept has an *extension*, which are the many phenomena or states of affairs to which the concept is applied. A conceptual term, on the other hand, is the piece of language that international lawyers use to refer to a concept in speech or writing. A conceptual term has *meaning*, much like any other term used by speakers of a language. Part of the meaning of a conceptual term are the many phenomena or states of affairs to which this term can be used to refer.

Importantly, since a concept and a conceptual term are two different things, a single term can be used to stand for different concepts. Think, for example, of 'the continental shelf'. In some contexts, this term can be used to stand for the section of the seabed adjacent to a coast 'that slopes down gradually from the low-water mark to the depth, averaging about 130 metres, at which the angle of the declination increases markedly'.[4] In other contexts, it can be used to stand for the seabed and subsoil of the submarine areas that extend beyond the territorial sea of a state 'throughout the natural prolongation of its land territory to the outer edge of the continental margin, or to a distance of 200 nautical miles from the baselines from which the breadth of the territorial sea is measured'.[5] In the reverse, a single concept can be represented by different terms. Think, for example, of the two terms '*jus dispositivum*' and 'ordinary international law', which both represent the great number of international norms that do not have the status of *jus cogens* and, thus, permit derogation.

[3] Ibid.

[4] Robin Churchill and Alan Lowe, *The Law of the Sea*, 3rd edition (Manchester: Manchester University Press, 1999), 141.

[5] United Nations Convention on the Law of the Sea, Montego Bay, 10 December 1982, in force 16 November 1994, 1833 U.N.T.S. 397, Art. 76.

These observations help to establish a proper methodology for our inquiries into the use of different concepts by different groups of international lawyers. If someone refers to a set of concepts used among a group of international law specialists as distinct, as we do in the title of this section, then this is because these specialists make different mental representations of the world than other international lawyers. Obviously, we can only observe these differences indirectly – through the use of conceptual terms by different groups of international lawyers. If different groups of international lawyers use a conceptual term to refer to partly different phenomena or states of affairs, as we will assume, this allows the inference that these groups of lawyers make different mental representations of the world.

Section 5.2 will provide altogether four examples of such divergences. In this sub-section, we will focus attention on the concept of a *jus cogens* norm. As noted in the vast literature on *jus cogens*, international lawyers have widely different opinions about the extension of this concept.[6] While they do not seem to have any issues with the term '*jus cogens*' as such, it is evident that they have widely different ideas of the characteristics that serve to justify a proposition that some particular norm or norms have the status of *jus cogens*. On further scrutiny, this is the result of their widely different ideas of the source of *jus cogens* obligations. The main dividing line is that between the legal positivists and the legal idealists.[7]

To illustrate, consider the suggestion that an international norm (N) is a *jus cogens*. As legal positivists are bound to argue, the *jus cogens* status of N derives from the existence of the second order norms of the *jus cogens* regime, and from the application of these norms to situations of conflict involving N.[8] By the 'second order norms of the *jus cogens* regime', we mean those norms that specify the legal consequences ensuing from the postulated superiority of *jus cogens* rules over ordinary international law. Examples include all those in the below list:

- If a treaty is in conflict with a rule of *jus cogens* created prior to the conclusion of the treaty, then the treaty shall be void.[9]

[6] See Ulf Linderfalk, *Understanding* Jus Cogens *in International Law and International Legal Discourse* (Cheltenham: Edward Elgar Publishing Limited, 2020), 7–19.

[7] See Section 3.5.

[8] See Linderfalk, *Understanding* Jus Cogens, 65–80.

[9] See Vienna Convention on the Law of Treaties, Vienna, 23 May 1969, in force 27 January 1980, 1155 U.N.T.S. 331, Art. 53.

- If the purport of a reservation to a treaty is in conflict with the a rule of *jus cogens*, then that reservation shall be void.[10]
- If a resolution adopted by an international organization is in conflict with a rule of *jus cogens*, then that resolution shall be void.[11]

The second order norms of the *jus cogens* regime classify as customary international law. They do not themselves have the status of *jus cogens*, but are ordinary international law.[12] It follows that the *jus cogens* status of N is the result of the operation of the ordinary processes creating and modifying customary international law.[13]

From the point of view of legal positivism, consequently, a proposition classifying a norm N as *jus cogens* will have to be justified in the very same way as any proposition claiming the existence of a rule of customary international law – by showing that it can be inferred from the practice and *opinio juris* of states.[14] It has to be shown, first, that states generally do not derogate from N and that they generally do not modify N by means other than the creation of new *jus cogens* norms. Secondly, it has to be shown that states widely subscribe to the opinion that there is in customary international law an authoritative set of second order norms, by virtue of which no derogations from N are permitted, and modifications of N can be accomplished only by the creation of new *jus cogens* norms.[15]

Legal idealists have a markedly different idea of the characteristics that serve to justify a proposition that some particular norm or norms have the status of *jus cogens*. For legal idealists, *jus cogens* obligations are entailed by the commitment of the international legal community to work for the realization of some presupposed legal ideal.[16] Legal idealists have different ideas of what this particular ideal might be. Common examples range from values typically associated with the concept of law

[10] See Guide to Practice on Reservations to Treaties, Report of the International Law Commission on the work of its Sixty-third Session, U.N. Doc. A/66/10, 43 (principle 4.4.3).

[11] See, for example, *Application of the Convention on the Prevention and Punishment of the Crime of Genocide (Bosnia and Herzegovina v. Serbia and Montenegro)*, Further Requests for the Indications of Provisional Measures, Separate Opinion of Judge Lauterpacht, [1993] I.C.J. Rep. 325, 440.

[12] See Linderfalk, *Understanding* Jus Cogens, 80.

[13] Ibid., at 73–80.

[14] Ibid., at 112–113.

[15] Ibid.

[16] Ibid., at 86–87.

such as justice, legality, and the maintenance of international public order, to abstruse states of affairs such as the essential dignity of the individual, the well-being of all members of the international society, the creation of the conditions that are necessary for people to be able to satisfy their basic aspirations, and the accommodation of the common basic needs of human beings.[17] These differences apart, what all legal idealists have to establish to justify a proposition that an international norm (N) is *jus cogens* is the existence of a very particular instrumental relationship between the posited legal ideal and the legal consequences ensuing from the conferral of a *jus cogens* status on N. They have to show that realization of the presupposed legal ideal is impossible as long as international law permits derogation from N and modification of N by means other than the creation of a new norm of *jus cogens.*[18]

The legal idealists' conception of a *jus cogens* norm is more common among some camps of international lawyers than others. It is especially common among those lawyers that specialize in international human rights law and international criminal law. These are all enterprises that stress the organization of human society and the conditions of human life. In so doing, they resonate well with the ideals, upon which many legal idealists build their theory of law and *jus cogens* conception. Symptomatically, in *Prosecutor v. Anto Furundžija*, a Trial Chamber of ICTY referred to the 'principle of respect for human dignity', which it insisted is 'the basic underpinning and indeed the very raison d'être of international humanitarian law'.[19]

In the same vein, in the *South West Africa Case*, Judge Tanaka recalled the origin of the principle of the protection of human rights, which, as he described it, 'derived from the concept of man as a person and his relationship with society which cannot be separated from universal human nature'.[20] It is not surprising that many lawyers specializing in international human rights law and international criminal law find the idealist's conception of *jus cogens* more appropriate.

[17] Ibid., at 87–92.

[18] Ibid., at 113–114.

[19] *Prosecutor v. Furundžija*, Trial Chamber, Judgment Case No. IT-95-17/1-T, 10 December 1998, para. 183.

[20] *South West Africa Case (Liberia v. South Africa; Ethiopia v. South Africa)*, Dissenting Opinion of Judge Tanaka, [1996] I.C.J. Rep. 297.

5.2.2 *The Concept of a Conflict of Two Rules*

The concept of a conflict of two rules is essential for the application of conflict norms, such as any of those in the list below:

- 'Each Party . . . undertakes not to enter into any international engagement in conflict with this Treaty'.[21]
- 'This Convention shall prevail, as between States Parties, over the Geneva Conventions on the Law of the Sea of 29 April 1958'.[22]
- 'When all the parties to the earlier treaty are parties also to the later treaty but the earlier treaty is not terminated or suspended in operation under Article 59, the earlier treaty applies only to the extent that its provisions are compatible with those of the later treaty'.[23]

All of these norms apply on the condition of the existence of a conflict of two rules. International lawyers conceive of this condition differently. These different conceptions of a normative conflict come hand in hand with two different theories of law, much like the different conceptions of *jus cogens.*[24] We will refer to these theories as 'legal positivism' and 'legal idealism'.

Whether we conceive of a normative conflict from the perspective of legal positivism or legal idealism, a conflict of two rules is characterized by a very particular kind of situation: for a duty-holder, two norms are equally applicable relative to some particular time and particular conduct or state of affairs; for some reason, the duty-holder cannot apply both and so is forced to make a choice. The important differences between the legal positivist's and the legal idealist's respective conception of a normative conflict are revealed by their respective responses to the following three questions: (1) What, precisely, is this choice that the duty-holder is facing? (2) Why does this choice have to be made? and (3) What does a conflict norm help to achieve when applied to the situation?

For the legal positivist, the choice that the duty-holder is facing is one between logically inconsistent obligations. A choice must be made because, if two rules impose logically inconsistent obligations, the duty-holder cannot possibly perform both. For legal positivists, conflict norms

[21] North Atlantic Treaty, Washington, D.C., 4 April 1949, in force 24 August 1949, 34 U.N.T.S. 243, Art. 8.

[22] Art. 311 of the United Nations Convention on the Law of the Sea.

[23] Art. 30(3) of the 1969 Vienna Convention on the Law of Treaties.

[24] See Section 5.2.1.

help to ensure a legal system free of all logical contradictions. Thus, legal positivists would define the concept of a conflict of two rules according to either of the below two propositions:

'In the relationship between a duty-holder (P) and a right-holder (Q), there is a conflict between two rules (R_1 and R_2), if, and only if, it is the case that: (a) R_1 and R_2 are equally applicable relative to some particular time or time period; (b) R_1 and R_2 are equally applicable relative to a particular conduct or state of affairs; and (c) the obligations, which R_1 and R_2 impose on P relative to this particular conduct or state of affairs, are logically inconsistent'.

'For a duty-holder (P), there is a conflict between two rules (R_1 and R_2), if, and only if, it is the case that: (a) R_1 and R_2 are equally applicable relative to some particular time or time period; (b) R_1 and R_2 are equally applicable relative to a particular conduct or state of affairs; and (c) the obligations, which R_1 and R_2 impose on P relative to this particular conduct or state of affairs, are logically inconsistent'.

As we have argued extensively elsewhere, the former of the two definitions applies when both of the conflicting rules express obligations of a bilateral nature. The latter definition applies when at least one of the two conflicting rules establish obligations *erga omnes* or *erga omnes partes*.[25]

For the legal idealists, a conflict of two rules involves a choice between different and irreconcilable results.[26] Say that a rule imposes an obligation on a state (S) to enable an individual to manifest his religious belief in worship together with other people, whereas another rule imposes an obligation on S to ensure the protection of public health and safety. In a situation where a fatal pandemic disease is quickly spreading, the performance of these obligations may involve a choice between different and irreconcilable results. This is so, if enabling an individual to manifest his religious belief in worship together with other people impedes the protection of public health and safety, and enabling the protection of public health and safety impedes the manifestation by an individual of his religious belief in worship together with other people. If, in such situations, a choice between obligations must be made, it is because the duty-holder cannot possibly act for the realization of both results. For the legal idealists, international conflict norms serve to pick out the one result that brings us closer to the realization of the presupposed legal ideal.

[25] See Ulf Linderfalk, *The International Legal System as a System of Knowledge* (Cheltenham: Edward Elgar Publishing Limited, 2022), 96–99.

[26] Ibid., at 99–101.

It is apt to describe the idealist's definition of a conflict between rules in terms of their purposes. A purpose is a desired state of affairs, as, for example, the freedom of individuals to manifest their religious belief in worship together with other people, or the protection of public health and safety. If a purpose is conferred on a rule, then it is because lawmakers expect that the performance of its obligations will enable, rather than impede, the realization of some such state of affairs. For legal idealists, these observations translate into the below definition:

For a duty-holder (P), there is a conflict between two rules (R_1 and R_2), if, and only if, it is the case that: (a) R_1 and R_2 are equally applicable relative to some particular time or time period; (b) R_1 and R_2 are equally applicable relative to a particular conduct or state of affairs; and (c) performance of the obligation which R_1 imposes on P will enable the realization of the purpose of R_1 but impede the realization of the purpose of R_2, and performance of the other obligation will enable the realization of the purpose of R_2 but impede the realization of the purpose of R_1.

This definition would seem to work in effect to ensure that the positivist's definition of a conflict between rules does not lead to undesirable outcomes. For legal idealists, a legal ideal will sometimes serve to render a rule of positive law invalid. In the same way, a legal ideal will sometimes prompt idealists to conclude that there is indeed a conflict between two rules, although legal positivists would think otherwise.[27]

The legal positivist's and legal idealist's conceptions of a normative conflict would seem to resonate differently with different groups of international lawyers. A case in point is international environmental law specialists, who more often than many other international lawyers construct their arguments based on the latter conception. Nele Matz discusses the example of Article 8 of the Convention on Biological Diversity, which would seem to require, in some cases, that coastal states establish areas of environmental protection in waters where they exercise resources jurisdiction. Such areas, she maintains, will impede the realization of an important purpose of the United Nations Convention on the Law of the Sea – free navigation in all territorial seas and exclusive economic zones.[28] Other environmental law specialists have brought attention to the necessity of reconciling multilateral environmental treaties with international trade agreements to avoid potential conflicts from

[27] Ibid., at 101–104.

[28] Rüdiger Wolfrum and Nele Matz, *Conflicts in International Environmental Law* (Berlin: Springer, 2003), 22.

materializing. In many cases, they contend, environmental treaties require legislation, which threatens to impede important purposes of international trade law, such as non-discrimination and the elimination of quantitative trade restrictions.[29]

The legal idealist's conception of a normative conflict is result-oriented, in contrast to the legal positivist's conception, which is only concerned with the internal structure of the international legal system.[30] Thus, the legal idealist's conception of a normative conflict resonates well with the categorization of international environmental law as a special regime. As we pointed out in Chapter 4, this categorization entails the assumption that international environmental law specialists do what they do based on the idea that some certain state of affairs is desirable. International environmental law specialists have certainly reason to regard the legal idealist's conception of a normative conflict as the more appropriate.

5.2.3 *The Concept of Effective Control*

The concept of control is a commonly used concept in general international law, as it has been included as one of the criteria for wrongful acts to be attributed to states in the ILC Articles on State Responsibility: 'The conduct of a person or group of persons shall be considered an act of State under international law if the person or group of persons is in fact acting on the instructions of, or under the direction or control of, that State in carrying out the conduct'.[31]

As is the case with the concept of *jus cogens*, discussed in Section 5.2.1, most international lawyers who refer and use the concept of 'control' do not seem to have any issues with the term itself but evidently have

[29] See, for example, Duncan Brack, 'Reconciling the GATT and Multilateral Environmental Agreements with Trade Provisions: The Latest Debate' (1997) 6 *Review of European, Comparative & International Environmental Law* 112–120; Steve Charnovitz, 'Multilateral Environmental Agreements and Trade Rules' (1996) 26 *Environmental Policy & Law* 163–169; Shannon Hudnall, 'Towards a Greener International Trade System: Multilateral Environmental Agreements and the World Trade Organization' (1996) 29 *Columbia Journal of Law & Social Problems* 175–216; Christina Voigt, *Sustainable Development as a Principle of International Law* (Leiden: Martinus Nijhoff Publishers, 2008).

[30] As sometimes said, positivists think of law as a form of social order valuable in its own right. See Linderfalk, *Understanding* Jus Cogens, 51.

[31] Articles on the Responsibility of States for Internationally Wrongful Acts, 28 January 2002, U.N. Doc. A/RES/56/83, Annex, Art. 8.

different ideas of the features which that concept encompasses. This is the case especially on the degree of control that is required. The main cause for this difference lies in the differing ideas that various communities have on the precise purpose of the concept in a variety of fields in international law. These different ideas about the features of the concept are not always clearly spelled out, but if we take the decisions of several international courts and tribunals on the question, we can see that there is a rather clear dividing line between general international courts, international criminal courts and decisions of (some) arbitral tribunals in ISDS.

As a starting point, the Commentary to Article 8 of the ILC Articles confirms that the article broadly covers two situations: instructions or direction or control.[32] In general terms, it should be noted that 'instructions', 'direction', or 'control' in themselves are insufficient to establish attribution – the 'instructions', 'direction' or 'control' must 'relate to the conduct which is said to have amounted to an internationally wrongful act'.[33] Also, there should be 'a specific factual relationship between the person or entity engaging in the conduct and the State'.[34] In both cases, the 'instructions', 'direction' or 'control' need to relate to the specific acts in question. While 'instructions' can be slightly more easily detected and proven, the criteria of direction or control are more complex,[35] notably in light of the degree of control and this is precisely the point on which the concept has been used distinctively.

The best representation of the perspective from general international law is the decision of the ICJ in the *Nicaragua* case. In that case, the ICJ set a rather high threshold for the required control and held that the acts of paramilitary groups could not be attributed to the United States because it did not have 'effective control' over the group. The ICJ explained that:

> even the general control by the [United States] over a force with a high degree of dependency on it, would not in [itself] mean, without further evidence, that the United States directed or enforced the perpetration of the acts contrary to human rights and humanitarian law alleged by the

[32] Draft Articles on Responsibility of States for Internationally Wrongful Acts with Commentaries, Report of the International Law Commission on the work of its Fifty-third Session, (2001) II-2 *Yearbook of the International Law Commission* 1, commentary to art. 8, para. 1.

[33] Ibid., at para. 8.

[34] Ibid., at para. 1.

[35] Ibid., at commentary to art. 5, para. 3.

> applicant State. [. . .] For this conduct to give rise to legal responsibility of the United States, it would in principle have to be proved that that State had effective control of the military or paramilitary operations in the course of which the alleged violations were committed.[36]

The relevant 'test' was subsequently confirmed by the ICJ in other decisions, chiefly the *Genocide* case *(Bosnia and Herzegovina v. Serbia and Montenegro).*[37]

As has been widely discussed, a different test has been devised by other courts and tribunals in order to assess the required 'control'. The ICTY Appeals Chambers in the *Tadić* case argued that a distinction should be made between 'individuals acting on behalf of a State without specific instructions, from that of individuals making up an organized and hierarchically structured group, such as a military unit or, in case of war or civil strife, armed bands of irregulars or rebels'.[38] The ICTY Appeals Chamber then argued that in for the attribution to a State of acts of armed groups 'it is sufficient to require that the group as a whole be under the overall control of the State'.[39]

While one could argue that this is merely a different interpretation of the same concept, the interesting point, which is often overlooked, is that the ICTY Appeals Chamber explicitly relied on a different *concept*. The Appeals Chamber indeed supported its perspective, in addition to relying on other cases, on the idea that

> the whole body of international law on State responsibility is based on *a realistic concept of accountability*, which disregards legal formalities and aims at ensuring that States entrusting some functions to individuals or groups of individuals must answer for their actions, even when they act contrary to their directives.[40]

This point was moreover taken up by Antonio Cassese, who was a member of the ICTY Appeals Chambers in the *Tadić* case, in a subsequent scholarly article, in which he criticized the case law of the ICJ on this point. He not only considered that the Court mistakenly claimed that the 'effective control' test was part of customary law. He also

[36] *Military and Paramilitary Activities in and Against Nicaragua (Nicaragua v. United States of America)*, [1986] I.C.J. Rep. 14, para. 115.

[37] *Application of the Convention on the Prevention and Punishment of the Crime of Genocide (Bosnia and Herzegovina v. Serbia and Montenegro)*, [2007] I.C.J. Rep. 43, para. 399.

[38] *Prosecutor v. Tadić*, Appeals Chamber, Judgment Case No. IT-94-1, 2 October 1995, para. 120.

[39] Ibid.

[40] Ibid., at para. 121 (emphasis added).

re-emphasized that, in reality, the ICTY relied on a different *concept* of responsibility altogether, similar to the position taken by the ICTY Appeals Chamber itself. He reiterates that the position taken by the ICTY Appeals Chamber relies on a different concept in line with

> a basic principle underpinning the whole body of rules and principles on state responsibility: states may not evade responsibility towards other states when they, instead of acting through their own officials, use groups of individuals to undertake actions that are intended to damage, or in the event do damage, other states; if states so behave, they must answer for the actions of those individuals, even if such individuals have gone beyond their mandate or agreed upon tasks – lest the worst abuses should go unchecked. This is the rationale behind the rule providing that whenever persons lawfully acting on behalf of a state exceed their authority or contravene state instructions, the state is nonetheless answerable for such actions.[41]

Moreover, the ICTY, as noted, also considered that in any event different norms apply in case of private individuals and organized groups, which also, of course, hints at the use of different concepts, or at least different features of the broader concept of 'control'. The important aspect, however, is the use by the ICTY Appeals Chamber of '*a realistic concept of accountability*' based on 'aims at ensuring that States entrusting some functions to individuals or groups of individuals must answer for their actions'. The use of this concept seems, in fact, tailored towards regimes such as IHL and international criminal law – as is visible from the quote of Cassese above. In fact, the ICTY Appeals Chamber emphasized that the test it had developed was specific to the attribution of the conduct of 'military or paramilitary groups'.[42] This might indeed explain why the ICJ has not used the same concept as the ICTY, instead seeking to posit a general principle of international law applicable irrespective of any specific regime. Despite the difference in the specific circumstances and facts of both cases, and the different mandates of both the ICTY Appeals Chamber and the ICTY, the above does clearly show that in applying the control concept or test, both were addressing an issue of state responsibility and attribution of conduct. This is also why the ICTY Appeals Chamber itself and Antonio Cassese have emphasized that they

[41] Antonio Cassese, 'The *Nicaragua* and *Tadić* Tests Revisited in Light of the ICJ Judgment on Genocide in Bosnia' (2007) 18 *European Journal of International Law* 649–668, 654.

[42] Ibid., at para. 124.

were using different concepts in relation to the same question of attribution of conduct.

5.3 The Use of a Distinct Terminology

5.3.1 Terms That Have No Use Outside of the Activities of a Group of Specialists

A terminology is a body of terms to which people ascribe particular meanings. Hence, if someone refers to a terminology used among a group of international law specialists as distinct, it can be so for two different reasons:

1. Because terms have no use outside of the activities of that group.
2. Because terms, while they are not as such unique for the activities of a group of international law specialists, have a unique meaning.

This observation helps to understand the difference between a distinct terminology and a distinct set of concepts, which was the topic of Section 5.2. In a terminology used among a group of international law specialists, most are 'conceptual terms' – they are terms that specialists use to refer to some or other concept.[43] A concept is a mental representation. In ontological terms, it is distinct from the pieces of language that people use when they refer to it in speech or writing. That said, in an investigation of the repertoire of a group of international law specialists, if no further limitations are being made, there will certainly be overlaps between the part of that study that pertains to its terminology and the part that pertains to its set of concepts. As we observed in Section 5.2, it is by observing that international law specialists ascribe a different meaning to a conceptual term than other people that we get to know that these specialists make different mental representations of the world. Consequently, to the extent that a terminology is distinct because it is a body of terms with a unique meaning, a distinct terminology will reflect much the same repertoire as a distinct set of concepts. Considering this overlap, we have decided to limit our examples in this section to such terms that have no use outside of the activities of a group of international law specialists.

[43] See Section 5.2.1.

A term does not necessarily correspond to a single word. It may also consist of a combination of two or more words if people ascribe to that combination a meaning that they cannot explain merely by reference to the lexical meaning of the single words and the rules of grammar. To illustrate, consider well-established compounds such as *ginger ale*, *sponge cake*, or *the United Nations*. This concept of a 'term' is important to understand when considering the concept of a distinct terminology. In legal terminology generally, there are indeed single words that have no use outside of the activities of lawyers, such as 'cession', 'estoppel', 'arbitrator' or 'justiciable', but they are not very common.[44] More often, if a term has no use outside of the activities of a group of international law specialists, this is because it combines words in a unique way. Examples include:

- In the terminology of law of the sea specialists, 'the Irish formula' and 'the extended continental shelf'
- In the terminology of international criminal law specialists, 'core crimes' and 'joint criminal enterprise'
- In the terminology of international human rights law specialists, 'margin of appreciation' and 'remedial secession'
- In the terminology of lawyers specializing in the law of international dispute settlement, 'incidental jurisdiction' and 'the optional clause system'
- In the terminology of international space law specialists, 'launching state' and 'envoy of mankind'
- In the terminology of lawyers specializing in international investment law, 'umbrella clauses' and 'foreign portfolio investment'

Acronyms are a related phenomenon that very few people use outside of a specific group of international law specialists. Think of 'MEA', for example, or 'MIT', or again 'LOAC'.[45]

These terms are all used for technical purposes to describe a phenomenon or state of affairs that is uniquely relevant for the activity of a group

[44] This may have something to do with the nature of legal language, which is parasitical on other languages – on everyday language as much as on technical languages other than that of law itself. On this topic, see Jerzy Wróblewski, 'Legal Language and Legal Interpretation' (1985) 4 *Law and Philosophy* 239–255, at 240–243.

[45] Readers unacquainted with these terms may want to know that 'MEA' stands for *multilateral environmental treaty*, that 'MIT' stands for multilateral investment treaty, and that 'LOAC' stands for *the law of armed conflict*.

of international law specialists. In all cases, they indicate the existence of a need of the international law specialists that use them. Whether we talk about lawyers specializing in the law of the sea, international criminal law or the law of international dispute settlement, specialists believe that by using terms such as 'the Irish formula', 'core crimes' or 'the optional clause system', they will be able to do what they do more easily. This is why they consider the use of these terms appropriate.

5.4 The Use of Distinct Methods

5.4.1 Compensation and the Ways of Calculating Interest

The question of compensation in international law can be used as a good example to showcase the use of distinct methods across various special regimes. As such, the principles relating to compensation in general international law are relatively straightforward. The secondary rules on reparation for internationally wrongful acts are well established in international law and codified in the ILC Articles on State Responsibility. Reparation in international law is governed by two fundamental principles, enunciated by the PCIJ in its decisions in the *Chorzów Factory* case.[46] The first principle is that 'the breach of an engagement involves an obligation to make reparation in an adequate form'.[47] The second principle is the principle of 'full reparation', which implies that reparation must be made so as to re-establish the situation as it was before the breach has since long been recognized in international law:

> The essential principle contained in the actual notion of an illegal act – a principle which seems to be established by international practice and in particular by the decisions of arbitral tribunals – is that reparation must, as far as possible, wipe out all the consequences of the illegal act and re-establish the situation which would, in all probability, have existed if that act had not been committed.[48]

These principles are reflected in Article 31 of the ILC Articles on State Responsibility, which state that 'the responsible State is under an obligation to make full reparation for the injury caused by the internationally wrongful act'. Such injury includes 'any damage, whether material or

[46] *Factory at Chorzów*, [1928] P.C.I.J. (ser. A) No. 9; *Factory at Chorzów*, [1928] P.C.I.J. (ser. A) No. 17.
[47] [1928] P.C.I.J. (ser. A) No. 17, 21.
[48] Ibid., at 47.

moral, caused by the internationally wrongful act of a State'.[49] The general principles in respect of reparation contained in the ILC Articles have been held to represent the customary law principles in relation to reparation.[50]

That a breach of an international obligations results in the obligation for the State to provide reparation for the damage caused by the breach is relatively unequivocal, as is the principle that reparation should re-establish the situation as it was before the breach. The question remains, however, which *form* of reparation is most adequate in case of breach of investment protection treaties and which method can be used to calculate or evaluate the compensation that has been awarded. In relation to the form of reparation, Article 34 of the ILC Articles provides that full reparation for the injury caused by an internationally wrongful act can take the form of 'restitution, compensation and satisfaction, either singly or in combination'. Compensation, very often termed 'damages' should cover 'any financially assessable damage including loss of profits insofar as it is established'.[51]

Let us look at compensation and the way in which interest is calculated in particular. There is first of all a different conception of the way in which compensation is dealt with by courts and tribunals. The generalist perspective can be shown through the case law of the ICJ. In the relatively recent case of *Certain Activities Carried Out by Nicaragua in the Border Area (Costa Rica v. Nicaragua)*, the Court had first established the responsibility of Nicaragua and determined that compensation was owed by it to Costa Rica. However, the Court had (as it frequently does) decided that the parties should first seek to settle the question of the compensation owed through negotiations for a period of twelve months.[52] Similar decisions were taken by arbitral tribunals in inter-state disputes, such as the decision of the Arbitral Tribunal in the *Enrica*

[49] Draft Articles on Responsibility of States for Internationally Wrongful Acts with Commentaries, Art. 31(2).

[50] See James Crawford, 'State Responsibility', in Rüdiger Wolfrüm (ed.), *Max Planck Encyclopedia of Public International Law* (Oxford: Oxford University Press, 2012), para. 31.

[51] Draft Articles on Responsibility of States for Internationally Wrongful Acts with Commentaries, Art. 36(2).

[52] See *Certain Activities Carried Out by Nicaragua in the Border Area (Costa Rica v. Nicaragua) and Construction of a Road in Costa Rica along the San Juan River (Nicaragua v. Costa Rica)*, [2015] I.C.J. Rep. 665, para. 229(5)(b).

Lexie case.[53] Other courts and tribunals will directly deal with the claim in compensation and leave little room for the parties to agree on the compensation to be awarded. This is notably the case in investor–state arbitration.[54]

Second, and more important for our purpose here, there is a significant difference in the methods used to calculate interests on the compensation awarded. Although, as explained, the main principles are well established, we see that certain special regimes have developed their own distinct method of calculating and awarding interests on the compensation awarded. Here too, the principle has been enshrined in the ILC Articles on States Responsibility, which provide in Article 38 the following:

1. Interest on any principal sum due under this chapter shall be payable when necessary in order to ensure full reparation. The interest rate and mode of calculation shall be set so as to achieve that result.
2. Interest runs from the date when the principal sum should have been paid until the date the obligation to pay is fulfilled.

The principle clearly leaves room for interpretation, as the award of interest is in principle accepted 'when necessary in order to ensure full reparation', and the rate and mode of calculation is left open. Among others, the question of whether interest should be awarded, and whether compound interest can or should be awarded shows different methods used in different regimes. On the question of compound interest, the Commentary to the ILC Articles explicitly mentions that

> the general view of courts and tribunals has been against the award of compound interest, and this is true even of those tribunals which hold claimants to be normally entitled to compensatory interest. [. . .] [G]iven the present state of international law, it cannot be said that an injured State has any entitlement to compound interest, in the absence of special circumstances which justify some element of compounding as an aspect of full reparation.[55]

[53] *The 'Enrica Lexie' Incident (Italy v. India),* PCA Case No. 2015-28, Award, 21 May 2020, para. 1089.

[54] See generally Christina Beharry (ed.), *Contemporary and Emerging Issues on the Law of Damages and Valuation in International Investment Arbitration* (Leiden: Brill Nijhoff, 2018).

[55] Draft Articles on Responsibility of States for Internationally Wrongful Acts with Commentaries, commentary to Art. 38, paras. 8–9.

A good starting point here also is the practice of the ICJ, which has largely followed the ILC Commentary. In its judgement on compensation in the recent case *Certain Activities Carried Out by Nicaragua in the Border Area (Costa Rica* v. *Nicaragua)*, the Court recalled that

> in the practice of international courts and tribunals, pre-judgement interest may be awarded if full reparation for injury caused by an internationally wrongful act so requires. Nevertheless, interest is not an autonomous form of reparation, nor is it a necessary part of compensation in every case.[56]

Based on this principle, and without much reasoning, the Court decided to award pre-judgement interest on the awarded compensation, at an annual interest rate fixed at 4 per cent.[57] In other cases, such as *Armed Activities on the Territory of the Congo (Democratic Republic of the Congo* v. *Uganda)*, the ICJ had not considered it necessary to award any pre-judgement interest as the Court noted that 'in determining the amount to be awarded for each head of damage, it has taken into account the passage of time'.[58] In *Ahmadou Sadio Diallo (Republic of Guinea v. Democratic Republic of the Congo)*, the Court similarly had refused to order any pre-judgement interest on the compensation awarded.[59]

Generally, the same core principles are adhered to in special regimes, that is the principle that pre-judgement interest may be awarded when necessary in order to ensure full reparation (in line with Article 38 ILC Articles). This is the case also in investor–state arbitration.[60] Investment treaty tribunals had initially followed the same route as the ICJ, which is to award compensation without detailed reasoning, nor explaining the specific method used to calculate the compensation and award interest.[61] This over time has developed substantially and it is safe to say that

[56] *Certain Activities Carried out by Nicaragua in the Border Area (Costa Rica v. Nicaragua)*, [2018] I.C.J. Rep. 15, para. 151.

[57] Ibid., at para. 153.

[58] *Armed Activities on the Territory of the Congo (Democratic Republic of the Congo* v. *Uganda)*, Reparations, [2022] I.C.J. Rep. 13, para. 401.

[59] *Ahmadou Sadio Diallo (Republic of Guinea v. Democratic Republic of the Congo)*, Compensation, [2012] I.C.J. Rep. 343, para. 56.

[60] See Mark Beeley, 'Approaches to the Award of Interest', in Christina Beharry, *Contemporary and Emerging Issues on the Law of Damages and Valuation in International Investment Arbitration* (Leiden: Brill Nijhoff, 2018), 377.

[61] See Irmgard Marboe, 'Reparation Cases: Applicable Principles in International Investment Arbitration', in Hélène Fabri and Edoardo Stoppioni (eds.), *International Investment Law: An Analysis of the Major Decisions* (Oxford: Hart Publishing, 2022), 443.

investment treaty tribunals have developed a regime-specific method of awarding and calculating interest on the awarded compensation. Aside from adhering to the principle and the fact there is generally speaking more reasoning on the quantification of the compensation and interest, the practice of arbitral tribunals in investor–state arbitration does show that they have used a distinct method of appreciation of the damage caused to the investor, and hence the compensation to be awarded. In doing so, they have taken a completely different approach to the question of the method used to calculate interest as part of the compensation.

Not only is there a clear favourable attitude towards the automatic award of pre-judgement interest, but the method of calculating the interest also differs from the practice and method used by the ICJ as discussed above. As one author has put it: 'the true battleground has shifted from the question of whether interest should be awarded at all to one of how much interest should be awarded, and on what basis'.[62]

The habitual practice in international law, as showcased by the several decisions of the ICJ discussed above, is to award simple interest, which is reflected also in the commentary to the ILC Articles.[63] Arbitral tribunals in investor–state arbitration, however, overwhelmingly award compound interest. A recent survey shows that this is the case in around 89 per cent of the decisions.[64] The reason behind the award of compound interest is the belief that this method of calculating interest is the only way to achieve full reparation (*restitutio in integrum*) for an aggrieved party. It is based on a pure economic approach to the questions of damage and compensation, which some have argued is 'necessary to make interest truly compensatory'.[65] Awarding simple interest, then, is considered to be a 'source of misgivings by many lawyers and thus by many tribunals'.[66] Importantly, the shift to awarding compound interest is a clear evidence of a regime-specific method of calculating the appropriate compensation to achieve full reparation. The practice, it has been noted, has been 'internalized by tribunals' and the counsel appearing before

[62] Beeley, 'Approaches to the Award of Interest', 377.

[63] Draft Articles on Responsibility of States for Internationally Wrongful Acts with Commentaries, commentary to Art. 38, para. 8. See also *Anaconda-Iran, Inc. v. Iran*, [1986] 13 Iran-U.S. Cl. Trib. Rep. 199, 235.

[64] Beeley, 'Approaches to the Award of Interest', 378.

[65] Ibid., at 389.

[66] Ibid., at 389.

them who are increasingly considered to be willing to 'engage with financial concepts underpinning the award of interests'.[67]

5.5 The Use of Distinct Forms of Argument

5.5.1 Arguments of 'Soft Law' in Legal Reasoning

The use of 'soft-law' in legal reasoning can be seen, perhaps, as something that would transpire throughout all legal regimes in a relatively similar manner. For one, the distinction between what is law and what is not should be relatively clear and unfirm in the minds of lawyers and hence in their legal reasoning. At least, such would be the view of positivists who consider soft law to be a misnomer as 'law is either hard or not law at all'.[68] Soft law, as a consequence, is or should be largely irrelevant in legal reasoning as it merely encapsulates suggested courses of action or behaviour falling short of any normative rule of law. The positivist view is well represented in the practice of courts and tribunals which typically only render a decision based on an established source of law in the positivist sense. The arbitral tribunal in the *OSPAR Arbitration* thus refused to apply 'soft law', safe for interpretation purposes, as Ireland had asked the tribunal to do:

> the Tribunal agrees with Ireland's proposal to 'draw on current international law and practice' [. . .], but only insofar as such law and practice are relevant and hence admissible under Article 31(3)(c) and (d) of the Vienna Convention. However, the Tribunal has not been authorized to apply 'evolving international law and practice' and cannot do so.[69]

Yet other perspectives have precisely criticized this binary approach to law, especially when used in legal argumentation. Both hard and soft norms, or hard and soft arguments would not be a proper categorization of the sources of law. The boundaries that have been set to delimit the sources of law from those that are not, nor hard law from soft law, would not take into account 'the particular content of the norms whose source is being considered'.[70] As David Kennedy further explains, the question

[67] Ibid., at 391.

[68] Jean d'Aspremont, 'Softness in International Law: A Self-Serving Quest for New Legal Materials' (2008) 19 *European Journal of International Law* 1075–1093, 1076.

[69] *Dispute Concerning Access to Information Under Article 9 of the OSPAR Convention, Ireland v. United Kingdom*, PCA Case No. 2001-03, Final Award, 2 July 2003, para. 101.

[70] David Kennedy, 'The Sources of International Law' (1987) 2 *American University International Law Review* 1–97, 11.

is not necessarily which norms are considered to be hard law or soft law, as they result in endless arguments about the authority of international law, which in essence is thus an argumentative tool. He explains in relation to the distinction between hard and soft law:

> In sources argument, one characteristically seeks to convince someone that a state which does not currently believe it to be in its interests to follow a given norm should do so anyway. In sources argument, one characteristically seeks to convince someone that a state which does not currently believe it to be in its interests to follow a given norm should do so anyway. Sources rhetoric provides two rhetorical or persuasive styles which we might call 'hard' and 'soft'. A 'hard' argument will seek to ground compliance in the 'consent' of the state to be bound. A 'soft' argument relies upon some extraconsensual notion of the good or the just. Of course there is no a priori reason to divide the 'sources' of law, or the persuasive reasons for compliance into these two categories. Indeed, it is difficult to classify the various classic sources as either 'hard' or 'soft', and it seems intuitively obvious that fulfilling promises is an important dimension of justice and vice versa.[71]

In the field of human rights, and in particular the human rights responsibility of corporations, the reference to and use of soft norms has, however, taken a central role, reflecting an idealist stance on the question which contrasts mostly with the positivist perspective on the authority of soft law. For example, legal instruments adopted so far in the regulation of corporate activity do not impose direct obligations on corporations,[72] but rather have focused on 'soft' obligations, conceivably as a consequence of the absence of corporations' international legal personality and therefore the inadequacy of traditional legal instruments to regulate such activity. There are a large number of non-binding instruments, such as the Global Compact, the ILO Tripartite Declaration of Principles concerning Multinational Enterprises and Social Policy and the OECD Guidelines for Multinational Enterprises. This, however, has not hindered certain authors from precisely relying on those soft norms in arguing that these do carry 'legal authority'. In relation to 'Norms on the Responsibilities of Transnational Corporations and Other Business Enterprises with Regard to Human Rights', adopted by the Human Rights Commission's Sub-Commission on the Promotion and

[71] Ibid., at 20.

[72] See also Sarah Joseph, 'Pharmaceutical Corporations and Access to Drugs: The "Fourth Wave" of Corporate Human Rights Scrutiny' (2003) 25 *Human Rights Quarterly* 425–452, 438.

Protection of Human Rights in 2003,[73] some authors have argued that despite their voluntary nature:

> The legal authority of the Norms derives principally from their sources in treaties and customary international law, as a restatement of international legal principles applicable to companies.[74]

The ideal to be achieved by the adoption of such norms is that the power of business enterprises in the world 'must be confronted, and that the human rights obligations of business enterprises, in particular, must be addressed'.[75] The need, then, for a 'regulation' is justified by the 'abundant reasons why the legal regulation of TNC's activities at all levels of impact is sought, ought to be sought, and is sometimes achieved'.[76] Of course, it is precisely because of the absence of any 'hard' law on the human rights responsibility of corporations that soft law arguments are abundantly present in international legal discourse. Yet, the specific argumentative practices in this specific field are quite contrasting to other fields where the very notion of soft law plays a rather marginal role, safe for arguments that in actual fact relate to the same soft law norms in the context of corporate social responsibility.[77]

5.5.2 *Arguments of Justice*

Arguments of justice abound in legal argumentations, notably in the context of international courts and tribunals – the very notion of justice indeed is to a large extent inherent in the set-up of courts and tribunals. Arguments of 'justice' therefore also infuse legal argumentation in relation to other courts and tribunals. It is most of all notable that the ICJ carries in its name the idea that 'justice' is the core *rationale* of the

[73] Draft Norms on the Responsibilities of Transnational Corporations and Other Business Enterprises with Regard to Human Rights, 30 May 2003, U.N. Doc. E/CN.4/Sub.2/2003/12.

[74] David Weissbrodt and Muria Kruger, 'Norms on the Responsibilities of Transnational Corporations and Other Business Corporations and Other Business Enterprises with Regard to Human Rights' (2003) 97 *The American Journal of International Law* 901–922, 913.

[75] Ibid., at 921.

[76] David Kinley and Junko Tadaki, 'From Talk to Walk: The Emergence of Human Rights Responsibilities for Corporations at International Law' (2004) 44 *Virginia Journal of International Law* 931–1023, 933.

[77] See generally Giovana Adinolfi, 'Soft Law in International Investment Law and Arbitration' (2021) 1 *The Italian Review of International and Comparative Law* 86–112.

Court's work. The ICJ's predecessor, the PCIJ perhaps even more so had the notion of 'international justice' reflected in its name. To that extent, it is beyond doubt that even beyond special regimes such as international criminal law as we will discuss later, the idea of 'justice' is present in legal argumentation. That notion of 'justice', however, was not necessarily very present in the debates surrounding the creation of the PCIJ or the ICJ. The attention at that time was more focused on 'war prevention'[78] than 'justice'. The ICJ too was considered important to provide a system of enforcement against those states who would breach the law and avoid recourse to force.

Certain regimes, however, are more prone to such arguments than others and certain communities also tend to rely more on arguments of justice than others.

A positivist perspective would emphasize the benefit of courts and tribunals to the overall enforcement of international law as a legal system. Positivists tend to focus on the 'need' for courts and tribunals as a method of enforcement of (international) law and hence as a demonstration of the legal validity of the norms in question and the existence of law as law. Kelsen, among others, considered that the availability and acceptance of other methods of enforcement in international law was sufficient for the recognition of international law as a legal system. Kelsen did not consider that international law was not law because of the absence of a compulsory method of settlement since there were modes of enforcement, such as reprisals and self-help.[79] However, he too advocated for the concentration of efforts 'to bring about an international treaty concluded by as many States as possible [. . .] establishing an international court endowed with compulsory jurisdiction'.[80] Justice then is equated to the enforcement of legal obligations.

The distinction between positivists and idealists, however, is clear when looking at the arguments behind the 'need' or 'necessity' of international courts and tribunals. International courts and tribunals offer effective legal remedies for breaches of international law, thereby not

[78] Wilhelm G. Grewe, *The Epochs of International Law* (Berlin: De Gruyter, 2000), 616.

[79] See, for example, Hans Kelsen, *Pure Theory of Law*, Max Knight (translator), 2nd edition (Berkeley: University of California Press, 1967). For a discussion, see Alexander Somek, 'Kelsen Lives' (2007) 18 *European Journal of International Law* 409–451. For a recent account of positivism and its nuances, see Jörg Kammerhofer, 'International Legal Positivism', in Florian Hoffman and Anne Orford (eds.), *The Oxford Handbook of the Theory of International Law* (Oxford: Oxford University Press, 2016), 407–426.

[80] Kelsen, *Pure Theory of Law*, 397.

only complementing the positivist notion of a legal system, but in the idealist's view contributing to international law's function in furthering the ideal or value of peace.[81] Idealist perspectives most often emphasize the overall benefit of the increased access to justice, and the idealist claim then becomes inextricably linked to the ideal of 'justice at the international level':

> The gradual realization – that we witness, and have the privilege to contribute to, nowadays – of the old ideal of justice at international level has been revitalizing itself, in recent years, with the reassuring creation and operation of the multiple contemporary international tribunals. [. . .] Nowadays, the international community fortunately counts on a wide range of international tribunals, adjudicating cases that take place not only at the *inter-State* level, but also at the *intra-State* level. This invites us to approach their work from the correct perspective of the *justiciable* themselves, and brings us close to their common mission of securing the realization of international justice, either at the *inter-State* or at the *intra-State* level. [. . .] Each international tribunal operates in the ambit of its own jurisdiction, but all undertake in harmony their common mission of imparting justice.[82]

If we look at the special regimes themselves, we also see abounding arguments of justice. Certain regimes, however, are more than others permeated by such arguments. In regimes such as the WTO, the acceptance of submitting disputes to the jurisdiction of courts and (arbitral) tribunals does not often coincide with arguments of justice. Rather, states accepting the competence of a court or tribunal often is done to receive the specific benefits that such acceptance entails through a cost–benefit analysis. In the specific context of dispute settlement under the WTO, not settling disputes would impact the free flow of goods – such as the drop in import and export or economic countermeasures. This, in turn, has prompted states to accept a compulsory method of settling disputes. Arguments of justice in this context seem less relevant, if not entirely irrelevant. It has, for example, often been explained that the reason behind the adoption of the WTO Dispute Settlement Understanding

[81] See, for example, Gentian Zyberi, 'The Interpretation and Development of International Human Rights Law by the International Court of Justice', in Martin Scheinin (ed.), *Human Rights in 'Other' International Courts* (Cambridge: Cambridge University Press, 2019), 28–61.

[82] Antônio Augusto Cançado Trindade, 'Prologue: An Overview of the Contribution of International Tribunals to the Rule of Law', in Geert De Baere and Jan Wouters (eds.), *The Contribution of International and Supranational Courts to the Rule of Law* (Cheltenham: Edward Elgar Publishing Limited, 2014), 3–5.

resided in the clear legal framework for the conduct of international trade including a functioning and efficient dispute settlement system.[83] Others have explained that dispute settlement is 'essential for the effective functioning of the WTO and for maintaining a proper balance between the rights and obligations of its members'.[84] The same holds true in respect of investor–state arbitration. The main reason underlying the signature of an investment treaty with an arbitration clause giving foreign investors direct access to arbitration still is that such a treaty stimulates foreign investment and capital flows between the signatory states. There is little reference to the need to achieve 'justice', although as said at the very start of the section, ideas of justice in the sense of upholding the rule of law or providing enforcement mechanisms for international legal obligations to a certain extent are inherent in all judicial or arbitral processes.

Conversely, arguments of justice are abundant in legal argumentation in the field of international criminal law. International criminal courts and tribunals, such as the International Criminal Court (ICC), are tasked with establishing the international criminal responsibility of individuals and hence their decisions cannot as such be seen as settling international disputes as is the case of other courts and tribunals such as the WTO regime mentioned above. This is perhaps why in this specific regime the establishment of a court or tribunal is more often justified by arguments of justice. Bill Schabas has notably explained that the move to the creation of international courts and tribunals lies in the 'increasing focus on promoting accountability and challenging impunity'.[85] Fatou Bensouda also argued in 2008, when she was Deputy Prosecutor of the ICC, that the Rome Statute establishing the ICC not only was an effort to 'address impunity at the international level' but also that both the ICC and the various ad hoc and special criminal courts and tribunals 'signalled the conviction of the international community that justice is an intrinsic component of durable peace'.[86]

[83] Valerie Hughes, 'The Institutional Dimension', in Daniel Bethlehem, Isabelle Van Damme, Donald McRae and Rodney Neufeld, *The Oxford Handbook of International Trade Law* (Oxford: Oxford University Press, 2009), 271.

[84] Peter van den Bossche and Werner Zdouc, *The Law and Policy of the World Trade Organization*, 4th edition (Cambridge: Cambridge University Press, 2019), 102.

[85] William Schabas, 'International Criminal Courts', in Cesare Romano, Karen Alter and Yuval Shany, *The Oxford Handbook of International Adjudication* (Oxford: Oxford University Press, 2014), 211.

[86] Fatou Bensouda, 'Justice, Reconciliation and the Role of the ICC', 6 February 2008, www.idea.int/sites/default/files/speeches/Justice-Reconciliation-and-the-Role-of-the-International-Criminal-Court-ICC-PDF.pdf.

5.6 The Use of Distinct Theories, Principles and Doctrines

5.6.1 The Clean Slate Principle

The clean slate principle pertains to an issue referred to by the ILC as 'the succession of states in respect of treaties'.[87] Succession, in this context, means 'the replacement of one State by another in the responsibility for the international relations of territory'.[88] It occurs in different situations: when a territory that was earlier dependent on a state for its international relations obtains independence; when two or more states merge so as to form a new state; when the territory of one state is incorporated in that of another; or when parts of the territory of a state separate to form one or more new states. In all of these situations, the question arises whether and to what extent the treaties that were applicable to the predecessor(s) shall be applicable to the successor(s). According to the clean slate principle, a new state should be free to decide itself by which treaties it shall be bound. Stated the other way around, a new state should not be bound by a treaty if it has not specifically agreed to apply it.[89] Commentators invoke two separate reasons to explain this proposition:

- *The sovereign freedom of states.* A new state should have as much of a right to determine its contractual obligations as its predecessor(s).[90]
- *The idea of treaty relations as personal.* When a state expresses its consent to be bound by a treaty, it does this relative to the other parties, but not to any third state.[91] To a new state, thus, the treaties concluded by the predecessor(s) are *res inter alios acta.*

For the determination of whether a successor state shall be bound by a treaty entered into by a predecessor state, the clean slate principle may be important, but it is certainly not absolute. International law recognizes the need to depart from the principle depending on such things as the way in which the successor state was created and the topic of a treaty.

87 See Vienna Convention on Succession of States in Respect of Treaties, Vienna, 23 August 1978, in force 6 November 1996, 1946 U.N.T.S., 3.

88 Ibid., at Art. 2(1)(b).

89 Malcolm Shaw, *International Law*, 7th edition (Cambridge: Cambridge University Press, 2014), 708; Antônio Augusto Cançado Trindade, *International Law for Humankind. Towards a New Jus Gentium* (Leiden: Martinus Nijhoff Publishers, 2010), 469.

90 Akbar Rasulov, 'Revisiting State Succession to Humanitarian Treaties: Is There a Case for Automaticity?' (2003) 14 *European Journal of International Law* 141–170, 148.

91 See *Eritrea/Yemen – Sovereignty and Maritime Delimitation in the Red Sea*, [1998] 114 I.L.R. 1, 48.

A well-known example are agreements, which establish either a boundary or a line delimiting the maritime zones of two or more states. According to customary international law, such treaties are subject to automatic succession – they are as much applicable to the successor state as they were applicable to the predecessor.[92] As the ICJ confirmed in *Gabčíkovo-Nagymaros Project*, customary international law makes a similar exception for 'other territorial regimes' – agreements that establish rights and obligations relating to the use of a territory.[93] Commentators typically justify these two exceptions by reference to two considerations, one of which is political and the other structural:

- *The need to maintain territorial stability.*[94] If the replacement of one state by another would cause these treaties to lapse, the law of state succession would not be an instrument of peaceful change but a source of dangerous friction.[95]
- *The special character of boundary/delimitation agreements and territorial regimes.* These are treaties, which typically create objective regimes; thus, they have an effect *erga omnes.*[96] Hence, if succession occurs in respect of a territory affected by such a treaty, the successor is not properly speaking a 'third state'.[97]

Strong voices have argued for a departure from the clean slate principle also in the case of so-called humanitarian treaties.[98] Humanitarian treaties, in the sense of this suggestion, are not only those that provide for the protection of civilians and other persons *hors de combat* in armed

[92] See Art. 11 of the Vienna Convention on Succession of States in Respect of Treaties.

[93] *Gabčíkovo-Nagymaros Project*, [1977] I.C.J. Rep. 7, para. 123. Compare Art. 12 of the Vienna Convention on Succession of States in Respect of Treaties. This specific case concerned the succession of Slovakia to the Agreement between Czechoslovakia and Hungary on the Construction of the Gabčikovo Nagymaros Project.

[94] Shaw, *International Law*, 701.

[95] See Draft Articles on Succession of States with Commentaries, (1974) II-1 *Yearbook of the International Law Commission* 174, 199.

[96] See *Eritrea/Yemen – Sovereignty and Maritime Delimitation in the Red Sea*, 48.

[97] Draft Articles on Succession of States with Commentaries, 204.

[98] See *Application of the Convention on the Prevention and Punishment of the Crime of Genocide (Bosnia and Herzegovina v. Yugoslavia)*, Preliminary Objections, Separate Opinion of Judge Weeramantry, [1996] I.C.J. Rep. 640, 642. See also Rasulov, 'Revisiting State Succession to Humanitarian Treaties', 143–144; Matthew Craven, 'The *Genocide* Case, the Law of Treaties and State Succession' (1997) 68 *British Yearbook of International Law* 127–163, 155.

conflict, but also those that provide for the protection of human rights.[99] Hence, at a meeting of chairpersons of the different UN human rights treaty bodies, held between 19 and 24 September 1994, attendants emphasized:

> they were of the view that successor States were automatically bound by obligations under international human rights instruments from the respective date of independence and that observance of the obligations should not depend on a declaration of confirmation made by the Government of the successor State.[100]

In his Separate Opinion appended to the 1996 Judgement of the ICJ in the *Bosnia Genocide Case*, Judge Weeramantry forcefully argued that the 'principle of automatic succession' that applied to 'a large range' of humanitarian treaties, should apply a fortiori to the Genocide Convention.[101] In 1997, subsequent to the dissolution of both the Federal Republic of Yugoslavia and the Soviet Union, the Human Rights Committee commented with respect to the continuity of rights enshrined in the International Covenant on Civil and Political Rights:

> The rights enshrined in the Covenant belong to the people living in the territory of the State party. The Human Rights Committee has consistently taken the view, as evidenced by its long-standing practice, that once the people are accorded the protection of the rights under the Covenant, such protection devolves with territory and continues to belong to them, notwithstanding change in government of the State party, including dismemberment in more than one State or State succession or any subsequent action of the State party designed to divest them of the rights guaranteed by the Covenant.[102]

In its judgement of 20 February 2001 in the *Čelebići Case*, the International Tribunal for the Former Yugoslavia (Appeals Chamber) considered the succession of Bosnia-Herzegovina to the 1949 Geneva Conventions. It noted the declaration of succession deposited by the

[99] See, for example, *Application of the Convention on the Prevention and Punishment of the Crime of Genocide*, Separate Opinion of Judge Weeramantry, 651.

[100] Status of the International Covenants on Human Rights, Succession of States in Respect of Treaties, Report of the Secretary General, 28 November 1994, U.N. Doc. E/CN.4/1995/80, 4.

[101] *Application of the Convention on the Prevention and Punishment of the Crime of Genocide*, Separate Opinion of Judge Weeramantry, 642.

[102] Human Rights Council, CCPR General Comment No. 26: Continuity of Obligations, U.N. Doc. CCPR/C/21/Rev.1/Add.8/Rev.1, para. 4.

Government of Bosnia and Herzegovina on 31 December 1992.[103] It quoted Article 23, paragraph 1 of the 1978 Vienna Convention on the Succession of States with Respect to Treaties. According to this provision, 'a newly independent State which makes a notification of succession . . . shall be considered a party to the treaty from the date of the succession of States or from the date of entry into force of the treaty, whichever is the later date'.[104] Importantly, the Chamber then quickly added:

> The Appeals Chamber is of the view that irrespective of any findings as to formal succession, Bosnia and Herzegovina would in any event have succeeded to the Geneva Conventions under customary law, as this type of convention entails automatic succession, i.e., without the need for any formal confirmation of adherence by the successor State. It may be now considered in international law that there is automatic State succession to multilateral humanitarian treaties in the broad sense, i.e., treaties of universal character which express fundamental human rights.[105]

Commentators often explain this departure from the clean slate principle in terms reminiscent of the reasons invoked in favour of the automatic succession of boundary/delimitation agreements and territorial regimes. As insisted by Judge Weeramantry, automatic succession contributes to 'global stability'.[106] It is particularly important during periods of transition, he says:

> [T]he break-up of states has often been accompanied by atrocities of the most brutal and inhuman kind, practised on a scale that defies quantification. To leave a lacuna in the continuity of the law or any vagueness in the perception of that continuity would be fraught with danger to the most cherished values of civilization.[107]

Apart from the concern for global stability, commentators invoke 'the special character' of humanitarian treaties,[108] which, as they emphasize, do not confer rights on any states but on individuals. Thus, the

[103] *Prosecutor v. Mucič et al.*, Judgment, Case No. IT-96-21-A, 20 February 2001, para. 109.
[104] Ibid., at para. 110.
[105] Ibid., at para. 111.
[106] *Application of the Convention on the Prevention and Punishment of the Crime of Genocide*, Separate Opinion of Judge Weeramantry, 648.
[107] Ibid., at 650–651. See, similarly, Menno Kamminga, 'State Succession in Respect of Human Rights Treaties' (1996) 7 *European Journal of International Law* 469–484, 470.
[108] Ibid., at 484; Cançado Trindade, *International Law for Humankind*, 471–472. This proposition is acknowledged and commented upon by: Akbar Rasulov, 'Revisiting State Succession to Humanitarian Treaties: Is There a Case for Automaticity?' (2003)

replacement of one state by another in a treaty relationship does not imply any vesting of rights in extraneous third parties. As Judge Weeramantry infers, '[t]he principle that *res inter alios acta* are not binding . . . does not therefore apply to such conventions'.[109]

In the context of this book, we would like to highlight yet another explanation offered by proponents of the automatic succession of humanitarian treaties. This explanation does not compare with any of those offered in favour of the automatic succession of boundary/delimitation agreements and territorial regimes, which is why it attracts our attention. As proponents suggest, the object of humanitarian treaties requires automatic succession. The Separate Opinion of Judge Shahabuddeen to the ICJ judgement in the *Bosnia Genocide Case* articulates this idea very neatly, although, for obvious reasons, this Opinion is confined to the Genocide Convention specifically. The eminent Judge quotes the Advisory Opinion of the International Court in *Reservations to the Convention on Genocide*:

> The Convention was manifestly adopted for a purely humanitarian and civilizing purpose. It is indeed difficult to imagine a convention that might have this dual character to a greater degree, since its object on the one hand is to safeguard the very existence of certain human groups and on the other to confirm and endorse the most elementary principles of morality. In such a convention the contracting States do not have any interests of their own; they merely have, one and all, a common interest, namely, the accomplishment of those high purposes which are the raison d'être of the convention. Consequently, in a convention of this type one cannot speak of individual advantages or disadvantages to States, or of the maintenance of a perfect contractual balance between rights and duties. The high ideals which inspired the Convention provide, by virtue of the common will of the parties, the foundation and measure of all its provisions.[110]

14 *European Journal of International Law* 141–170, at 151–152; Craven, 'The *Genocide* Case', at 155.

[109] *Application of the Convention on the Prevention and Punishment of the Crime of Genocide*, Separate Opinion of Judge Weeramantry, 651. See similarly, Kamminga, 'State Succession in Respect of Human Rights Treaties', 472–473; Shaw, *International Law*, 711.

[110] *Advisory Opinion on Reservations to the Convention on Genocide*, [1951] I.C.J. Rep. 15, 23; *Application of the Convention on the Prevention and Punishment of the Crime of Genocide (Bosnia and Herzegovina v. Yugoslavia)*, Preliminary Objections, Separate Opinion of Judge Shahabuddeen, [1996] I.C.J. Rep. 634, 635.

He continues:

> I think that the object and purpose of the Genocide Convention required parties to observe it in such a way as to avoid the creation of such a break in the protection which it afforded. The Convention could not be read as meaning that a Party, which was bound under the Convention to apply its jurisdictional provisions for the protection of the 'human groups' inhabiting a given area, was allowed to regard itself as liberated from those provisions in relation to a successor State by reason of the fact that that particular area was now comprised within the territory of the successor State ... To effectuate its object and purpose, the Convention would fall to be construed as implying the expression of a unilateral undertaking by each party to the Convention to treat successor States as continuing as from independence any status which the predecessor State had as a party to the Convention.[111]

As we believe, this reasoning is reflective of the idea of IHL and international human rights law as special regimes. To the extent of humanitarian treaties, IHL and international human rights specialists find the clean slate principle inappropriate. They do this for several reasons. One of them is the object and purpose of humanitarian treaties. The clean slate principle does not cohere with the state of affairs that IHL and international human rights specialists are pursuing: the universal application of the standards that humanitarian treaties embody.

5.6.2 *The Theory of Autonomous Concepts*

The language of the European Convention on Human Rights is imbued with terms that would seem to refer to concepts of domestic law. Prominent examples include 'normal civic obligations',[112] 'the lawful arrest or detention of a person',[113] 'alcoholics',[114] 'criminal offence',[115]

[111] Ibid., at 635–636.

[112] Convention on the Prevention and Punishment of the Crime of Genocide, Paris, 9 December 1948, in force 12 January 1951, 78 U.N.T.S. 277, Art. 4, para. 3(d). For further consideration of this concept, see, for example, Case No. 13580/88, *Schmidt v. Germany*, [1994] ECHR 18, para. 23.

[113] Art. 5, para. 1(f) of the Genocide Convention. For further consideration of this concept, see, for example, Case No. 62892/12, *Karimov v. Russia*, First Section, Judgment of 28 May 2014, para. 177.

[114] Art. 5, para. 1(e) of the Genocide Convention. For further consideration of this concept, see, for example, Case No. 26629/95, *Litwa v. Poland*, [2000] ECHR 141, paras. 60–61.

[115] Art. 6(2) of the Genocide Convention. For further consideration of this concept, see, for example, Case No. 5100/71, *Engel v. The Netherlands*, [1976] ECHR 3, para. 81.

'penalty',[116] 'association',[117] 'expulsion',[118] 'responsibilities of a private law character',[119] and 'marriage'.[120] The European Court of Human Rights has established a very particular approach to the interpretation of these terms. Scholars refer to it as 'the theory of autonomous concepts'.[121] According to this theory, terms such as any of those in the list of examples enjoy a status of semantic independence.[122] The meaning that domestic law and legal practice ascribe to them is certainly not irrelevant for the way in which they should be understood in the context of the European Convention.[123] It cannot be, since, typically, this is their ordinary meaning and thus a frame of reference throughout the entire process of interpretation of these instruments.[124] In effect, what the theory of autonomous concepts does is to confirm the importance of other means of interpretation. Even though it is indeed very difficult to think of a *criminal offence* or a *penalty* without regard to domestic law and legal practice, the domestic legal meaning of a term is never itself decisive if, for example, the context or the object and purpose of the European Convention suggest that it be understood differently.

[116] Art. 7 of the Genocide Convention. For further consideration of this concept, see, for example, Case No. 19359/04, *M v. Germany*, IHRL 3709 (ECHR 2009), para. 120.

[117] Art. 11 of the Genocide Convention. For further consideration of this concept, see, for example, Case No. 25088/94, *Chassagnou v. France*, [2000] 29 EHRR 615, para. 100.

[118] Art. 4 of Protocol 4 of the Genocide Convention. For further consideration of this concept, see, for example, Case Nos. 8675/15, 8697/15, *N.D. and N.T. v. Spain*, [2020] ECHR 142, para. 185.

[119] Protocol 7 to the European Convention for the Protection of Human Rights and Fundamental Freedoms, Strasbourg, 22 November 1984, in force 1 November 1988, European Treaty Series No. 117, Art. 5.

[120] Ibid.

[121] See, for example, George Letsas, 'The Truth in Autonomous Concepts: How to Interpret the ECHR' (2004) 15 *European Journal of International Law* 279–305, 282; Andrew Legg, *The Margin of Appreciation in International Human Rights Law: Deference and Proportionality* (Oxford: Oxford University Press, 2012), 111. The approach is sometimes also referred to as 'autonomous interpretation'. See, for example, Franz Matscher, 'Methods of Interpretation of the Convention', in Ronald St. J. Macdonald, Franz Matscher and Herbert Petzold (eds.), *The European System for the Protection of Human Rights* (Dordrecht: Martinus Nijhoff, 1993), 70–73.

[122] Letsas, 'The Truth in Autonomous Concepts', 282; Clare Ovey and Robin White, *Jacobs & White, European Convention on Human Rights*, 3rd edition (Oxford: Oxford University Press, 2002), 31.

[123] See, emphatically, Rudolf Bernhardt, 'Thoughts on the Interpretation of Human Rights Treaties', in Franz Matscher and Herbert Petzold (eds.), *Protecting Human Rights: The European Dimension: Studies in Honour of Gérard J Wiarda* (Köln: Heymanns, 1988), 67.

[124] See Arts. 31–32 of the 1969 Vienna Convention on the Law of Treaties.

Now, references to domestic legal concepts is nothing unique for the European Convention. It can be found in many international treaties. Consider, for example, the UN Convention on Jurisdictional Immunities of States and Their Property, which uses terms such as 'witness',[125] 'contract of employment',[126] 'immovable property',[127] 'intellectual property',[128] 'attachment or arrest',[129] and 'the central bank'.[130] This Convention allows for some interesting comparisons, since in the interpretation of terms such as these, lawyers tend to defer largely to their meaning in domestic law and legal practice.[131] It is evident that in the interpretation of the UN Convention on Jurisdictional Immunities of States and Their Property, little place is reserved for something like a theory of autonomous concepts. This observation raises a crucial question. Why do judges of the European Court of Human Rights think of the theory of autonomous concept as appropriate for the understanding of the European Convention, when obviously international lawyers do not think it of it as appropriate in other legal contexts? The answer would seem to reside in the characterization of European human rights law as a special regime. Judges of the European Court believe that the theory of autonomous concept helps them to realize some certain desirable state of affairs. To illustrate this proposition, consider the two judgements of the European Court in *Engel v. The Netherlands* and *Chassagnou v. France*.

In *Engel and Others v. The Netherlands*,[132] four conscripted soldiers complained over the penalties for offences against military discipline that had been passed on them by their respective commanding officers. The applicants argued that the proceedings before the military authorities

125 Ibid., at Art. 8.
126 Ibid., at Art. 11.
127 Ibid., at Art. 13.
128 Ibid., at Art. 14.
129 Ibid., at Art. 18.
130 Ibid., at Art. 21.
131 See, for example, Hazel Fox, *The Law of State Immunity*, 3rd edition (Oxford: Oxford University Press, 2015); Roger O'Keefe and Christian Tams (eds.), *The United Nations Convention on Jurisdictional Immunities of States and Their Property: A Commentary* (Oxford: Oxford University Press, 2013). See also Draft Articles on Jurisdictional Immunities of States and Their Property, with Commentaries, (1991) II-2 *Yearbook of the International Law Commission* 13.
132 *Engel v. The Netherlands*.

were not in conformity with the requirements of Article 6 of the European Convention. The Government, for its part, claimed that disciplinary measures did not come within the extension of a 'criminal charge' in the sense of Article 6. This gave the Court reason to clarify the importance of the distinction made in all contracting states between disciplinary and criminal proceedings:

> It must thus be asked whether or not the solution adopted in this connection at the national level is decisive from the standpoint of the Convention. Does Article 6 (art. 6) cease to be applicable just because the competent organs of a Contracting State classify as disciplinary an act or omission and the proceedings it takes against the author, or does it, on the contrary, apply in certain cases notwithstanding this classification?[133]

To answer this question, the Court introduced the idea that criminal charge was an autonomous concept. A sovereign state is free, it said, to maintain or establish a distinction between criminal law and disciplinary law, and to draw the dividing line as it sees fit. For purposes of the application of the European Convention, however, this freedom is exercised subject to certain conditions:

> If the Contracting States were able at their discretion to classify an offence as disciplinary instead of criminal, or to prosecute the author of a 'mixed' offence on the disciplinary rather than on the criminal plane, the operation of ... [Article 6] would be subordinated to their sovereign will. A latitude extending thus far might lead to results incompatible with *the purpose and object of the Convention.*[134]

In *Chassagnou and Others v. France,*[135] the applicants were owners of landholdings in Western France. They complained over the compulsory inclusion of their land in the hunting grounds of a local hunting association – an *Associations communales de chasse agréées* ('ACCA'). Similarly, they complained over the obligation to join this association, although, as members of the anti-hunting movement, they strongly disapproved of its objectives. They submitted that they had suffered an infringement of their right to freedom of association, in the sense of Article 11 of the European Convention. The Government maintained that the hunting organization in the case was in fact not an association

[133] Ibid., at para. 80.
[134] Ibid., at para. 81. Italics are added.
[135] *Chassagnou v. France.*

but 'public-law para-administrative institution', as it called itself.[136] The Court noted that, in French law, the question whether ACCAs are governed by private or public law had not yet been settled. It continued in terms similar to its findings in *Engel and Others v. The Netherlands*:

> the question is not so much whether in French law ACCAs are private associations, public or para-public associations, or mixed associations, but whether they are associations for the purposes of Article 11 of the Convention.
>
> If Contracting States were able, at their discretion, by classifying an association as 'public' or 'para-administrative', to remove it from the scope of Article 11, that would give them such latitude that it might lead to results incompatible with the object and purpose of the Convention, which is to protect rights that are not theoretical or illusory but practical and effective [. . .].[137]

As it concluded:

> The term 'association' therefore possesses an autonomous meaning; the classification in national law has only relative value and constitutes no more than a starting point.[138]

[136] Ibid., at para. 98.
[137] Ibid., at para. 100.
[138] Ibid.

6

Special Regimes and the Fragmentation of International Law

6.1 Summary of All Findings

This book is essentially an inquiry into the concept of a special regime. In Chapter 1, we started this inquiry by asking two questions:

Question (1): What are the defining features that allow international lawyers to think about a segment of the international legal system as a special regime separate from other special regimes and from general international law?
Question (2): What is the significance of having identified a segment of the international legal system as a special regime?

As we argued in Sections 1.2 and 1.3 of that same chapter, neither of these questions can be answered categorically. For the same reasons as lawyers disagree about the proper definition of the concept of international law, not only do they assume different definitions of the concept of a special regime, but they also ascribe a different significance to having identified an entity as one that belongs to the extension of this concept. Thus, depending on the theory of law that a lawyer endorses, he or she may conceive of the concept of a special regime in either of the below three ways:

1. A *special regime* is a collection of norms, the pedigree or logical form of which somehow distinguishes it from other parts of international law with respect to some, but not all, of its several features. The concept helps international lawyers to understand and to describe social facts in a logically coherent fashion.
2. A *special regime* is a collection of norms, which address either a set of similar facts or a set of similar legal consequences. The concept helps international lawyers to think and talk about detected differences in legal practice in an economic fashion.

3. A *special regime* is a community of practice in the sense of Etienne Wenger – it is distinguishable because of the basic normative presuppositions of community members. The concept helps international lawyers to understand and describe social facts in a way that coheres with their commitment to give time and energy to the realization of some presupposed legal ideal or ideals.

This conclusion builds on three basic assumptions:

1. A special regime is a subpart of the international legal system.
2. The significance of having identified an entity as one that belongs to the extension of a special regime is dependent on the defining features of this concept. This is why the answer to Question (2) is as much dependent on a theory of law as the answer to Question (1).
3. All theories of law come hand in hand with a very distinct conception of a legal system. This is why, throughout this book, we have referred to the three conceptions of a special regime as 'the legal positivist's', 'the legal realist's' and 'the legal idealist's' conception, respectively.

There are considerable differences among the legal positivist's, the legal realist's and the legal idealist's conceptions of a special regime. Most importantly, the three conceptions place their emphasis on different aspects of legal structure, and they further the realization of different results. This observation raises questions about their relative utility. In Section 1.4, we expressed a preference for the legal idealist's conception of a special regime. As we insisted, this conception is very useful inasmuch as it helps to manage and control the effect of legal fragmentation to an extent that the legal positivist's and the legal realist's conceptions do not.

The legal idealist's conception of a special regime directs attention to the social context that distinguishes the activities of different groups of international law specialists, and, more precisely, their normative presuppositions. Many international lawyers and scholars would conceive of this focus as a problem. They would consider themselves ill-equipped to engage with any relationship between human beings and their social context. A study of this relationship, they would insist, requires the methodology and expertise of a sociologist. In Section 1.4, we challenged this position. We believe that it builds on a misconception of the task needed to justify a suggestion that some subpart of the international legal system is a special regime. This task, we insisted, is not significantly different from many investigations that classically trained legal scholars are already conducting, more or less as a matter of course.

We recognize that this is a bold proposition that needs further justification. To meet this need, in Chapter 2, we outlined the further details of Etienne Wenger's theory of communities of practice. According to Wenger, a community of practice is characterized by the presence of three structural elements: there must be a mutual engagement of community members; community members must be engaged in a joint enterprise; and they must have a shared repertoire.[1] In Section 2.2, we explored how this theory translates to the context of international law and our analysis of the legal idealist's conception of a special regime. We suggested that it be interpreted to mean that in a special regime (X):

1. X law specialists believe that it is desirable that they join forces and collaborate in the pursuit of some particular enterprise.
2. X law specialists do what they do based on the idea that some certain state of affairs is desirable.
3. X law specialists consider the use of certain rhetorical tools appropriate.

In Section 2.3, we drew up the contours of a methodology that may help to establish the existence of such normative presuppositions. We suggested that they be studied as implicit in the actual conduct of community members, based on the assumption that these members act rationally and that they recognize the appropriateness of their own action.

To illustrate the practical operation of this methodology, in Chapters 3–5, we conducted a series of case studies. Each chapter highlighted a different structural element. Thus, in Chapter 3, we addressed the suggestion that for a special regime to exist, there must be a mutual engagement of community members. As we argued, in the context of international law, a mutual engagement among a group of international law specialists can be inferred from their participation in a distinct legal discourse, and from their further specialization and distinct way of ascribing functions to legal agents. As our case studies illustrated, more specifically, it can be inferred from:

- the publication of specialized international law journals;
- the way of organization of conferences and workshops;
- the creation of inter-governmental organization;

[1] See Section 2.1.

- the work of NGOs;
- the specialized research profile of international scholars and description of chairs;
- their separation of tasks or division of labour;
- the function that they ascribe to the judiciary and to the international legal scholar.

In Chapter 4, we addressed the suggestion that for a special regime to exist, community members must be engaged in a joint enterprise. In the context of international law, to claim that a group of international law specialists is engaged in a joint enterprise is to assert that they do what they do based on the idea that some certain state of affairs is desirable. As we argued, in the context of international law, the existence of such a presupposition can be inferred from the actual pursuit of those specialists of a distinct state of affairs, and the way in which they perform assignments. As our case studies illustrated, more specifically, it can be inferred from:

- the way in which specialists exercise discretion;
- the way in which specialists understand the principle of legal certainty;
- the effect that specialists ascribe to invalid declarations and reservations;
- the way in which specialists apply the concept or principle of sustainable development;
- the extent to which specialists accept *amicus curiae* participation and submissions;
- the approach of specialists to rules of legal interpretation;
- the way in which specialists apply the principle of *jura novit curia*;
- the extent to which specialists exercise incidental jurisdiction;
- the way in which the specialists conduct proportionality assessments;
- the role that the specialists ascribe to teleological reasoning in treaty interpretation.

In Chapter 5, we addressed the suggestion that for a special regime to exist, community members must have a shared repertoire. In the context of international law, to claim that a group of international law specialists have a shared repertoire is to assert that they consider the use of certain rhetorical tools appropriate. As we argued, in the context of international law, the existence of such a presupposition can be inferred from:

- the actual use by specialists of distinct concepts, such as the concept of a *jus cogens* norm, the concept of a conflict of two rules, or the concept of effective control;

- the actual use by specialists of a distinct terminology;
- the actual use by specialists of a distinct method, such as the way of calculating interest on compensation;
- the actual use by specialists of distinct form of arguments, such as arguments of 'soft-law', or arguments of justice;
- the actual use by specialists of distinct theories, principles and doctrines, such as the clean slate principle, or the theory of autonomous concepts.

6.2 Is Specialization a Threat to the Unity of the International Legal System?

6.2.1 The Fragmentation Debate Revisited

In this second section of the concluding chapter of our book, we will address one of the really big questions associated with the proliferation of special regimes in international law and legal practice: how can the development towards an increasingly more specialized and diversified international law be combined with the fundamental idea of international law as a single legal system? We touched upon this question in Chapter 1, although very briefly. As we indicated, our analysis of the concept of a special regime will help lawyers come to grips with precisely this question. We will devote the remainder of this chapter to explaining this proposition.

As we mentioned in Chapter 1, over the last thirty or so years, international law and legal practice have become increasingly specialized and diversified. Symptomatically, international lawyers no longer think of the international legal system as an indivisible whole, but as something that can be better described by reference to the many different segments making up this system. Lawyers refer to these segments in some cases as 'special regimes' and in others as 'general international law'. They are all elements of the international legal system, although lawyers regard them as more or less distinct from one another and refer to them by distinct names such as 'international environmental law', 'international criminal law', 'diplomatic law', 'international human rights law' and so forth.

When, in 2002, the ILC established a study group to examine the difficulties arising from the fragmentation of international law,[2] members

[2] Report of the work of the International Law Commission at its fifty-fourth session, 29 April–7 June and 22 July–16 August 2002, U.N. Doc. A/57/10, paras. 492–494.

of the Commission regarded the proliferation of special regimes as one of the important causes of this much-debated phenomenon. Already Gerhard Hafner, who had earlier been tasked to conduct a 'feasibility study' of the topic, referred to the phenomenon as one that threatens to seriously 'undermine any tendency towards a homogeneous international law and system'.[3] According to him, the proliferation of special regimes jeopardizes 'the coherence of international law'.[4] It leads to 'topic autonomy',[5] and thus poses a threat to 'the unity of international law' itself.[6]

The Final Study of the ILC Study Group described the phenomenon as '[t]he splitting up of the law into highly specialized "boxes" that claim relative autonomy from each other and from general international law'.[7] Among other things, it examined it relative to the concept of a self-contained regime so-called.[8] As it asserted, the proliferation of special regimes creates problems of coherence in international law, as '[v]ery often new rules or regimes develop precisely in order to deviate from what was earlier provided by the general law'.[9] Just as Gerhard Hafner had done, the Study Group warned that 'when such deviations become general and frequent, the unity of the law suffers'.[10]

These descriptions reveal an implicit assumption: in the course of time, the development towards an increasingly specialized and diversified international law may serve to separate the many special regimes from the international legal system and transform them into legal systems of their own. We would like to challenge this assumption. When you conceive of a special regime as a community of practice, as we do, the

[3] Gerhard Hafner, 'Risks Ensuing from Fragmentation of International Law', in Official Records of the General Assembly, fifty-fifth session, Supplement No. 10, U.N. Doc. A/55/10, at 148.

[4] Ibid., at 146, with reference to: Ian Brownlie, 'Problems Concerning the Unity of International Law', in A. Giuffrè (ed.), *Le droit international à l'heure de sa codification. Études en l'honneur de Roberto Ago*, 4 vols., vol. I (Milan: Dott, 1987), 156.

[5] Ibid., at 146.

[6] Ibid., at 149.

[7] Fragmentation of International Law: Difficulties Arising from the Diversification and Expansion of International Law, Report of the Study Group prepared for the fifty-eighth session of the International Law Commission, 1 May–9 June and 3 July–11 August 2006, UN Doc A/CN.4/L.702, para. 8.

[8] Fragmentation of International Law: Difficulties Arising from the Diversification and Expansion of International Law, Report of the Study Group prepared for the fifty-eighth session of the International Law Commission, 1 May–9 June and 3 July–11 August 2006, U.N. Doc A/CN.4/L.682, Corr. 1 and Add. 1, see especially paras. 123–190.

[9] Ibid., at para. 15.

[10] Ibid.

proliferation of special regimes does not have the disintegrating effect that members of the ILC seem to assume. This suggestion builds on three distinct propositions:

(1) Different theories of law correspond to different conceptions of an international legal system. In analogy to the legal positivist's, the legal realist's and the legal idealist's conceptions of a special regime, we will refer to them as the legal positivist's, the legal realist's and the legal idealist's conceptions of an international legal system.
(2) These conceptions can all be described as systems of knowledge-that.
(3) Whereas the legal idealist's conception of an international legal system can also be described as a system of knowledge-how, the legal positivist's and the legal realist's conceptions cannot.

In Sections 6.2.2–6.2.3, we will explain these three propositions. In the concluding Section 6.2.5, we will spell out in more detail why they entail our suggestion – that the proliferation of special regimes does not pose any threat to the unity of the international legal system.

6.2.2 Knowledge-That and Knowledge-How

Our argument suggests that the legal positivist's, the legal realist's and the legal idealist's conceptions of an international legal system all be described as systems of knowledge. The important upshot is the suggestion that they be described as systems of knowledge in different senses. While, according to us, the legal positivist's and the legal realist's conceptions of an international legal system should be characterized as systems of knowledge-that, the legal idealist's conception should be described as the combination of a system of knowledge-that and knowledge-how. The explanation of this proposition requires further engagement with the concept of knowledge itself. It presupposes an answer to a much-discussed issue in epistemology: what is the difference between knowledge-that and knowledge-how, and how are these different kinds of knowledge related? In this section, we will briefly explain how we position ourselves relative to this issue.

In epistemology textbooks, philosophers remind us to distinguish between two kinds of knowledge. The first kind is knowledge of facts. Since belief in the existence of a factual state of affairs can be represented by a logical proposition, and since propositions are commonly stated in the form 'It is the case that …', philosophers refer to this kind of knowledge as *knowledge-that*. It is the kind of knowledge that we acquire when we learn that Ferrari is an Italian race car, for example, or that people in different countries celebrate Christmas on different days or again that international law imposes on states the obligation to abstain from sending military troops to invade the territory of other countries. The second kind of knowledge is what you need to have to be able to say, truthfully, that you know how to carry out a practical task, such as cook spaghetti, play the guitar, grow sweet potato in a cold climate, drive a Ferrari or argue a case before a court of law.[11] To distinguish this kind of knowledge from knowledge-that, philosophers refer to it as *knowledge-how*.

The concept of knowledge-how goes back to the writing of Aristotle, who distinguished between *epistêmê* (that is, scientific knowledge or knowledge-that) and *technê* (knowledge of craft or knowledge-how). The relationship between knowledge-how and knowledge-that was brought to serious scrutiny for the very first time in 1946 by analytical philosopher Gilbert Ryle in a paper presented to the Aristotelian Society.[12] In this paper, Ryle defended two propositions: (1) that knowing-how must be treated as a faculty distinct from knowing-that, and not reducible to it, as commonly assumed at that time; and (2) that knowing-how in fact presupposes knowing-that. These propositions presuppose a definition of the two concepts that are their focus – knowledge-that and knowledge-how. Ryle's conception of knowledge-that is simple enough – it is the orthodox knowledge about facts. His conception of knowledge-how is slightly more difficult to grasp.

For Ryle, clearly, knowledge-how implies an ability.[13] Thus, if you know how to swim, you have the ability to swim. Ability, however, is not enough. In the same way as a lucky guess cannot represent a piece of knowledge-that,[14] there is a sense in which someone, who does something just once by pure chance, still does not know how to do it – like staying afloat by merely waving your arms. This is why Ryle introduces a second requirement: 'When a person knows how to do things of a certain sort his performance is in some way governed by principles, rules,

[11] See, for example, Jane Roland, 'On "Knowing How" and "Knowing That"' (1958) 67 *The Philosophical Review* 379–388, 380.

[12] Gilbert Ryle, 'Knowing How and Knowing That: The Presidential Address' (1945–1946) *Proceedings of the Aristotelian Society* 1–16.

[13] Ibid., at 8.

[14] See, for example, Mylan Engel Jr, 'Epistemic Luck', in *Internet Encyclopedia of Philosophy*, https://iep.utm.edu/epi-luck.

standards or criteria'.[15] This requirement does not imply that a person who knows how to swim, for example, should be able to articulate explicitly all those norms that govern swimming. What it does imply, Ryle emphasizes, is an ability to distinguish between correct and incorrect swimming.[16]

German philosopher Stefan Brandt recently published an article, in which he develops Ryle's understanding of the concept of know-how.[17] As Brandt argues, Ryle was wrong in assuming that knowledge-how in all cases implies an ability. Brandt illustrates this point by giving two examples: 'A seamstress with arthritis may still know how to make a dress, although she is not able to do it anymore, and an athletic coach may know how to perform certain routines although he was never able to perform them himself'.[18] If Brandt is correct – and his two examples are certainly very convincing – then the sole emphasis in a definition of the concept of knowledge-how should be on the second of Ryle's two requirements. Thus, Brandt suggests that we modify Ryle's definition. In the case of the previous example (swimming), it would read something like the following:

> A person knows how to swim if and only if: (a) he or she knows what swimming is; and (b) he or she is able to arrive at correct situation-specific judgments about how to swim successfully.[19]

Condition (a), Brandt explains, might be taken by many readers to be implied by condition (b). It is nevertheless included to ensure that we do not think of a person as one who knows how to do something, if that person himself or herself does not grasp what kind of activity is involved. Thus, a person does not know how to play chess, for example, if he or she does not know that chess is a game played according to certain rules with the purpose of winning.[20]

Having now what seems to be a solid definition of the two concepts of knowledge-how and knowledge-that, we are able to understand better the difference between them. The difference lies in the way in which knowledge can be measured or assessed. Knowledge-that is something that a

15 Ryle, 'Knowing How and Knowing That', 8–9.
16 Ibid.
17 Stefan Brandt, 'Ryle on Knowing How: Some Clarifications and Corrections' (2020) 29 *European Journal of Philosophy* 152–167.
18 Ibid., at 161.
19 Ibid.
20 Ibid., at 162.

person either possesses or not. You either know that Ferrari is an Italian race car, or you do not. Knowledge-how, on the other hand, comes in degrees: you can be a more or less proficient swimmer or defence counsel, just as you can be more or less skilled at cooking spaghetti or sewing clothes. Thus, unlike knowledge-that, knowledge-how cannot be stated in terms of logical propositions.

These observations explain the description that Ryle offered in his 1946 paper of the relationship between knowledge-how and knowledge-that. Knowledge-how is a distinct faculty that cannot be reduced to or defined in terms of knowledge-that. We can sometimes say correctly of someone that he knows how to perform an activity, say swimming, although he is not able to cite any general rules, principles or instructions about this activity. In the reverse, we can sometimes say correctly of someone that he *does not* know how to swim, although he can indeed cite such rules, principles or instructions.[21] Knowing how to do something is not exhibited by citing the rules governing that activity, but by correct situation-specific judgements. On the other hand, the specific judgements in which knowledge-how is exercised will always have propositional content. If you know how to play chess, for example, your instructions to a beginner may read something like the following propositions:

- 'The king moves exactly one square horizontally, vertically, or diagonally'.
- 'A rook moves any number of vacant squares horizontally or vertically'.
- 'A bishop moves any number of vacant squares diagonally'.[22]

In this sense, knowledge-how presupposes knowledge-that, and this is exactly what Ryle argued.[23]

6.2.3 The International Legal System as a System of Knowledge-That

Our argument suggests that the legal positivist's, the legal realist's and the legal idealist's conceptions of an international legal system all be described as systems of knowledge-that. The explanation of this proposition requires further engagement with the conditions for saying correctly that you possess a piece of knowledge of this kind. We have earlier

[21] Ibid., at 155.
[22] Erich Schiller, *Official Rules of Chess*, 2nd edition (Las Vegas: Cardoza Publishing, 2003), 17–19.
[23] Ryle, 'Knowing How and Knowing That', 15–16.

referred to knowledge-that as knowledge of facts – as a belief in the existence of a factual state of affairs that can be represented by a logical proposition. A few further distinctions would now have to be added.

Legal knowledge is a cognitive achievement.[24] It is the result of a mental process of sorts, manifested in a specific kind of attitude of an individual to either a proposition or a set of propositions. Epistemologists refer to this attitude as a *belief*.[25] To possess a piece of legal knowledge is to *believe* that some certain legal state of affairs obtains. A person may believe, for example, that international law imposes on states the obligation to abstain from sending military troops to invade the territory of other countries. If an individual does not believe that this legal state of affairs obtains, he cannot *know* it.[26]

Belief is of course not a sufficient condition for knowing. In philosophy textbooks, it is standard to define knowledge as a justified true belief.[27] According to this definition, a person (S) knows something (p), if and only if: (i) p is true; (ii) S believes that p; and (iii) S has good reasons for believing that p.[28] If p is made to stand for the proposition that the Earth is flat, for example, then this proposition will for S represent a piece of knowledge if and only if: (i) S believes that the Earth is flat; and (ii) it is true that the Earth is flat, and (iii) S has good reasons to believe that the Earth is flat.

The requirement that a proposition must be true derives from the mere character of what we would like to think that the proposition represents – a fact.[29] For the same reason as a false proposition cannot represent a fact, no belief in false propositions can be defined as knowledge possessed by any person. Another way of putting this is to say that people cannot know things about which they are wrong. It is primarily because of the requirement of truth that no person can be said to know that the Earth is flat.

24 See, for example, Matthias Steup and Ram Neta, 'Epistemology', in Edward Zalta (ed.), *The Stanford Encyclopedia of Philosophy* (Online, Spring 2020 Edition), https://plato.stanford.edu/archives/spr2020/entries/epistemology.

25 It is commonplace among epistemologists to distinguish between knowing facts (or knowing *that*), knowing *how*, and knowing *individuals*. Ibid., at 6–8. We are assuming throughout that legal knowledge is a matter of knowing facts.

26 See, for example, J. J. Ichikawa and Matthias Steup, 'The Analysis of Knowledge', in Edward Zalta (ed.), *The Stanford Encyclopedia of Philosophy* (Online, Summer 2018 Edition), https://plato.stanford.edu/archives/sum2018/entries/knowledge-analysis.

27 Ibid., at 2.

28 Ibid.

29 Ibid., at 2–3.

The requirement that a person must have good reasons to believe whatever he or she happens to believe would seem to be necessary to fill the gap that would otherwise be left between knowledge and the truth. Truth is a matter of how things are and not of how they can be established to be.[30] Thus, when we say that only beliefs in true propositions can be referred to as knowledge, we are not saying anything about how anyone can access that truth. If knowing something means to have a certain access to the truth – which is what the terminology assumes – a definition of knowledge must include an element that can (at least tentatively) guarantee that access. This is what the requirement of justification supposedly does.[31]

Now, what does this requirement mean precisely? What does it mean to say, for example, that a person has good reasons to believe that international law imposes on states the obligation to abstain from sending military troops to invade the territory of other countries? This question is indeed fundamental for the consideration of the effect that the proliferation of special regimes may have on the unity of the international legal system. Yet, it impresses on us the need to engage with some of the most contentious of issues addressed in epistemology. We will try to make our line of argument as plain and easily accessible as possible. Since we have dealt with issues of epistemic justification in our previous writing,[32] we will limit ourselves to just summarizing, in two paragraphs, how we position ourselves relative to some of the contentious points.

The justification of a belief held by an individual is dependent on the structure of the entire system of beliefs that this same individual possesses.[33] The fact that single beliefs are not arbitrarily pieced together, but arranged as a unitary whole ('a system of knowledge'),[34] presupposes the existence of two kinds of beliefs. Not only do people hold first-order beliefs, thinking, for example, that a certain legal states of affairs obtains. They also hold second-order beliefs: they have a certain idea of how first-order beliefs should be fitted together. Hence, it is a first necessary

[30] Ibid., at 3.

[31] Because of luck, a belief can be unjustified yet true; and because of human fallibility, a belief can be justified yet false. This is why truth and justification are two separate conditions of knowledge.

[32] Ulf Linderfalk, *The International Legal System as a System of Knowledge* (Cheltenham: Edward Elgar Publishing Limited, 2022), 10–15.

[33] Ibid., at 10.

[34] Ibid.

condition for the justification of a first-order belief relative to any person that the second-order beliefs held by that same person allow it.[35]

The justification of a belief is also dependent on factors that are external to a believer's mind.[36] These factors vary with the context in which knowledge is being sought, as for example international legal discourse.[37] Hence, if, for some individual, the internal justification of a single belief about international law is dependent on the second-order structural beliefs held by that same person, these second-order structural beliefs will have to enjoy recognition by other participants in international legal discourse, or else the belief will not classify as a piece of knowledge. Put differently, international legal discourse presupposes some notion of how single pieces of knowledge of international law should be fitted together. We have referred to this as a 'conception of an international legal system'.[38]

The legal positivist's, the legal realist's and the legal idealist's conceptions of an international legal system all enjoy recognition among the community of international lawyers and scholars.[39] If any confirmation is needed, readers may consult our previous book, *The International Legal System as a System of Knowledge*,[40] which provides plenty of examples. For all three conceptions, legal norms are a constitutive element of the international legal system, although, of course, legal positivists, legal idealists and legal realists understand the concept of a legal norm differently. For legal positivists and legal idealists, a legal norm is a reason for action and a basis for justification of legal decisions. It guides the behaviour of its addressees because of the legal obligations that it imposes. For legal realists, a legal norm remains no more than a piece of language. It never entails any obligations. Instead, it guides the behaviour of its addressees because of its grammatical form and referential meaning.

In the case of all three conceptions of an international legal system, legal knowledge is a belief in the existence of a factual state of affairs

35 Ibid., at 11–12.
36 Ibid., at 12.
37 Ibid., at 13–15.
38 On this concept, see ibid., at 16–18.
39 Symptomatically, international law textbooks refer to 'legal positivism', 'legal idealism' and 'legal realism' as the three schools of thought that dominate international legal discourse. See, for example, G. J. H. Van Hoof, *Rethinking the Source of International Law* (Deventer: Kluwer Law and Taxation Publishers, 1983), 29.
40 Linderfalk, *The International Legal System*.

represented by a proposition. Again, different lawyers would articulate this proposition differently. Legal positivists and legal idealists would articulate the proposition in terms of an obligation. For example: 'International law imposes upon Russia the obligation to abstain from sending military troops to invade the territory of Ukraine.' Legal realists would articulate it in terms of a prediction of the legal consequences of a set of facts. For example: 'If Russian troops invade the territory of Ukraine, then international legal decision-makers are likely to find that Russia has acted wrongfully, and, thus, that Russia must immediately redraw all troops, that it must make full reparation for the injury that its action has caused, and that it must offer appropriate assurances and guarantees of non-repetition.' Still, for all three conceptions of an international legal system, legal knowledge is propositional. This is to say that they are all conceptions of a system of knowledge-that.

6.2.4 The International Legal System as Knowledge-How

Our previous analysis of the concepts of knowledge-how and knowledge-that highlighted several distinguishing features. Based on these observations, we will now make a comparison of the legal idealist's conception of an international legal system with that of the legal positivists or the legal realists. A comparison suggests that we describe the legal idealist's conception as a system of knowledge-how, in contrast to the legal positivist's and the legal realist's conceptions, which can only be described as systems of knowledge-that. Consider the following three defining features of knowledge-that and knowledge-how:

> *(1) Whereas knowledge-that is knowledge about facts, knowledge-how is the kind of knowledge that you need to have to be able to carry out practical tasks.*

From the point of view of the legal positivist's and the legal realist's conception of an international legal system, international law does not include any normative elements akin to ideals. International law is a set of norms, and a set of norms only. The existence of these norms is a matter of social fact. In the case of the legal positivists, more specifically, the existence of a legal norm is inherent in the occurrence of a past event – the conclusion of an international agreement or the adoption of a decision by an international organization – to the extent that the basic criteria of the legal system identify it as an act of law-making. In the case of the legal realists, the existence of a legal norm is inherent in the occurrence of past events, to the extent that these events can be thought to have an influence on future legal decision-making. From the point of view of the legal positivist and the legal idealists, people know the law if they have knowledge of these facts.

For legal idealism, law is a social practice. One of the characteristic features of a social practice is the idea among its participants that there is something that makes this practice worthwhile. Thus, law does not exist for its own sake. It exists because of the presence of some or other idea, either of what law should be like, or of what the legal project should achieve. We have referred to this idea as an ideal – a state of affairs presented by a group of people as something desirable and worth aspiring to. This explains the essence of the legal idealist's conception of law: compliance with the law is never a goal in itself; what ultimately counts is always whether the law helps to realize the assumed legal ideal, and, if so, to what extent. Legal idealists think of legal knowledge in the same way. People know the law if they are able to make situation-specific judgements about how to apply it to realize the assumed legal ideal.

> *(2) Knowledge-that is something that a person either possesses or not, in contrast to knowledge-how, which comes in degrees.*

From the point of view of the legal positivist's and the legal realist's conception of the international legal system, legal knowledge is the belief in the existence of a factual state of affairs. In the case of the legal positivists, more specifically, it is a belief in the occurrence of an event, which basic criteria of the legal system identify as an act of law-making. In the case of the legal realists, it is a belief in events that they predict will have an influence on future legal decision-making. These states of affairs can be represented by logical propositions. Such propositions are either true or false. Hence, from the point of view of the legal positivist's and the legal realist's conception of the international legal system, legal knowledge does not come in degrees – you either possess it, or you do not.

Legal idealists think of norms as means to realize the ideal set for the legal project. People know the law if they are able to make situation-specific judgements about how to apply it to realize the assumed legal ideal. This ability presupposes knowledge of the factual consequences of applying individual norms relative to the ideal. Such knowledge is not easy to obtain. Legal norms do not operate in a vacuum. Their effect is always more or less dependent on a context. This context includes other individual norms of the same legal system. Consider, for example, the principle of the freedom of the high seas. Whether and to what extent the application of this principle will serve to accommodate an ideal such as the accommodation of the basic needs of human beings will depend on the existence and scope of application of other norms concerning navigational safety, for example, or the conservation of fish stocks or again the control of pollution by dumping or from sea-bed activities. Even more importantly, the context of operation of norms includes the world at large. Clearly, the realization of legal ideals is not served by legal means exclusively but also by means that are outside of law proper. In the case of many societies, for example, a right to liberty and security of person may be needed to accommodate the basic needs of all human beings, but the realization of this same ideal may also be dependent on factual conditions, such as the supply of water and foodstuffs. The interesting thing to acknowledge is the frequent interaction of norms with their factual context. Interaction may take many different forms,[41] as illustrated by the following three examples:

- Some legal norms serve the realization of an ideal only on the condition of the existence of some factual circumstances. For example, the right to participate in cultural life laid down in Article 15 of the International Covenant on Economic, Social and Cultural Rights will not lead to the realization of any well-being of community members if there are no cultural activities to begin with.[42]
- Some factual circumstances are unable to serve the realization of an ideal independently of the law. Normally, the translation of documents into another language has no bearing on the realization of justice, for example. However, when translation occurs in the context of judicial proceedings involving a foreign national charged with a criminal offence, because of the right to a fair trial and the principle of equality of arms,[43] a different assessment will no doubt have to be made.
- Many legal norms help to alleviate the effect of factual circumstances, which serve to impede the realization of an ideal. For example, if certain methods of fishing threaten the extinction of some species of

[41] I admit to having used the below three examples in my previous writing. See Ulf Linderfalk, *Understanding* Jus Cogens *in International Law and International Legal Discourse* (Cheltenham: Edward Elgar Publishing Limited, 2020), 128–129.

[42] International Covenant on Economic, Social and Cultural Rights, New York, 16 December 1966, in force 3 January 1976, 993 U.N.T.S. 3.

[43] See, for example, Convention for the Protection of Human Rights and Fundamental Freedoms, as amended by Protocols Nos. 11 and 14, Rome, 4 November 1950, European Treaty Series No. 5, Art. 6.

fish, and the continued existence of these species serve to accommodate the basic needs of human beings, then in order not to compromise the ideal altogether, the conclusion of an agreement on the total abolishment of these methods may be necessary.

As these examples make apparent, the factual consequences of applying individual norms relative to an assumed legal ideal are not easily determined. When an idealist says that he has knowledge of the factual consequences of applying a legal norm relative to an assumed legal ideal, clearly, he does not mean knowledge in any absolute sense. The kind of knowledge assumed is one that can be possessed only partly. The person may be an expert with extensive previous experience of the application of a norm, but he can never know it to the full.

(3) Knowing-how supposes knowledge-that, but it is not reducible to it.

The difference between the three conceptions of an international legal system is well illustrated relative to the exercise of a legal discretion. Discretion is a power conferred by a lawmaker on a legal decision-maker. It enables the legal decision-maker to make decisions in conformity with a legal rule, while giving at the same time this person or institution the possibility to choose between diverse courses of action.[44] For example, Article 5 of the Interim Accord of 13 September 1995 between Greece and FYROM may impose on the Greek and FYROM Governments an obligation to 'continue negotiations' with a view to settling outstanding differences over the name of the latter country. Yet, it may confer upon them the discretion to decide how, precisely, negotiations are to be conducted and when.[45] A legal decision-maker 'exercises discretion' when it avails itself of a decision-making power so framed.

From the point of view of the legal positivist's and the legal realist's conception of an international legal system, legal knowledge is a belief in the existence of a legal norm or set of legal norms. Such a belief can be either true or false: either a legal norm exists, or it does not. This approach to legal knowledge gives legal positivist and legal realists limited possibility to criticize the exercise of a discretion. As long as a

[44] On the concept of legal discretion, see Ulf Linderfalk, 'The Exercise of Discretion in International Law: Why Constraining Criteria Have a Proper Place In the Analysis of Legal Decision-Making' (2019) 62 *German Yearbook of International Law* 407–430.

[45] *Application of the Interim Accord of 13 September 1995 (The Former Republic of Macedonia v. Greece)* [2011] I.C.J. Rep. 644, paras. 127–138.

legal decision-maker stays within the scope of what law allows, every decision will be equally good.

From the point of view of legal idealism, people know the law if they are able to make situation-specific judgements about how to apply it to realize the assumed legal ideal. Suppose that a norm leaves to decision-makers to choose between four different courses of action. Legal idealists would not say that people know this norm just because they can tell us that four courses of action can be taken. They would insist that people tell us which of these four courses of action is best aligned with the assumed legal ideal.

6.2.5 *Conclusions*

In Section 6.2.1, we ventured a very bold suggestion: when you conceive of a special regime as a community of practice, the proliferation of special regimes does not pose any threat to the unity of the international legal system. Sections 6.2.2–6.2.4 explained the three propositions that form the basis of this suggestion:

(1) The legal positivist's, legal realist's and legal idealist's conceptions of international law correspond to three different conceptions of an international legal system.
(2) These conceptions can all be described as systems of knowledge-that.
(3) Whereas the legal idealist's conception of an international legal system can also be described as a system of knowledge-how, the legal positivist's and the legal realist's conceptions cannot.

In this concluding section of Chapter 6, we will tie things together and spell out in more detail how these three propositions support our argument.

We would like to begin with reminding readers of the definition that we established already at the outset of this book: a special regime is a subpart or segment of the international legal system. This definition applies alike to the legal positivist's, the legal realist's and the legal idealist's conception of a special regime. Hence, if the legal idealist's conception of an international legal system can be described as a combination of a system of knowledge-that and a system of knowledge-how, this is bound to affect also the legal idealist's conception of a special regime.

In our understanding, the crucial difference between the many special regimes in international law is not that they represent different sets of knowledge-that, but that different international law specialists have different ways of carrying out their legal tasks. To illustrate, consider international environmental law and the law of the sea. There is, of course, something that we can refer to as knowledge-that of international environmental law and the law of the sea, and we typically expect of specialists of these fields of law that they possess it. However, this is not the knowledge that distinguishes international environmental law from the law of the sea, or specialists of the one field from specialists of the other. It cannot be, for the same reason as knowledge of the law of the sea in many cases presupposes knowledge of international environmental law, and vice versa. If any example is needed, consider Article 216, paragraph 1 of the United Nations Convention on the Law of the Sea:

> Laws and regulations adopted in accordance with this Convention and applicable international rules and standards established through competent international organizations or diplomatic conference for the prevention, reduction and control of pollution of the marine environment by dumping shall be enforced: (a) by the coastal State with regard to dumping within its territorial sea or its exclusive economic zone or onto its continental shelf; (b) by the flag State with regard to vessels flying its flag or vessels or aircraft of its registry; (c) by any State with regard to acts of loading of wastes or other matter occurring within its territory or at its off-shore terminals.[46]

The knowledge that distinguishes international environmental law from the law of the sea is rather the *knowledge-how* that specialists develop over time by actively engaging in the discourse specific for each branch. Thus, in our understanding, the difference between international environmental law and the law of the sea is not any greater than that between different schools of chess. What distinguishes different schools of chess is not their different knowledge of the rules of chess, but their different ways of playing chess within the framework of what these rules allow. In the same way, what distinguishes lawyers specializing in different branches of international law are the different ways in which they carry out their tasks *within the legal framework*.

This understanding squares well with how Wenger addresses the concepts of knowledge and learning in his book. Learning for him is a process by which knowledge is produced.[47] Knowledge, in turn, 'is a

[46] United Nations Convention on the Law of the Sea, Montego Bay, 10 December 1982, in force 16 November 1994, 1833 U.N.T.S. 397.

[47] See Section 2.1.

matter of competence with respect to valued enterprises – such as singing in tune, discovering scientific facts, fixing machines, writing poetry, being convivial, growing up as a boy or a girl, and so forth'.[48] For Wenger, clearly, knowledge is not propositional knowledge, but knowledge-how. The focus of his entire book is on *how to do things* in a community of people.

The case studies that we conducted in Chapters 3–5 paint a similar picture. If there is a theme that connects all of these studies, it is not that different international law specialists apply different norms to solve common legal problems. The theme is rather that different specialists have different ideas of how to properly do things when law does not offer sufficient guidance. Guidance is lacking, in some cases, because an issue is altogether outside of the scope of the law, as in the case of the publication of journals,[49] the organization of conferences and workshops[50] and the use of a distinct terminology.[51] In other cases, guidance is lacking because law leaves decision-makers a discretion, such as to determine the effect of invalid reservations and declarations,[52] how to conduct a proportionality assessment[53] or to choose between ascribing to a treaty concept an autonomous meaning or a meaning that remains dependent on domestic law and legal practice.[54]

Two important conclusions follow from this understanding of a special regime. First, and importantly, the legal idealist's conception of a special regime is compatible with all of the legal positivist's, legal realist's and legal idealist's conceptions of an international legal system, although for different reasons. It is compatible with the legal positivist's and legal realist's conceptions of an international legal system because they are systems of knowledge of a fundamentally different kind – they are systems of knowledge-that, whereas the idealist's conception of a special regime focuses on knowledge-how. The legal idealist's conception of an international legal system, in contrast, can indeed be described as a system of knowledge-how, just like the idealist's conception of a special regime. Certainly, the idealist's conception of an international legal

[48] Etienne Wenger, *Communities of Practice. Learning, Meaning and Identity* (Cambridge: Cambridge University Press, 1998), 4.
[49] See Section 3.2.1
[50] See Section 3.2.2.
[51] See Section 5.3.
[52] See Section 4.2.4.
[53] See Section 4.3.3.
[54] See Section 5.6.3.

system presupposes that legal tasks be carried out in a way that does not always agree with what a specialist would think correct. However, this does make the two conceptions incompatible. It is to allow for precisely such differences that idealists need the concept of a special regime in the first place. As they would contend, 'if the practice of international norms is to be of any help for the realisation of the presupposed legal ideal or ideals, we have to accept that different contexts of law sometimes require different solutions to similar problems'.[55]

Secondly, as far as the legal idealist's conception of a special regime is concerned, the development towards an increasingly more specialized and diversified international law does not pose any threat to the fundamental idea of international law as a single legal system. It cannot, for reasons already noted:

- As far as the legal idealist's conception of a special regime is concerned, a special regime is a system of knowledge in a different sense than the legal positivist's and the legal realist's conception of an international legal system. Thus, from the point of view of these two conceptions, in no way does the proliferation of special regimes in international law affect the international legal system.
- The concept of a special regime is what the legal idealists need to explain why similar tasks should sometimes be carried out differently. Thus, from the point of view of the legal idealist's conception of a special regime, the proliferation of special regimes in international law does indeed affect the international legal system, but only in a positive way – it increases the efficacy of international law relative to the assumed legal ideal.

These important conclusions bring us back to the real threat posed by the increasingly specialized and diversified international law. While the proliferation of special regimes in international law does not itself put in danger the idea of international law as a single legal system, it is not free of problems. As we expressed in Chapter 1,

> Because of the increasing specialization and diversification of international law, specialists are experiencing increasingly greater difficulty with understanding the reasoning of other specialists and their particular solutions to legal problems. Generalists are having similar problems with understanding the specialists, and vice versa.[56]

[55] See Section 1.3.
[56] Section 1.4.

This is the vexing problem of cross-border communication. It is acute because '[w]hen lawyers cannot any more understand each other, all that they will see is incorrect thought and behaviour'.[57] Such understandings have a devastating effect on the rationality of legal communication. This is why we suggested that something should be done to improve communication across the borders of the different special regimes: 'a doctrine must be developed that can explain why, sometimes, specialists in different fields of law do similar things differently'.[58] It was with precisely this need in mind that we initiated the writing of this book. Future will tell whether we have succeeded.

[57] Ibid.
[58] Ibid.

LIST OF SOURCES

Articles, Book Chapters, and Monographs

Adinolfi, Giovana, 'Soft Law in International Investment Law and Arbitration' (2021) 1 *The Italian Review of International and Comparative Law* 86–112.

Ammann, Odile, *Domestic Courts and the Interpretation of International Law: Methods and Reasoning Based on the Swiss Example* (Leiden: Koninklijke Brill NV, 2020).

Andenäs, Mads & Björge, Eirik (eds.), *A Farewell to Fragmentation: Reassertion and Convergence in International Law* (Cambridge: Cambridge University Press, 2015).

Andrade Lage, Délber & Brant, Leonardo Nemer Caldeira, 'The Growing Influence of Non-Governmental Organizations: Chances and Risks' (2008) III-1 *Anuário Brasileiro de Direito Internacional* 79–93.

Bacchus, James, 'Not in Clinical Isolation', in Gabrielle Marceau (ed.), *A History of Law and Lawyers in the GATT/WTO: The Development of the Rule of Law in the Multilateral Trading System* (Cambridge: Cambridge University Press, 2015).

Barker, J. Craig, 'International Court of Justice: "Jurisdictional Immunities of the State (Germany v. Italy)" Judgment of 3 February 2012' (2013) 62 *International and Comparative Law Quarterly* 741–752.

Barnhoorn, L. & Wellens, Karel (eds.), *Diversity in Secondary Rules and the Unity of International Law* (The Hague: Nijhoff, 1995).

Bartsch, Kerstin & Elberling, Björn, '*Jus Cogens* vs. Immunity, Round Two: The Decision of the European Court of Human Rights in the Kalogeropoulou et al. v. Greece and Germany Decision' (2003) 4 *German Law Journal* 477–491.

Beeley, Mark, 'Approaches to the Award of Interest', in Christina Beharry (ed.), *Contemporary and Emerging Issues on the Law of Damages and Valuation in International Investment Arbitration* (Leiden: Brill Nijhoff, 2018).

Beharry, Christina (ed.), *Contemporary and Emerging Issues on the Law of Damages and Valuation in International Investment Arbitration* (Leiden: Brill Nijhoff, 2018).

Bernhardt, Rudolf, 'Thoughts on the Interpretation of Human Rights Treaties', in Franz Matscher & Herbert Petzold (eds.), *Protecting Human Rights: The European Dimension: Studies in Honour of Gérard J Wiarda* (Cologne: Heymanns, 1988).

Beyerlin, Ulrich, 'Sustainable Development', in Rüdiger Wolfrum (ed.), *The Max Planck Encyclopedia of Public International Law* (Oxford: Oxford University Press, 2013).

Beyerlin, Ulrich & Marauhn, Thilo, *International Environmental Law* (Oxford: Hart, 2011).

Bianchi, Andrea, 'Gazing at the Crystal Ball (Again): State Immunity and *Jus Cogens* beyond Germany v. Italy' (2013) 4 *Journal of International Dispute Settlement* 1–19.

Blakemore, Dianne, *Understanding Utterances: Introduction to Pragmatics* (Hoboken: Wiley, 1992).

Boudreault, François, 'Identifying Conflicts of Norms: The ICJ Approach in the Case of the "Jurisdictional Immunities of the State (Germany v. Italy: Greece Intervening)"' (2012) 25 *Leiden Journal of International Law* 1003–1012.

Boyle, Alan & Chinkin, Christine, *The Making of International Law* (Oxford: Oxford University Press, 2007).

Brack, Duncan, 'Reconciling the GATT and Multilateral Environmental Agreements with Trade Provisions: The Latest Debate' (1997) 6 *Review of European, Comparative & International Environmental Law* 112–120.

Brandt, Stefan, 'Ryle on Knowing How: Some Clarifications and Corrections' (2020) 29 *European Journal of Philosophy* 152–167.

Brownlie, Ian, 'Problems concerning the Unity of International Law', in A. Giuffrè (ed.), *Le droit international à l'heure de sa codification: Études en l'honneur de Roberto Ago*, 4 vols., vol. I (Milan: Dott, 1987).

Cançado Trindade, Antônio Augusto, *International Law for Humankind: Towards a New Jus Gentium* (Leiden: Martinus Nijhoff, 2010).

'Prologue: An Overview of the Contribution of International Tribunals to the Rule of Law', in Geert De Baere & Jan Wouters (eds.), *The Contribution of International and Supranational Courts to the Rule of Law* (Cheltenham: Edward Elgar, 2014).

Cannizzaro, Enzo, 'The Role of Proportionality in the Law of International Countermeasures' (2001) 12 *European Journal of International Law* 889–916.

Cassese, Antonio, 'The *Nicaragua* and *Tadić* Tests Revisited in Light of the ICJ Judgment on Genocide in Bosnia' (2007) 18 *European Journal of International Law* 649–668.

Charnovitz, Steve, 'Multilateral Environmental Agreements and Trade Rules' (1996) 26 *Environmental Policy & Law* 163–169.

Chi, Manjiao, *Integrating Sustainable Development in International Investment Law: Normative Incompatibility, System Integration and Governance Implications* (New York: Routledge, 2018).

Christoffersen, Jonas, *Fair Balance: Proportionality, Subsidiarity and Primarity in the European Convention on Human Rights* (Leiden: Martinus Nijhoff, 2009).

Churchill, Robin & Lowe, Alan, *The Law of the Sea*, 3rd ed. (Manchester: Manchester University Press, 1999).

Clark, Tim, 'The Teleological Turn in the Law of International Organisations' (2021) 70 *International and Comparative Law Quarterly* 533–567.

Cordero Moss, Giuditta, 'Tribunal's Powers versus Party Autonomy', in Peter Muchlinski, Frederico Ortino, & Christoph Schreuer (eds.), *The Oxford Handbook of International Investment Law* (Oxford: Oxford University Press, 2009).

Coyle, Sean, 'Positivism, Idealism and the Rule of Law' (2006) 26 *Oxford Journal of Legal Studies* 257–288.

Craven, Matthew, 'The *Genocide* Case, the Law of Treaties and State Succession' (1997) 68 *British Yearbook of International Law* 127–163.

Crawford, James, 'State Responsibility', in Rüdiger Wolfrüm (ed.), *Max Planck Encyclopedia of Public International Law* (Oxford: Oxford University Press, 2012).

d'Aspremont, Jean, 'Softness in International Law: A Self-Serving Quest for New Legal Materials' (2008) 19 *European Journal of International Law* 1075–1093.

Dam-de Jong, Daniëlla, 'Who Is Targeted by the Council's Sanctions? The UN Security Council and the Principle of Proportionality' (2020) 89 *Nordic Journal of International Law* 383–398.

De Brabandere, Eric, 'Arbitral Decisions as a Source of International Investment Law', in Tarcisio Gazzini & Eric De Brabandere (eds.), *International Investment Law* (Leiden: Koninklijke Brill NV, 2012).

Investment Treaty Arbitration as Public International Law: Procedural Aspects and Implications (Cambridge: Cambridge University Press, 2014).

'(Re)Calibration, Standard-Setting and the Shaping of Investment Law and Arbitration' (2018) 59 *Boston College Law Review* 2607–2634.

'Coherence, Consistency, and the Reform of Investment Treaty Arbitration', in Daniel Franchini, Russell Buchan & Nicholas Tsagourias (eds.), *The Changing Character of International Dispute Settlement* (Cambridge: Cambridge Academic, 2023).

de la Rasilla, Ignacio, 'A Very Short History of International Law Journals (1869–2018)' (2018) 29 *European Journal of International Law* 137–168.

de Londras, Fiona & Dzehtsiarou, Kanstantsin, 'Grand Chamber of the European Court of Human Rights, A, B & C v. Ireland, Decision of 17 December 2010' (2013) 62 *International and Comparative Law Quarterly* 250–262.

Dörr, Oliver, 'Article 31', in Oliver Dörr & Kirsten Schmalenbach (eds.), *Vienna Convention on the Law of Treaties: A Commentary* (Heidelberg: Springer, 2012).

Dzehtsiarou, Kanstantsin, 'European Consensus and the Evolutive Interpretation of the European Convention on Human Rights' (2011) 12 *German Law Journal* 1730–1745.

Eatwell, Tatyana, 'Selling the Pass: Habeas Corpus, Diplomatic Relations and the Protection of Liberty and Security of Persons Detained Abroad' (2013) 62 *International and Comparative Law Quarterly* 727–739.

Espósito, Carlos, '*Jus Cogens* and Jurisdictional Immunities of States at the International Court of Justice: A Conflict Does Exist' (2011) 21 *Italian Yearbook of International Law* 161–174.

'Of Plumbers and Social Architects: Elements and Problems of the Judgment of the International Court of Justice in the Jurisdictional Immunities of the State' (2013) 4 *Journal of International Dispute Settlement* 439–456.

Feichtner, Isabel, 'Realizing Utopia Through the Practice of International Law' (2012) 23 *European Journal of International Law* 1143–1157.

Fenwick, Mark & Wrbka, Stefan, 'The Shifting Meaning of Legal Certainty', in Mark Fenwick & Stefan Wrbka (eds.), *Legal Certainty in a Contemporary Context* (Singapore: Springer, 2016).

Fisher-Lescano, Andreas & Teubner, Gunther, 'Regime Collisions: The Vain Search for Legal Unity in the Fragmentation of Global Law' (2004) 25 *Michigan Journal of International Law* 999–1046.

Fitzmaurice, Gerald, 'Hersch Lauterpacht – The Scholar as Judge' (1961) 37 *British Yearbook of International Law* 1–71.

Fontanelli, Filippo & Björge, Eirik, 'International Court of Justice, "Application of the Interim Accord of 13 September 1995 (the Former Yugoslav Republic of Macedonia v. Greece)" Judgment of 5 December 2011' (2012) 61 *International and Comparative Law Quarterly* 775–784.

Fox, Hazel, *The Law of State Immunity* (Oxford: Oxford University Press, 2002).

The Law of State Immunity, 3rd edition (Oxford: Oxford University Press, 2015).

Gagliani, Gabriele, 'The International Court of Justice and Cultural Heritage: International Cultural Heritage Law Through the Lens of World Court Jurisprudence?', in Anne-Marie Carstens & Elizabeth Varner (eds.), *Intersections in International Cultural Heritage Law* (Oxford: Oxford University Press, 2020).

Gardiner, Richard, *Treaty Interpretation*, 2nd edition (Oxford: Oxford University Press, 2008).

Gehring, Markus & Kent, Avidan, 'International Investment Agreements and the Emerging Green Economy: Rising to the Challenge', in Freya Baetens (ed.), *Investment Law within International Law: Integrationist Perspectives* (Cambridge: Cambridge University Press, 2013).

Genin, Vincent, *Le laboratoire belge du droit international* (Brussels: Académie royale de Belgique, 2018).

Gillespie, Alexander, *Conservation, Biodiversity and International Law* (Cheltenham: Edward Elgar Publishing Limited, 2011).

Giorgetti, Chiara & Pollack, Mark (eds.), *Beyond Fragmentation: Cross-Fertilization, Co-operation and Competition among International Courts and Tribunals* (Cambridge: Cambridge University Press, 2022).

Green, Michael, 'Hans Kelsen and the Logic of Legal Systems' (2003) 54 *Alabama Law Review* 365–413.

'Legal Realism as a Theory of Law' (2005) 46 *William and Mary Law Review* 1915–2000.

Grewe, Wilhelm G., *The Epochs of International Law* (Berlin: De Gruyter, 2000).

Hafner, Gerhard, 'Pros and Cons Ensuing from Fragmentation of International Law' (2004) 25 *Michigan Journal of International Law* 849–863.

Heere, Wybo (ed.), *From Government to Governance: The Growing Impact of Non-State Actors on the International and European Legal System* (The Hague: T.M.C. Asser Press, 2004).

Hennebel, Ludovic, 'Le rôle des Amici Curiae Devant la Cour Européenne des Droits de L'Homme' (2007) 71 *Revue Trimestrielle des Droits de l'Homme* 641–668.

Higgins, Rosalyn, *Problems and Process: International Law and How We Use It* (Oxford: Oxford University Press, 1994).

'"The Rule of Law: Some Sceptical Thoughts" Lecture Given at the British Institute for International and Comparative Law 16 October 2007', in Rosalyn Higgins (ed.), *Themes and Theories*, vol. II (Oxford: Oxford University Press, 2009).

Himma, Kenneth, 'Legal Positivism', in *Internet Encyclopedia of Philosophy*, https://iep.utm.edu/legalpos.

Hjørland, Birger, 'Concept Theory' (2009) 60 *Journal of the American Society for Information Science and Technology* 1519–1536.

Horowitz, Jodi, 'Regina v. Bartle and the Commissioner of Police for the Metropolis and Others Ex Parte Pinochet: Universal Jurisdiction and Sovereign Immunity for Jus Cogens Violations' (1999) 23 *Fordham International Law Journal* 489–527.

Howse, Robert, 'The World Trade Organization 20 Years On: Global Governance by Judiciary' (2016) 27 *European Journal of International Law* 9–77.

Hudnall, Shannon, 'Towards a Greener International Trade System: Multilateral Environmental Agreements and the World Trade Organization' (1996) 29 *Columbia Journal of Law & Social Problems* 175–216.

Hughes, Valerie, 'The Institutional Dimension', in Daniel Bethlehem, Isabelle Van Damme, Donald McRae, & Rodney Neufeld (eds.), *The Oxford Handbook of International Trade Law* (Oxford: Oxford University Press, 2009).

Humphreys, Stephen, 'Climate Change: Too Complex for a Special Regime' (2016) 34 *Journal of Energy & Natural Resources Law* 51–56.

Ichikawa, J. J. & Steup, Matthias, 'The Analysis of Knowledge', in Edward Zalta (ed.), *The Stanford Encyclopedia of Philosophy* (Summer 2018 Edition), https://plato.stanford.edu/archives/sum2018/entries/knowledge-analysis.

Jeutner, Valentin, *The Reasonable Person: A Legal Biography* (Cambridge: Cambridge University Press, 2024).

Joseph, Sarah, 'Pharmaceutical Corporations and Access to Drugs: The "Fourth Wave" of Corporate Human Rights Scrutiny' (2003) 25 *Human Rights Quarterly* 425–452.

Joyner, Daniel & Roscini, Marco (eds.), *Non-Proliferation Law as a Special Regime: A Contribution to Fragmentation Theory in International Law* (Cambridge: Cambridge University Press, 2012).

Kammerhofer, Jorg, 'International Legal Positivism', in Florian Hoffmann & Anne Orford (eds.), *Oxford Handbook of International Legal Theory* (Oxford: Oxford University Press, 2016), 407–426.

Kamminga, Menno, 'State Succession in Respect of Human Rights Treaties' (1996) 7 *European Journal of International Law* 469–484.

Kaufmann-Kohler, Gabrielle, 'Arbitral Precedent: Dream, Necessity or Excuse?' (2007) 23 *Arbitration International* 357–378.

Kelsen, Hans, *Pure Theory of Law*, Max Knight (translator), 2nd edition (Berkeley: University of California Press, 1967).

Kennedy, David, 'The Sources of International Law' (1987) 2 *American University International Law Review* 1–97.

Kinley, David & Tadaki, Junko, 'From Talk to Walk: The Emergence of Human Rights Responsibilities for Corporations at International Law' (2004) 44 *Virginia Journal of International Law* 931–1023.

Kooijmans, Pieter, 'The ICJ in the 21st Century: Judicial Restraint, Judicial Activism, or Proactive Judicial Policy' (2007) 56 *The International and Comparative Law Quarterly* 741–753.

Koskenniemi, Martti, 'The Politics of International Law' (2009) 20 *European Journal of International Law* 7–19.

Koskenniemi, Martti & Leino, Päivi, 'Fragmentation of International Law: Post-Modern Anxieties' (2005) 15 *Leiden Journal of International Law* 553–579.

Krenc, Frédéric, '"Dire le droit", "rendre la justice". Quelle Cour européenne des droits de l'homme?' (2018) 2 *Revue trimestrielle des droits de l'homme* 311–346.

Laird, Ian & Askew, Rebecca, 'Finality Versus Consistency: Does Investor-State Arbitration Need an Appellate System' (2005) 7 *Journal of Appellate Practice and Process* 285–302.

Lanquetin, Marie-Thérèse, 'L'égalité entre hommes et femmes dans le régime spécial de retraite de fonctionnaires' (2002) 2 *Droit Social* 178–199.

Laurence, Stephen & Margolis, Eric, 'Concepts and Cognitive Science', in Eric Margolis & Stephen Laurence (eds.), *Concepts: Core Readings* (Cambridge: The MIT Press, 1999).

Legg, Andrew, *The Margin of Appreciation in International Human Rights Law: Deference and Proportionality* (Oxford: Oxford University Press, 2012).

Leiter, Brian, 'Rethinking Legal Realism: Towards a Naturalized Jurisprudence' (1997) 76 *Texas Law Review* 267–315.

Letsas, George, 'The Truth in Autonomous Concepts: How to Interpret the ECHR' (2004) 15 *European Journal of International Law* 279–305.

Lifante-Vidaln, Isabel, 'Is Legal Certainty a Formal Value?' (2020) 11 *Jurisprudence* 456–467.

Linderfalk, Ulf, *On the Interpretation of Treaties* (Dordrecht: Springer, 2007).

'The Application of International Legal Norms Over Time: The Second Branch of Intertemporal Law' (2011) 58 *Netherlands International Law Review* 147–172.

'The Principle of Rational Decision-Making: As Applied to the Identification of Normative Conflicts in International Law' (2013) 73 *Zeitschrift für ausländisches öffentliches Recht und Völkerrecht* 591–614.

'Cross-Fertilisation in International Law' (2015) 84 *Nordic Journal of International Law* 428–455.

'Philip Morris Asia Ltd. v. Australia: Abuse of Rights in Investor-State Arbitration' (2017) 86 *Nordic Journal of International Law* 403–419.

'What Are the Functions of the General Principles? Good Faith and International Legal Pragmatics' (2018) 78 *Zeitschrift für ausländisches öffentliches Recht und Völkerrecht* 1–32.

'The Exercise of Discretion In International Law – Why Constraining Criteria Have a Proper Place in the Analysis of Legal Decision-Making' (2019) 62 *German Yearbook of International Law* 407–430.

'Proportionality and International Legal Pragmatics' (2020) 89 *Nordic Journal of International Law* 422–437.

'The Legal Consequences of *Jus Cogens* and the Individuation of Norms' (2020) 33 *Leiden Journal of International Law* 893–909.

Understanding Jus Cogens in International Law and International Legal Discourse (Cheltenham: Edward Elgar Publishing Limited, 2020).

'Rational Reconstruction and International Legal Reasoning' (December 13, 2022) *SSRN*, Working Paper.

The International Legal System as a System of Knowledge (Cheltenham: Edward Elgar Publishing Limited, 2022).

'The Concept of an International Legal Concept' (2023) 12 *Cambridge International Law Journal* 177–189.

Lindroos, Anja, 'Addressing Norm Conflicts in a Fragmented Legal System: The Doctrine of *Lex Specialis*' (2005) 74 *Nordic Journal of International Law* 27–66.

Logister, Louis, 'Global Governance and Civil Society. Some Reflections on NGO Legitimacy' (2007) 3 *Journal of Global Ethics* 165–179.

Lowenfeld, Andreas, 'The ICSID Convention: Origins and Transformation' (2009) 38 *Georgia Journal of International and Comparative Law* 47–61.

Maher, Julie, 'Eweida and Others: A New Era for Article 9?' (2014) 63 *International and Comparative Law Quarterly* 213–233.

Mahmoudi, Said, *The Law of Deep Sea-Bed Mining* (Stockholm: Almqvist & Wiksell International, 1987).

Malanczuk, Peter, *Akehurst's Modern Introduction to International Law*, 7th edition (London: Routledge, 1997).

Marboe, Irmgard, 'Reparation Cases: Applicable Principles in International Investment Arbitration', in Hélène Fabri & Edoardo Stoppioni (eds.), *International Investment Law: An Analysis of the Major Decisions* (Oxford: Hart Publishing, 2022).

Margolis, Eric & Laurence, Stephen, 'The Ontology of Concepts: Abstract Objects or Mental Representations?' (2007) 41 *Noûs* 561–593.

Margolis, Eric & Laurence, Stephen, 'Concepts', in Edward Zalta & Uri Nodelman (eds.), *The Stanford Encyclopedia of Philosophy* (Summer 2010 Edition), http://plato.stanford.edu/archives/sum2010/entries/concepts.

Matscher, Franz, 'Methods of Interpretation of the Convention', in Ronald St. J. Macdonald, Franz Matscher, & Herbert Petzold (eds.), *The European System for the Protection of Human Rights* (Dordrecht: Martinus Nijhoff, 1993).

Maxeiner, James, 'Legal Certainty and Legal Methods: A European Alternative to American Legal Indeterminacy?' (2007) 15 *Tulane Journal of International & Comparative Law* 541–607.

McCaffrey, Stephen, *The Law of International Watercourses: Non-Navigational Uses* (Oxford: Oxford University Press, 2001).

McDougal, Myres, 'Law as a Process of Decision: A Policy-Oriented Approach to Legal Study' (1956) *Natural Law Forum*, Paper 6.

McLachlan, Campbell, 'The Principle of Systemic Integration and Article 31(3)(c) of the Vienna Convention' (2005) 54 *International and Comparative Law Quarterly* 279–320.

Mitchell, Andrew, 'Leave Your Hat On: Head of State Immunity and Pinochet' (1999) 25 *Monash University Law Review* 225–256.

'Proportionality and Remedies in WTO Disputes' (2006) 17 *European Journal of International Law* 985–1008.

Moeckli, Daniel, 'The Emergence of Terrorism as a Distinct Category of International Law' (2008) 44 *Texas International Law Journal* 157–183.

Möschel, Mathias, 'Jura Novit Curia and the European Court of Human Rights' (2022) 33 *European Journal of International Law* 631–650.

Murphy, Sean, 'The United States and the International Court of Justice: Coping with Antinomies', in Cesare Romano (ed.), *The Sword and the Scales: The*

United States and International Courts and Tribunals (Cambridge: Cambridge University Press, 2009).

O'Keefe, Roger & Tams, Christian (eds.), *The United Nations Convention on Jurisdictional Immunities of States and Their Property: A Commentary* (Oxford: Oxford University Press, 2013).

Orakhelashvili, Alexander, *Peremptory Norms in International Law* (Oxford: Oxford University Press, 2006).

'The Classification of International Legal Rules: A Reply to Stefan Talmon' (2013) 26 *Leiden Journal of International Law* 89–103.

Ovey, Clare & White, Robin, *Jacobs & White, European Convention on Human Rights*, 3rd edition (Oxford: Oxford University Press, 2002).

Parker, Matthew, 'The Origin of LL.M. Programs: A Case Study of the University of Pennsylvania Law School' (2018) 39 *University of Pennsylvania Journal of International Law* 825–887.

Paulsson, Jan, *International Arbitration and the Generation of Legal Norms: Treaty Arbitration and International Law* (Alphen aan den Rijn: Kluwer Law International, 2007).

Paulus, Andreas, '*Jus Cogens* in a Time of Hegemony and Fragmentation' (2005) 74 *Nordic Journal of International Law* 297–334.

Pauwelyn, Joost, *Conflict of Norms in Public International Law* (Cambridge: Cambridge University Press, 2003).

Pellet, Alain, 'Article 19: Formulation of a Reservation', in Olivier Corten & Pierre Klein (eds.), *The Vienna Conventions on the Law of Treaties: A Commentary*, vol. 1 (Oxford: Oxford University Press, 2011).

Peters, Anne, 'Realizing Utopia as a Scholarly Endeavour' (2013) 24 *European Journal of International Law* 533–552.

Pirker, Benedikt, *Proportionality Analysis and Models of Judicial Review: A Theoretical and Comparative Study* (Groningen: Europa Law Publishing, 2013).

Prost, Mario, *The Concept of Unity in Public International Law* (Oxford: Hart, 2012).

Raible, Lea, 'Incidental Jurisdiction in Human Rights Litigation: Surprising Absence and Rival Techniques' (2022) 116 *AJIL Unbound* 176–180.

Rasulov, Akbar, 'Revisiting State Succession to Humanitarian Treaties: Is There a Case for Automaticity?' (2003) 14 *European Journal of International Law* 141–170.

Rayfuse, Rosemary, 'Countermeasures and High Seas Fisheries Enforcement' (2004) 51 *Netherlands International Law Review* 41–76.

Non-Flag State Enforcement in High Seas Fisheries (Leiden: Koninklijke Brill NV, 2004).

Roland, Jane, 'On "Knowing How" and "Knowing That"' (1958) 67 *The Philosophical Review* 379–388.

Ross, Alf, 'Tû-tû' (1956–1957) 70 *Harvard Law Review* 812–825.

Ryle, Gilbert, 'Knowing How and Knowing That: The Presidential Address' (1945–1946) 46 *Proceedings of the Aristotelian Society* 1–16.

Schabas, William, 'International Criminal Courts', in Cesare Romano, Karen Alter, & Yuval Shany (eds.), *The Oxford Handbook of International Adjudication* (Oxford: Oxford University Press, 2014).

Schiller, Erich, *Official Rules of Chess*, 2nd edition (Cardoza Publishing, 2003).

Schreuer, Christoph, 'Three Generations of ICSID Annulment Proceedings', in Emmanuel Gaillard & Yas Banifatemi (eds.), *Annulment of ICSID Awards* (New York: Juris Publishing, 2004).

Shany, Yuval, 'Towards a General Margin of Appreciation Doctrine in International Law?' (2005) 16 *European Journal of International Law* 907–940.

Shaw, Malcolm, *International Law*, 7th edition (Cambridge: Cambridge University Press, 2014).

Shelton, Dinah, 'The Participation of Nongovernmental Organizations in International Judicial Proceedings' (1994) 88 *American Journal of International Law* 611–642.

'Normative Hierarchy in International Law' (2006) 100 *American Journal of International Law* 291–323.

'*Jura Novit Curia* in International Human Rights Tribunals', in Nerina Boschiero, Tullio Scovazzi, Cesare Pitea, & Chiara Ragni (eds.), *International Courts and the Development of International Law* (The Hague: T.M.C. Asser Press, 2013).

Siehr, Kurt, 'A Special Regime for Cultural Objects in Europe' (2003) 8 *Uniform Law Review* 551–564.

Simma, Bruno & Hernández, Gleider, 'Legal Consequences of an Impermissible Reservation to a Human Rights Treaty: Where Do We Stand?', in Enzo Cannizzaro (ed.), *The Law of Treaties Beyond the Vienna Convention* (Oxford: Oxford University Press, 2011).

Simma, Bruno & Pulkowski, Dirk, 'Of Planets and the Universe: Self-Contained Regimes in International Law' (2006) 17 *European Journal of International Law* 483–529.

Small, David, 'The Oil Platforms Case: Jurisdiction Through the—Closed—Eye of the Needle' (2004) 3 *The Law and Practice of International Courts and Tribunals* 113–124.

Somek, A., 'Kelsen Lives' (2007) 18 *European Journal of International Law* 409–451.

Spaak, Torben, 'Realism About the Nature of Law' (2017) 30 *Ratio Juris* 75–104.

Spoorenberg, Frank & Viñuales, Jorge, 'Conflicting Decisions in International Arbitration' (2009) 8 *The Law and Practice of International Courts and Tribunals* 91–113.

St John, Taylor, *The Rise of Investor-State Arbitration: Politics, Law and Unintended Consequences* (Oxford: Oxford University Press, 2018).

Stahn, Carsten & De Brabandere, Eric, 'The Future of International Legal Scholarship: Some Thoughts on "Practice", "Growth", and "Dissemination"' (2014) 27 *Leiden Journal of International Law* 1–10.

Steer, Cassandra & Hersch, Matthew (eds.), *War and Peace in Outer Space* (New York: Oxford University Press, 2021).

Stephens, Tim, 'International Courts and Sustainable Development: Using Old Tools to Shape a New Discourse', in Brad Jessup & Kim Rubenstein (eds.), *Environmental Discourses in Public and International Law* (Cambridge: Cambridge University Press, 2012), 195–217.

Steup, Matthias & Neta, Ram, 'Epistemology', in Edward Zalta (ed.), *The Stanford Encyclopedia of Philosophy* (Spring 2020 Edition), https://plato.stanford.edu/archives/spr2020/entries/epistemology.

Sugihara, Takane, 'The Principle of Jura Novit Curia in the International Court of Justice: With Reference to Recent Decisions' (2012) 55 *Japanese Yearbook of International Law* 77–109.

Sur, Serge, 'The State between Fragmentation and Globalization' (1997) 8 *European Journal of International Law* 421–434.

Taekema, Sanne, *The Concept of Ideals in Legal Theory* (The Hague: Kluwer Law International, 2010).

Talmon, Stefan, '*Jus Cogens* After Germany v. Italy: Substantive and Procedural Rules Distinguished' (2012) 25 *Leiden Journal of International Law* 979–1002.

Tams, Christian, *Enforcing Obligations Erga Omnes in International Law* (Cambridge: Cambridge University Press, 2005).

Taylor, Roger, '*Pinochet*, Confusion, and Justice: The Denial of Immunity in U.S. Courts to Alleged Torturers Who Are Former Heads of State' (2001) 24 *Thomas Jefferson Law Review* 101–120.

Thirlway, Hugh, 'Judicial Activism and the International Court of Justice', in Nisuke Ando, Edward McWhinney, & Rüdiger Wolfrum (eds.), *Liber Amicorum Judge Shigeru Oda*, 2 vols., vol. 1 (The Hague: Kluwer Law International, 2002).

The International Court of Justice (Oxford: Oxford University Press, 2016).

Trebilcock, Michael & Trachtman, Joel, *Advanced Introduction to International Trade Law* (Cheltenham: Edward Elgar Publishing Limited, 2020).

Tzeng, Peter, 'Incidental Jurisdiction', in Hélène Fabri (ed.), *The Max Planck Encyclopedia of International Procedural Law* (Oxford: Oxford University Press, 2022).

Valencia-Ospina, Eduardo, 'Non-Governmental Organizations and the International Court of Justice', in Tulio Treves, Alessandro Fodella, Attila

Tanzi, & Marco Frigessi di Rattalma (eds.), *Civil Society, International Courts and Compliance Bodies* (The Hague: T.M.C. Asser Press, 2005).

van Aaken, Anne & Lehman, Tobias, 'Sustainable Development and International Investment Law: A Harmonious View From Economics', in Roberto Echandi & Pierre Sauvé (eds.), *Prospects in International Investment Law and Policy* (Cambridge: Cambridge University Press, 2013).

van den Bossche, Peter & Zdouc, Werner, *The Law and Policy of the World Trade Organization*, 4th edition (Cambridge: Cambridge University Press, 2019).

Van den Eynde, Laura, 'Amicus Curiae: European Court of Human Rights (ECtHR)', in Hélène Fabri (ed.), *The Max Planck Encyclopedia of International Procedural Law* (Oxford: Oxford University Press, 2019).

Van Hoof, G. J. H., *Rethinking the Source of International Law* (Deventer: Kluwer Law and Taxation Publishers, 1983).

Van Meerbeeck, Jérémie, 'The Principle of Legal Certainty in the Case Law of the European Court of Justice: From Certainty to Trust' (2016) 41 *European Law Review* 275–288.

van Steenberghe, Raphaël, *Droit international humanitaire: Un regime special de droit international?* (Bruxelles: Bruylant, 2013).

Venzke, Ingo, *How Interpretation Makes International Law: On Semantic Change and Normative Twists* (Oxford: Oxford University Press, 2012).

Vidmar, Jure, 'Rethinking *Jus Cogens* After Germany v. Italy: Back to Article 53?' (2013) 60 *Netherlands International Law Review* 1–25.

Viljanen, Jukka, 'The Role of the European Court of Human Rights as a Developer of International Human Rights Law' (2008) 62/63 *Cuadernos constitutucionales de la Catedra Fadrique Furio Ceriol* 249–265.

Viñuales, Jorge, 'Cartographies imaginaires: Observations sur la portée juridique du concept de "régime spécial" en droit international' (2013) 140 *Journal du droit international* 405–425.

'Sustainable Development in International Law', in Lavanya Rajamani & Jacqueline Peel (eds.), *The Oxford Handbook of International Environmental Law*, 2nd edition (Oxford: Oxford University Press, 2019).

Voigt, Christina, *Sustainable Development as a Principle of International Law* (Leiden: Martinus Nijhoff Publishers, 2008).

Vöneky, Silja, 'Analogy in International Law', in Rüdiger Wolfrum (ed.), *The Max Planck Encyclopedia of Public International Law*, vol. 1 (Oxford: Oxford University Press, 2012), 374–380.

Vranes, Erich, 'The Definition of "Norm Conflict" in International Law and Legal Theory' (2006) 17 *European Journal of International Law* 395–418.

Weatherall, Thomas, '*Jus Cogens* and Sovereign Immunity: Reconciling Divergence in Contemporary Jurisprudence' (2014–2015) 46 *Georgetown Journal of International Law* 1151–1212.

Weissbrodt, David & Kruger, Muria, 'Norms on the Responsibilities of Transnational Corporations and Other Business Corporations and Other Business Enterprises with Regard to Human Rights' (2003) 97 *The American Journal of International Law* 901–922.

Wenger, Etienne, *Communities of Practice: Learning, Meaning, and Identity* (Cambridge: Cambridge University Press, 1998).

Wolfrum, Rüdiger & Matz, Nele, *Conflicts in International Environmental Law* (Berlin: Springer, 2003).

World Commission on Environment and Development, *Our Common Future* (Oxford: Oxford University Press, 1987).

Wróblewski, Jerzy, 'Legal Language and Legal Interpretation' (1985) 4 *Law and Philosophy* 239–255.

Young, Margaret (ed.), *Regime Interaction in International Law: Facing Fragmentation* (Cambridge: Cambridge University Press, 2012).

Zarbiyev, Fuad, 'Judicial Activism in International Law – A Conceptual Framework for Analysis' (2012) 3 *Journal of International Dispute Settlement* 247–278.

Zimmermann, Andreas, 'Sovereign Immunity and Violations of International *Jus Cogens*' (1995) 16 *Michigan Journal of International Law* 433–440.

Zyberi, Gentian, 'The Role and Contribution of International Courts in Furthering Peace as an Essential Community Interest', in Cecilia Bailliet (ed.), *Research Handbook on International Law and Peace* (Cheltenham: Edward Elgar, 2019), pp 424–448.

Judicial Decisions

International Court of Justice

Accordance with International Law of the Unilateral Declaration of Independence by the Provisional Institutions of Self-Government of Kosovo, Order, [2008] I.C.J. Rep. 409.

Advisory Opinion on Reservations to the Convention on Genocide, [1951] I.C.J. Rep. 15.

Ahmadou Sadio Diallo (Republic of Guinea v. Democratic Republic of the Congo), Compensation, [2012] I.C.J. Rep. 343.

Application of the Convention on the Prevention and Punishment of the Crime of Genocide (Bosnia and Herzegovina v. Serbia and Montenegro), [2007] I.C.J. Rep. 43.

Application of the Convention on the Prevention and Punishment of the Crime of Genocide (Bosnia and Herzegovina v. Serbia and Montenegro), Further Requests for the Indications of Provisional Measures, [1993] I.C.J. Rep. 3.

Application of the Convention on the Prevention and Punishment of the Crime of Genocide (Bosnia and Herzegovina v. Yugoslavia), Preliminary Objections, [1996] I.C.J. Rep. 595.

Application of the International Convention for the Suppression of the Financing of Terrorism and of the International Convention on the Elimination of All Forms of Racial Discrimination (Ukraine v. Russian Federation), Preliminary Objections, [2019] I.C.J. Rep. 558.

Application of the International Convention on the Elimination of All Forms of Racial Discrimination (Georgia v. Russian Federation), Preliminary Objections, [2011] I.C.J. Rep. 70.

Application of the Interim Accord of 13 September 1995 (The Former Republic of Macedonia v. Greece), [2011] I.C.J. Rep. 644.

Armed Activities on the Territory of the Congo (Democratic Republic of the Congo v. *Uganda)*, Reparations, [2022] I.C.J. Rep. 13.

Armed Activities on the Territory of the Congo (New Application: 2002) (Democratic Republic of the Congo v. Rwanda), Jurisdiction of the Court and Admissibility of the Application, [2006] I.C.J. Rep. 6.

Asylum Case (Colombia v. Peru), Oral proceedings-Documents-Correspondence, Part IV: Correspondence, [1950] I.C.J. Rep. 202.

Border and Transborder Armed Action (Nicaragua v. Honduras), Jurisdiction and Admissibility, [1988] I.C.J. Rep. 69.

Case Concerning Pulp Mills on the River Uruguay (Argentina v. Uruguay), [2010] I.C.J. Rep. 14.

Certain Activities Carried Out by Nicaragua in the Border Area (Costa Rica v. Nicaragua), [2018] I.C.J. Rep. 15.

Certain Activities Carried Out by Nicaragua in the Border Area (Costa Rica v. Nicaragua) and Construction of a Road in Costa Rica along the San Juan River (Nicaragua v. Costa Rica), [2015] I.C.J. Rep. 665.

Fisheries Case (United Kingdom v. Norway), [1951] I.C.J. Rep. 116.

Fisheries Jurisdiction (United Kingdom v. Zealand), [1974] I.C.J. Rep. 3.

Gabčíkovo-Nagymaros Project, [1977] I.C.J. Rep. 7.

International Status of South-West Africa, Advisory Opinion, [1950] I.C.J. Rep. 130.

Kasikili/Sedudu Island (Botswana/Namibia), [1999] I.C.J. Rep. 1045.

Maritime Delimitation in the Indian Ocean (Somalia v. Kenya), Preliminary Objections, [2017] I.C.J. Rep. 3.

Military and Paramilitary Activities in and Against Nicaragua (Nicaragua v. United States of America), [1986] I.C.J. Rep. 14.

Military and Paramilitary Activities in and Against Nicaragua (Nicaragua v. United States of America), Jurisdiction and Admissibility, [1984] I.C.J. Rep. 392.

Navigational and Related Rights (Costa Rica v. Nicaragua), [2009] I.C.J. Rep. 213.

Nuclear Tests (Australia v. France), [1974] I.C.J. Rep. 253.

Oil Platforms (Islamic Republic of Iran v. United States of America), [2003] I.C.J. Rep. 161.

Questions Relating to the Obligation to Prosecute or Extradite (Belgium v. Senegal), [2012] I.C.J. Rep. 99.

South West Africa Case (Liberia v. South Africa; Ethiopia v. South Africa), [1966] I.C.J. Rep. 6.

United States Diplomatic and Consular Staff in Tehran (United States v. Iran), [1980] I.C.J. Rep. 3.

Permanent Court of International Justice

Factory at Chorzów (Indemnities) [1928] P.C.I.J. (ser. A) No. 9.

Factory at Chorzów (Merits) [1928] P.C.I.J. (ser. A) No. 17.

Railway Traffic between Lithuania and Poland, [1931] P.C.I.J. (ser. A/B) No. 42.

Status of Eastern Carelia, [1923] P.C.I.J. (ser. B) No. 5.

European Court of Human Rights

Animal Defenders International v. United Kingdom, Appl. No. 48876/08, [2013] ECHR 362.

Bayatyan v. Armenia, Appl. No. 23459/03, IHRL 169 (ECHR 2011).

Belilos v. Switzerland, Appl. No. 10328/83 [1988] ECHR 4.

Brogan and Others v. United Kingdom, Appl. Nos. 1120984, 1123484, 1126684, 1138685, [1989] 11 EHRR 117.

Chapman v. United Kingdom, Appl. No. 27238/95, [2001] 33 EHRR 399.

Chassagnou v. France, Appl. No. 25088/94, [2000] 29 EHRR 615.

Engel v. The Netherlands, Appl. No. 5100/71, [1976] ECHR 3.

Evans v. United Kingdom, Appl. No. 6339/05, [2007] ECHR 264.

Frodl v. Austria, Appl. No. 20201/04, [2010] ECHR 508.

Goodwin v. United Kingdom, Appl. No. 28957/95, [2002] ECHR 588.

Grande Stevens v. Italy, Appl. No. 18640/10, [2014] ECHR 4.

Guerra and Others v. Italy, Appl. No. 14967/89, [1998] ECHR 7.

Ireland v. United Kingdom, Appl. 5310/71, [1978] ECHR 1.

Jeronovičs v. Latvia, Appl. No. 44898/10, [2016] IHRL 3954.

Karimov v. Russia, Appl. No. 62892/12, First Section, Judgment of 28 May 2014.

Kjeldsen v. Denmark, Appl. No. 5095/71, [1976] ECHR 6.

Klass and Others v. Germany, Appl. No. 5029/71, [1979–1980] 2 EHRR 214.

König v. Germany, Appl. No. 6232/73, IHRL 18 (ECHR 1978).

Korchuganova v. Russia, Appl. No. 75039/01, [2006] ECHR 602.

Litwa v. Poland, Appl. No. 26629/95, [2000] ECHR 141.

Loizidou v. Turkey, Appl. No. 15318/89, [1995] ECHR 10.

M v. Germany, Appl. No. 19359/04, IHRL 3709 (ECHR 2009).
Maaouia v. France, Appl. No. 39652/98, [2000] ECHR 455.
Mamatkulov and Askarov v. Turkey, Appl. No. 46827/99, [2005] ECHR 64.
N.D. and N.T. v. Spain, Appl. Nos. 8675/15, 8697/15, [2020] ECHR 142.
Otto-Preminger Institut v. Austria, Appl. No. 13470/87, [1994] 19 EHHR 34.
Perdigão v. Portugal, Appl. No. 24768/06, IHRL 1822 (ECHR 2010).
Rantsev v. Cyprus and Russia, Appl. No. 25965/04, IHRL 3632 (ECHR 2010).
Refah Partisi (The Welfare Party) v. Turkey, Appl. Nos. 41340/98, 41342/98, 41343/98, 41344/98, [2003] ECHR 87.
Rousk v. Sweden, Appl. No. 25/7/13, [2013] ECHR 746.
Schmidt v. Germany, Appl. No. 13580/88, [1994] ECHR 18.
Scoppola v. Italy (No 2), Appl. No. 10249/03, [2010] 51 EHRR 12.
Scoppola v. Italy (No 3), Appl. No. 126/05, [2012] ECHR 23.
Selmouni v. France, Appl. No. 25803/94, [1999] ECHR 66.
Sigurjónson v. Iceland, Appl. No. 16130/90, [1993] ECHR 264.
Soering v. United Kingdom, Appl. No. 14038/88, [1989] ECHR 14.
Stubbings v. United Kingdom, Appl. Nos. 22083/93, 22095/93, [1996] ECHR 44.
Ukraine v. Russia (Re Crimea), Admissibility, Appl. Nos. 20958/14 and 38334/18, [2020] ECHR 12.
United Communist Party of Turkey v. Turkey, Appl. No. 19392/92, [1998] ECHR 1.
Weber v. *Switzerland*, Appl. No. 11034/84, [1990] ECHR 13.

International Criminal Tribunal for the Former Yugoslavia

Prosecutor v. Furundžija, Trial Chamber, Judgment, Case No. IT-95-17/1-T, 10 December 1998.
Prosecutor v. Kunarac, Trial Chamber, Judgment, Case No. IT-96-23-T and IT-96-23/1-T, 22 February 2001.
Prosecutor v. Mucič et al., Judgment, Case No. IT-96-21-A, 20 February 2001.
Prosecutor v. Slobodan Milošević, Reasons for Decision on Refusal to Order Joinder, Case Nos. IT-99-37-AR73, IT-01-50-AR73, IT-01-51-AR73, 18 April 2002.
Prosecutor v. Tadić, Appeals Chamber, Defence Motion for Interlocutory Appeal on Jurisdiction Case No. IT-94-1, 2 October 1995.
Prosecutor v. Tadić, Appeals Chamber, Judgment Case No. IT-94-1, 2 October 1995.

Inter-American Court of Human Rights

Hilaire v. Trinidad and Tobago, Case 11.816, [2001] Inter. Am. Ct. H.R. (ser. C) No. 80.

YATAMA v. Nicaragua, [2005] Inter-. Am. Ct. H.R. (ser. C) No. 127.

International Tribunal for the Law of the Sea

The 'Arctic Sunrise' Case (Kingdom of the Netherlands v. Russian Federation), Provisional Measures, www.itlos.org/en/main/cases/list-of-cases/case-no-22.

Various Arbitration Tribunals

ADC Affiliate Limited and ADC & ADMC Management Limited v. Republic of Hungary, ICSID Case No. ARB/03/16, Award, 2 October 2006.

Air Services Agreement, [1978] 18 R.I.A.A. 417.

Anaconda-Iran, Inc. v. Iran, [1986] 13 Iran-U.S. Cl. Trib. Rep. 199.

Award in the Arbitration regarding the Iron Rhine ("Ijzeren Rijn") Railway between the Kingdom of Belgium and the Kingdom of the Netherlands, [2005] 27 U.N.R.I.A.A. 35.

BP Exploration Co (Libya) Ltd. v. The Government of the Libyan Arab Republic, [1979] 53 I.L.R. 297.

Burlington Resources v. Republic of Ecuador and Empresa Estatal Petróleos del Ecuador, ICSID Case No. ARB/08/5, Decision on Jurisdiction, 2 June 2010.

Dispute Concerning Access to Information Under Article 9 of the OSPAR Convention, Ireland v. United Kingdom, PCA Case No. 2001-03, Final Award, 2 July 2003.

Dispute Concerning Coastal State Rights in the Black Sea, Sea of Azov, and Kerch Strait (Ukraine v. the Russian Federation), PCA Case No. 2017-06, Award on Preliminary Objections, 21 February 2020.

Electrabel S.A. v. Republic of Hungary, ICSID Case No. ARB/07/19, Decision on Jurisdiction, Applicable Law and Liability, 30 November 2012.

Eritrea/Yemen – Sovereignty and Maritime Delimitation in the Red Sea, [1998] 114 I.L.R. 1.

Everest Estate LLC v. Russian Federation, PCA Case No. 2015-36, Award, 2 May 2018.

Iurii Bogdanov, Agurdino-Invest Ltd. and Agurdino-Chimia JSC v. Republic of Moldova, SCC Case No. 93/2004, Arbitral Award, 22 September 2005.

Klöckner Industrie-Anlagen GmbH v. United Republic of Cameroon and Société Camerounaise des Engrais, ICSID Case No. ARB/81/2, Decision of the *ad hoc* Committee, 3 May 1985.

M.C.I. Power Group L.C. and New Turbine Inc. v. Republic of Ecuador, ICSID Case No. ARB/03/6, Decision on Annulment, 19 October 2009.

Public Joint Stock Company 'State Savings Bank of Ukraine' (JSC Oschadbank) v. the Russian Federation, PCA Case No. 2016-14, Award, 26 November 2018, as cited by the European Court of Human Rights in Case Nos. 20958/14 and 38334/18, *Ukraine v. Russia (Re Crimea)*, Decision on Admissibility, 16 December 2020.

Saipem v. People's Republic of Bangladesh, ICSID Case No. ARB/05/7, Award, 30 June 2009.

The 'Enrica Lexie' Incident (Italy v. India), PCA Case No. 2015-28, Award, 21 May 2020.

Víctor Pey Casado and President Allende Foundation v. Republic of Chile, ICSID Case No. ARB/98/2, Award, 8 May 2008.

Wena Hotels Ltd. v. Arab Republic of Egypt, ICSID Case No. ARB/98/4, Decision on Annulment, 5 February 2002.

Domestic Courts

R v. Bow Street Metropolitan Stipendiary Department Magistrate, ex parte Pinochet Ugarte (No 3), [1999] 199 I.L.R. 261.

Treaties and Agreements (in Reverse Chronological Order)

Rome Statute of the International Criminal Court, Rome, 17 July 1998, in force 1 July 2002, 2187 U.N.T.S. 3.

Interim Accord between Greece and the Former Yugoslav Republic of Macedonia, New York, 13 September 1995, in force 13 October 1995, 1891 U.N.T.S. 7.

Understanding on Rules and Procedures for the Settlement of Disputes, in Agreement Establishing the World Trade Organization, Marrakesh, 15 April 1994, 1869 U.N.T.S. 401, Annex 2.

General Agreement on Tariffs and Trade, in Agreement Establishing the World Trade Organization, Marrakesh, 15 April 1994, 1867 U.N.T.S. 187.

European Convention on the Recognition of the Legal Personality of International Non-Governmental Organizations, Strasbourg, 24 April 1986, in force 1 January 1991, European Treaty Series No. 124.

Vienna Convention on the Law of Treaties Between States and International Organizations or Between International Organizations, Vienna, 21 March 1986, not in force, (1986) 25 ILM 543.

Protocol No. 7 to the European Convention for the Protection of Human Rights and Fundamental Freedoms, Strasbourg, 22 November 1984, in force 1 November 1988, European Treaty Series No. 117.

United Nations Convention on the Law of the Sea, Montego Bay, 10 December 1982, in force 16 November 1994, 1833 U.N.T.S. 397.

Vienna Convention on Succession of States in Respect of Treaties, Vienna, 23 August 1978, in force 6 November 1996, 1946 U.N.T.S. 3.

Statute of the River Uruguay, Salto, 26 February 1975, in force 18 September 1976, 1295 U.N.T.S. 331.

Vienna Convention on the Law of Treaties, Vienna, 23 May 1969, in force 27 January 1980, 1155 U.N.T.S. 331.

International Covenant on Economic, Social and Cultural Rights, New York, 16 December 1966, in force 3 January 1976, 993 U.N.T.S. 3.

Vienna Convention on Consular Relations, Vienna, 24 April 1963, in force 19 March 1967, 596 U.N.T.S. 261.

United Nations Conference on Trade and Development, 8 December 1962, U.N. Doc. A/RES/1785 (XVII).

Vienna Convention on Diplomatic Relations, Vienna, 18 April 1961, in force 24 April 1964, 500 U.N.T.S. 95.

Convention for the Protection of Human Rights and Fundamental Freedoms, as amended by Protocols Nos. 11 and 14, Rome, 4 November 1950, European Treaty Series No. 5.

Statute of the Council of Europe, London, 5 May 1949, in force 3 August 1949, 87 U.N.T.S. 103.

North Atlantic Treaty, Washington, D.C., 4 April 1949, in force 24 August 1949, 34 U.N.T.S. 243.

Convention on the Prevention and Punishment of the Crime of Genocide, Paris, 9 December 1948, in force 12 January 1951, 78 U.N.T.S. 277.

Statute of the International Court of Justice, San Francisco, 26 June 1945, in force 24 October 1945, XV U.N.C.I.O. 355.

Charter of the United Nations, San Francisco, 26 June 1945, in force 24 October 1945, XV UNCIO 335, amendments in 557 U.N.T.S. 143, 638 U.N.T.S. 308 and 892 U.N.T.S. 119.

Agreement between Great Britain and Germany, respecting Zanzibar, Heligoland, and the Spheres of Influence of the two Countries in Africa ("Heligoland-Zanzibar Treaty", or "Anglo-German Treaty"), Berlin, 1 July 1890, in force 1 July 1890, 51 *Das Staatsarchiv, Sammlung der offiziellen Aktenstücke zur Geschichte der Gegenwart* (Verlag von Duncker & Humblot, 1891), 151.

UN Documents (in Reverse Chronological Order)

Right to development in international investment law: Overview of the ongoing study by the Expert Mechanism on the Right to Development, 1 March 2022, U.N. Doc. A/HRC/EMRTD/5/CRP.2.

Report of Working Group III (Investor-State Dispute Settlement Reform) on the work of its thirty-ninth session, Vienna, 5–9 October 2020, U.N. Doc. A/CN.9/1044.

Possible reform of investor-State dispute settlement (ISDS): Consistency and related matters, Note by the Secretariat, 28 August 2018, U.N. Doc. A/CN.9/WG.III/WP.150.

Report of the International Law Commission, seventieth session, 30 April–1 June and 2 July–10 August 2018, U.N. Doc. A/73/10.

Third report on peremptory norms of general international law (*jus cogens*) by Dire Tladi, Special Rapporteur, 29 May 2018, U.N. Doc. A/CN.4/714/Corr.1, 68.

Report of the United Nations Commission on International Trade Law, fiftieth session, 3–21 July 2017, U.N. Doc. A/72/17.

Toye, John, UNCTAD at 50: A Short History (2014), U.N. Doc. UNCTAD/OSG/2014/1, https://unctad.org/system/files/official-document/osg2014d1_en.pdf.

Guide to Practice on Reservations to Treaties, Report of the International Law Commission on the work of its sixty-third session, U.N. Doc. A/66/10.

Fragmentation of International Law: Difficulties Arising from the Diversification and Expansion of International Law, Report of the Study Group prepared for the fifty-eighth session of the International Law Commission, 1 May–9 June and 3 July–11 August 2006, UN Doc A/CN.4/L.702.

Fragmentation of International Law: Difficulties Arising from the Diversification and Expansion of International Law, Report of the Study Group prepared for the fifty-eighth session of the International Law Commission, 1 May–9 June and 3 July–11 August 2006, U.N. Doc. A/CN.4/L.682, Corr.1 and Add.1.

Draft Norms on the Responsibilities of Transnational Corporations and Other Business Enterprises with Regard to Human Rights, 30 May 2003, U.N. Doc. E/CN.4/Sub.2/2003/12.

Report of the International Law Commission, fifty-fourth session, 29 April–7 June and 22 July–16 August 2002, U.N. Doc. A/57/10.

Report of the work of the International Law Commission at its fifty-fourth session, 29 April–7 June and 22 July–16 August 2002, U.N. Doc. A/57/10.

Articles on the Responsibility of States for Internationally Wrongful Acts, 28 January 2002, U.N. Doc. A/RES/56/83.

Draft Articles on the Responsibility of International Organizations with Commentaries, Report of the International Law Commission on the work of its sixty-third session, (2001) II-2 *Yearbook of the International Law Commission* 39.

Hafner, Gerhard, 'Risks Ensuing from Fragmentation of International Law', in Official Records of the General Assembly, fifty-fifth session, Supplement No. 10, U.N. Doc. A/55/10.

Draft Articles on Responsibility of States for Internationally Wrongful Acts with Commentaries, Report of the International Law Commission on the work of its fifty-third Session, (2001) II-2 *Yearbook of the International Law Commission* 1.

Human Rights Council, CCPR General Comment No. 26: Continuity of Obligations, U.N. Doc. CCPR/C/21/Rev.1/Add.8/Rev.1.

Status of the International Covenants on Human Rights, Succession of States in Respect of Treaties, Report of the Secretary General, 28 November 1994, U.N. Doc. E/CN.4/1995/80, 4.

Human Rights Committee, General Comment No. 24, 11 November 1994, U.N. Doc. CCPR/C/21/Rev.1/Add.6. Security Council Resolution 827, 25 May 1993, U.N. Doc. S/RES/827.

Fourth Report on State Responsibility, by Mr Gaetano Arangio-Ruiz, Special Rapporteur, Report of the International Law Commission on the work of its forty-fourth session, (1992) II-1 *Yearbook of the International Law Commission* 1.

Draft Articles on Jurisdictional Immunities of States and Their Property, with Commentaries, (1991) II-2 *Yearbook of the International Law Commission* 13.

Draft Articles on Succession of States with Commentaries, (1974) II-1 *Yearbook of the International Law Commission* 174.

Establishment of the United Nations Commission on International Trade Law, 17 December 1966, U.N. Doc. A/RES/2205 (XXI).

Other Documents

Amendments to the Rules of Procedure of the European Court of Human Rights, (1974) 17 *Yearbook of the European Convention on Human Rights* 30.

International Court of Justice, Practice Direction XII, *Acts and Documents No. 7*, 169.

Websites and Online Encyclopaedias

'Academic Forum on ISDS', www.jus.uio.no/pluricourts/english/projects/leginvest/academic-forum/.

'American Journal of International Law', www.cambridge.org/core/journals/american-journal-of-international-law.

'American Society of International Law: Primary Publications', www.asil.org/resources/primary-publications.

Amnesty International, 'What We Do', www.amnesty.org/en/what-we-do/.

'Business & Human Rights Journal', www.business-humanrights.org/en/latest-news/business-human-rights-journal.

'Cambridge English Dictionary', https://dictionary.cambridge.org/us/dictionary/english.

Center for International Environmental Law, 'Our Mission', www.ciel.org/about-us/our-mission/.

'Criminal Law Forum', www.springer.com/journal/10609.

Engel Jr., Mylan, 'Epistemic Luck', in *Internet Encyclopedia of Philosophy*, https://iep.utm.edu/epi-luck.

'European Journal of International Law', www.ejil.org/.

'Ingo Venzke, professor of International Law and Social Justice', www.uva.nl/en/content/news/professor-appointments/2018/08/ingo-venzke-professor-of-international-law-and-social-justice.html.

'International & Comparative Law Quarterly', www.cambridge.org/core/journals/international-and-comparative-law-quarterly.

'Journal du Droit International (Clunet)', www.worldcat.org/title/journal-du-droit-international-clunet/oclc/231026790.

'Journal of International Arbitration', https://kluwerlawonline.com/Journals/Journal+of+International+Arbitration/4.

'Journal of International Criminal Justice', https://academic.oup.com/jicj/pages/About.

'Journal of International Dispute Settlement', https://academic.oup.com/jids/pages/About.

'Journal on the Use of Force and International Law', www.tandfonline.com/action/journalInformation?show=aimsScope&journalCode=rjuf20.

'Leiden Journal of International Law', www.cambridge.org/core/journals/leiden-journal-of-international-law.

'London Review of International Law', https://academic.oup.com/lril/pages/About.

'Netherlands model Investment Agreement', 22 March 2019, https://investmentpolicy.unctad.org/international-investment-agreements/treaty-files/5832/download.

'Nordic Journal of International Law', https://brill.com/view/journals/nord/nord-overview.xml.

'P. (Panos) Merkouris, Prof', www.rug.nl/staff/p.merkouris/cv?lang=en.

'Prof. dr. L. (Liesbeth) Zegveld', https://acil.uva.nl/profile/z/e/l.zegveld/l.zegveld.html?origin=YU15UDmwSzGxsoxvNG1ACQ.

'Revue belge de droit international', https://rbdi.bruylant.be.

'Revue générale de droit international public (RGDIP)', www.ridi.org/adi/rgdip/home.htm.

'Society of International Economic Law', www.sielnet.org.

'Transnational Legal Theory', www.tandfonline.com/action/journalInformation?show=aimsScope&journalCode=rtlt20.

'WTO Bodies involved in the dispute settlement process', www.wto.org/english/tratop_e/dispu_e/disp_settlement_cbt_e/c3s3p1_e.htm.

Miscellaneous

Ambassador Lighthizer, Robert E., Office of the United States Trade Representative: Report on the Appellate Body of the World Trade Organization (February 2020).

Bensouda, Fatou, 'Justice, Reconciliation and the Role of the ICC', 6 February 2008, www.idea.int/sites/default/files/speeches/Justice-Reconciliation-and-the-Role-of-the-International-Criminal-Court-ICC-PDF.pdf.

European Court of Human Rights, 'Practical Guide on Admissibility Criteria', 28 February 2023, www.echr.coe.int/documents/admissibility_guide_eng.pdf.

Lee, Ricky, 'Creating a Practical Legal Framework for the Commercial Exploitation of Mineral Resources in Outer Space', PhD thesis, Murdoch University (2009).

Lenaerts, Koen, 'The European Court of Human Rights and the Court of Justice of the European Union: Creating Synergies in the Field of Fundamental Rights Protection', in *Solemn hearing for the opening of the Judicial Year* (26 January 2018).

Nolte, Georg, 'The European Court of Human Rights and the Sources of International Law', 23 September 2020, https://rm.coe.int/the-european-court-of-human-rights-and-the-sources-of-international-la/1680a05733.

Rules of the Court, European Court of Human Rights, Strasbourg, 23 June 2023, www.echr.coe.int/documents/rules_court_eng.pdf.

Van den Bossche, Peter, 'The Demise of the WTO Appellate Body: Lessons for Governance of International Adjudication?' (28 October 2021) *World Trade Institute*, Working Paper No. 02/2021, www.wti.org/research/publications/1333/the-demise-of-the-wto-appellate-body-lessons-for-governance-of-international-adjudication/.

Verbeek, Bart-Jaap, 'Organisaties lanceren platform voor kritische inspraak op blauwdruk Nederlandse investeringsverdragen', 31 May 2018, www.somo.nl/nl/organisaties-lanceren-platform-kritische-inspraak-op-blauwdruk-nederlandse-investeringsverdragen.

INDEX

For EU product safety concerns, contact us at Calle de José Abascal, 56–1°, 28003 Madrid, Spain or eugpsr@cambridge.org.

www.ingramcontent.com/pod-product-compliance
Lightning Source LLC
LaVergne TN
LVHW011813200926
848484LV00005B/1180
9781009543200